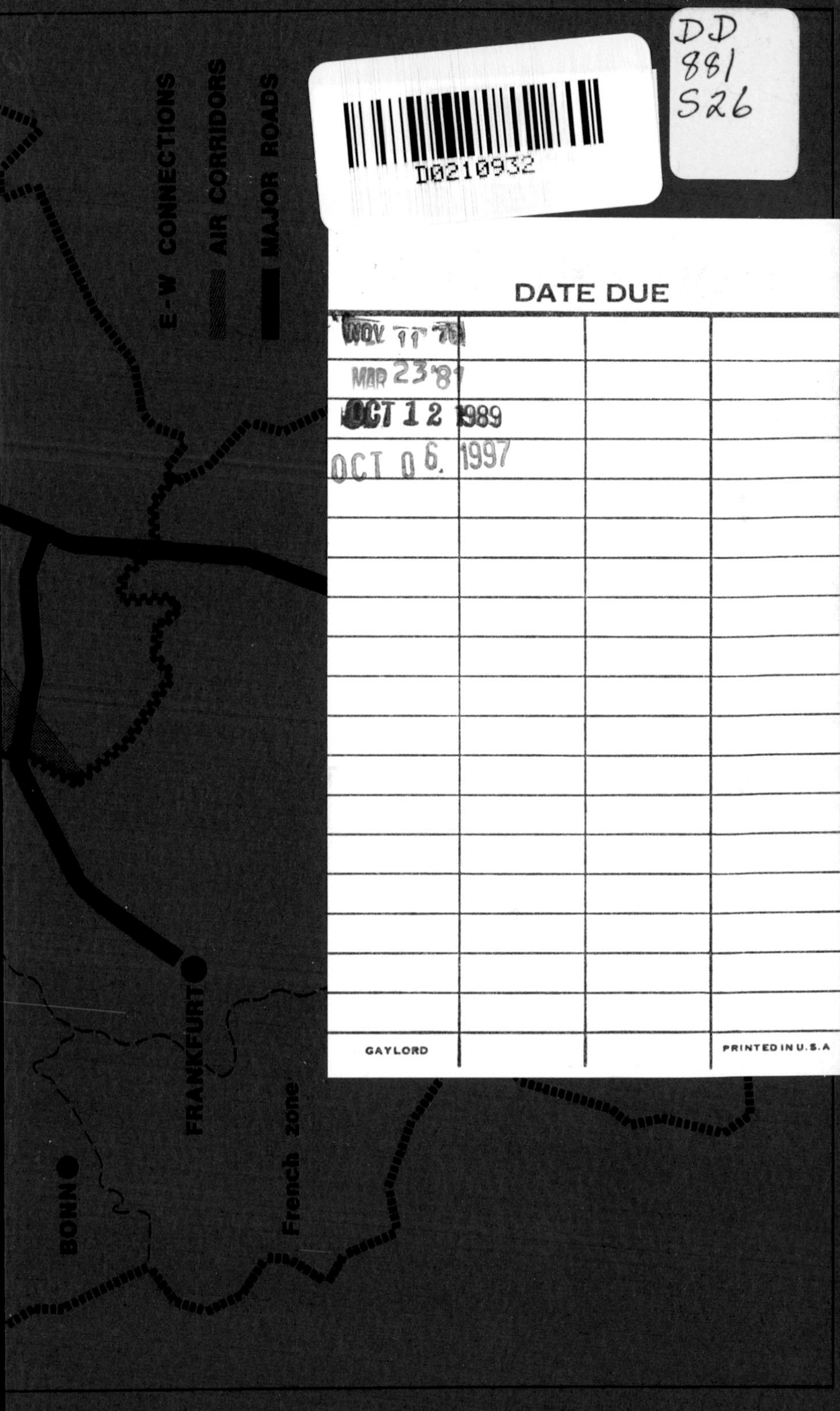
E-W CONNECTIONS
AIR CORRIDORS
MAJOR ROADS
FRANKFURT
BONN
French zone

THE
BERLIN
CRISIS
1958-1962

Jack M. Schick

THE
BERLIN
CRISIS
1958–1962

PHILADELPHIA

UNIVERSITY OF PENNSYLVANIA PRESS

1971

Printed in the United States of America

To NANCY

Map of Berlin, p. 164

CONTENTS

PREFACE

DURING HIS term of office, Dean Rusk, in one of his choice apocalyptic remarks, said: "When I go to sleep at night I try not to think about Berlin." Secretaries of state can easily dream nightmares about the risks of war over Berlin. Nowhere else is the United States more dependent on nuclear retaliation to ensure a national commitment. A holocaust, however, is not a desirable or usable means of defense. Yet any prospect of the Soviet Union seizing the city is equally undesirable. And there the matter rests, frozen in splendid ambiguity.

West Berlin, or Berlin-west—as the West Germans say to emphasize the unity of the city—is an enclave 110 miles behind the Iron Curtain, in the midst of a heavy military encampment. Twenty Soviet divisions, including ten tank divisions, and six East German divisions, including two tank and four motorized rifle divisions, supported by nuclear-armed bomber and fighter aircraft are deployed in East Germany. Headquarters of the Group of Soviet Forces in Germany (GSFG) is at Wünsdorf near East Berlin.[1] The garrisons of the Western powers in Berlin, manned by about 10,000 troops, and therefore outnumbered by Soviet divisions, still serve as a "trip wire" for Western retaliation. Berlin crises are tests of nerve and occur when Soviet leaders decide to apply pressure on the United States, exposed as it is in Berlin. Both sides move their armor and infantry, posturing for effect while their foreign ministries try to come to an understanding. For all the sincerity and real substance there is in the American commitment to the people of West Berlin, the location of the city behind the demarcation line separating West Germany and East Germany is an unfortunate circumstance Soviet leaders can use to embarrass an administration in Washington. American administrations have learned to live with periodic embarrassment about Berlin, but they regularly try to improve on the early decisions of 1945 that fixed the present status quo.

The occupation protocol of September 12, 1944, signed by the United States, Britain, and the Soviet Union, created the present

1. *The Military Balance, 1969–70*, Institute of Strategic Studies, London, 1969, pp. 7, 11, 13.

status quo in Central Europe. The three wartime allies concurred in this protocol even before the Yalta Conference of February 1945 occurred. Many critics of the present status quo mistakenly identify its origins with Yalta. The 1944 protocol divided Germany, like Caesar's Gaul, into three parts (zones) and Berlin correspondingly into three parts (sectors).[2] The Soviet zone encompassed Berlin, although the protocol specified a joint administration for "Greater Berlin." In the November 1944 amendment to the occupation protocol, Britain granted the United States control of Bremen and Bremerhaven on the North Sea and transit facilities between these ports and the American zone in southwestern Germany.[3] The United States in 1944 made no comparable arrangements with the Soviet Union for access to the American sector of Berlin. The explanation of this inconsistency lies in the structure of the occupation contemplated at the time. The occupation protocol allocated a zone to each of the three powers and anticipated separate administrations of the zones. The Berlin area, although divided into three sectors, was to be jointly occupied and administered by all three powers. For these reasons, the United States had to acquire access rights through the British zone by an amendment to the occupation protocol. It enjoyed access rights to Berlin as a party to the shared arrangement for the city.[4]

In the political environment created by the occupation protocol, neither General Dwight Eisenhower nor General Lucius Clay considered it necessary in early June 1945 to obtain specific assurances of access when they negotiated the arrival of American forces in Berlin with Soviet Marshal Georgi Zhukov. At another meeting, later in June, Marshal Zhukov implied that he regarded Western access to Berlin as a privilege granted by the Soviet Union to the Western powers rather than as a right inscribed in the occupation protocol.[5] He proposed they use one highway, one rail line, and one air cor-

2. United States Senate, Committee on Foreign Relations, *Documents on Germany, 1944–1961*, 87th Cong., 1st Sess. (Washington: Government Printing Office, 1961), pp. 1-3 (hereafter cited as *Documents*). The protocol was amended on July 26, 1945, to provide France a role in the occupation. *Ibid.*, pp. 3-5.
3. *Ibid.*, p. 4.
4. William M. Franklin, "Zonal Boundaries and Access to Berlin," *World Politics*, 16 (October 1963), 23. The four-power status of Berlin also derives from the agreement of November 14, 1944, on control machinery for Germany and Berlin. *Documents*, pp. 5-8.
5. Jean Edward Smith, *The Defense of Berlin* (Baltimore: The Johns Hopkins Press, 1963), p. 83.

ridor. Clay orally accepted Zhukov's proposal as a temporary one, expecting to discuss the issue further once the occupation government could be established. Clay felt later that the United States should have refused to withdraw the forces which had overrun parts of the Soviet zone until Berlin access arrangements were clearly settled.[6]

The earliest instance of access interruption occurred the first time American troops used the ground routes. On June 17, Colonel Frank Howley, under orders from Major General Floyd Parks—the designated American commandant for Berlin—moved a column of 500 troops and 120 vehicles, led by a Russian guide, across the Mulde River toward Berlin. A Soviet colonel intercepted them before they reached the main span of the Elbe River bridge. The Russian insisted that "the Berlin agreement" allowed no more than 37 officers, 50 vehicles, and 125 men to enter or leave Berlin. Howley protested that no such agreement existed and asked for the colonel's superior. The superior officer, his superior, and the colonel general superior to all of the Soviet officers on the scene were adamant. General Parks finally ordered excess men and baggage back to Halle and the column proceeded, the Soviet colonel furtively counting officers, vehicles, and men as it departed.

Subsequently, Colonel Howley went back and forth twice between Berlin and Halle. Each time, the Soviet colonel at the bridge demanded that the number of officers, vehicles, and men entering Berlin could not exceed the number going out to Halle. Howley recounts the colonel's objection when Howley brought in ten-ton trucks under the 37–50–125 ceiling:

> "No," he said loudly, "you cannot do that. You took out little trucks (meaning jeeps) and now you bring back big trucks. That's not in the agreement. Why do you bring back big trucks?"
>
> "Because that's what we need to carry food, tentage and supplies," I explained patiently.
>
> The Colonel thought a minute. "You do not have to bring the same trucks back, but if you take a small truck out you must bring a small truck back."
>
> That's where I blew my top. "To hell with that idea," I yelled at him. "It won't go with me. It isn't the agreement, and it

6. Lucius D. Clay, *Decision in Germany* (New York: Doubleday and Company, Inc., 1950), pp. 24-27.

isn't going to be that way. It can't work and it won't work. It's
a truck for a truck, whether it's a big truck or a little truck!"
The Colonel quieted down immediately. He asked, quite
meekly, to have a look inside to see if we carried any guns or
ammunition—which we didn't and forty-five minutes later I was
off through the twilight to Babelsberg and Berlin.[7]

The colonel's orders must have been terribly inflexible or he was an
extremely cautious subordinate. In any event, the Soviets, on Zhukov's
authority, gave up the road to Berlin very reluctantly and tried to
regulate Western force levels in Berlin as early as June 1945.

On July 1, 1945, when the United States Military Government
moved to Berlin, Red Army officers tried to halt the column. Howley's
troops honked them away or threw them bodily into the ditch. On
July 5, Zhukov had not relinquished formal control of the American
sector of Berlin. But by this time, the atmosphere arousing mutual
suspicion had its effect and Howley took over the sector for General
Parks in a dawn *fait accompli* to the surprise of the Russians, who
"don't get up until noon." The Soviets, if pressed hard, acknowledged
the occupation protocol. But they stiffly interpreted the implementing
details. This pattern of stiff but grudging acknowledgment of Western
rights in the city has not changed since 1945 when Colonel Howley
discovered it. The United States subsequently ignored the 37–50–125
ceiling, although it has accepted other rules.

In late 1945, the Western powers proposed to use six air corridors
including routes to Warsaw, Prague, and Copenhagen. They settled
for the three in operation today: Berlin-Hamburg, Berlin-Hannover,
Berlin-Frankfurt-am-Main. Each corridor is twenty miles wide. By
customary usage, flights do not exceed a 500-foot minimum or 10,000-
foot maximum altitude. No advance notice is required for civilian or
military flights, although Western air controllers usually inform the
Soviet air controller of impending flights. The four air controllers
sit in the four-power Berlin Air Safety Center. Actual control of
flights in the three corridors is directed by Western personnel at the
American air traffic control center at Tempelhof airfield.[8]

Temporary arrangements for the zones, Berlin access, and Ger-

---

7. Frank Howley, *Berlin Command* (New York: G. P. Putnam's Sons, 1950),
pp. 37-38.

8. *Documents*, pp. 63-72; John Ausland, "The Struggle over Access to West
Berlin," unpublished MS, 1966, p. 67.

many's frontiers froze into a seemingly permanent status quo in 1946 and 1947. The Soviet Union blockaded Berlin for eleven months in 1948–1949. The blockade served Stalin as a means of protesting currency reform sponsored by the United States, Britain, and France in the Western zones to revive the sluggish West German economy. The Soviets objected to currency reform because they expected it to produce a resurgence of German economic power.[9]

When the blockade took effect on June 24, 1948, neither Moscow nor Washington realized the full potential of an airlift. Neither wanted to risk a war through a dramatic confrontation on the road to Berlin. General Clay ordered an airlift of food and supplies on June 25.[10] The Soviets proposed restrictions to confine the air corridors to Western military use, reserved air space in the corridors for their own aircraft, and harassed incoming and outgoing planes.[11] In spite of Soviet opposition and weather hazards, the airlift succeeded. As spring approached, Moscow indicated a willingness to lift the blockade and to drop objections to currency reform.[12] The New York Agreement of May 4, 1949, terminated the blockade.[13] Although countered by the airlift, the Berlin blockade remains fixed in the minds of American administrations as what could happen again.

9. See the Soviet Military Governor's proclamation, his letters to General Clay, and his Order 111 on currency reform. Wolfgang Heidelmeyer and Günter Hindrichs (eds.), *Documents on Berlin, 1943–1963* (München: R. Oldenbourg Verlag, 1963), pp. 59-65 (hereafter cited as *Documents on Berlin*). The Soviets described the rail blockade as a "technical interruption of the railway line" requiring repairs "to be carried out as soon as possible." *Ibid.*, p. 66.

10. For a chart of total goods transported by airlift 1948–1949, see *Documents on Berlin*, p. 361; W. Phillips Davison, *The Berlin Blockade: A Study in Cold War Politics* (Princeton: Princeton University Press, 1958), p. 261.

11. Davison, *op. cit.*, pp. 65-68, 127, 154, 198-199; Zhukov had asserted in 1945 that the corridors should be used only for the military supply of Western garrisons in Berlin and that Soviet aircraft should also be allowed to fly in them. *Ibid, pp.* 35-37, 48-49. And, in fact, Soviet aircraft did fly in them to transport machinery reparations from West Germany in the immediate postwar years. Ausland, *op. cit.*, p. 72.

12. The negotiations between Soviet Ambassador Jakob Malik and United States Ambassador Philip Jessup at the United Nations laid the groundwork for lifting the blockade. *Documents*, pp. 88-90.

13. For the text, see *ibid.*, pp. 90-91; the New York Agreement restored the status quo ante except for the split in the Berlin city government occurring in August and September, 1948. For an account of Berlin city politics in the blockade period, see Philip Windsor, *City on Leave: A History of Berlin 1945–1962* (New York: Frederick A. Praeger, 1963), pp. 48-158.

The four-power Council of Foreign Ministers in June 1949 agreed to a communiqué which remains the most explicit statement to date about Western access to Berlin. Referring to the New York Agreement, the Ministers said:

> In order . . . to improve and supplement this and other arrangements as regards the movement of persons and goods and communications between the eastern zone and the western zones and between the zones and Berlin, and also in regard to transit, the occupation authorities, each in his own zone, will have an obligation to take the measures necessary to ensure the normal functioning and utilization of rail, water, and road transport for such movement of persons and goods and such communications by post, telephone, and telegraph.[14]

Since 1949, the United States has tried "to improve and supplement" existing access arrangements. It desires a written agreement. In the absence of one, it is forced to rely on implied rights of access, citing the protocols and other documentation from the early postwar period. For example, it uses the written agreement on Western access to Vienna, originally isolated like Berlin in a Soviet zone of occupation, as an analogy for Berlin access.[15] The State Department takes every occasion it can to urge Moscow to negotiate a written agreement.

The Department particularly wants to ensure civilian access and egress from West Berlin. Over 95 percent of the vehicular traffic is civilian. The city's economic viability depends upon an uninterrupted flow of goods and services. Air transportation normally provides only about 0.1 percent of the volume of goods flowing into West Berlin. In the Berlin crisis period, the volume of goods by tons transported to West Berlin divided as follows: 36 percent by road, 35 percent by canal, 29 percent by rail. The volume leaving West Berlin had a different pattern: 64 percent by road, 23 percent by canal, and 13 percent by rail. City exports are finished or semifinished goods suitable for road transport. Imports are industrial raw materials or bulk goods more suitable for water or rail.[16]

The Berlin-Helmstedt and Berlin-Hof *autobahnen* are the two major roadways connecting West Berlin and West Germany. A smaller road

14. *Documents*, p. 95.
15. Franklin, *op. cit.*, p. 31.
16. Berlin, JRO-Sonderkarte, Presse und Informationsamt des Landes Berlin, 1961.

runs to Hamburg. The rail links connect Berlin-Hamburg, Berlin-Hannover, Berlin-Frankfurt-am-Main and Berlin-Nürnberg. The Mittelland Kanal and others provide surface access for barge traffic. All these routes have been closed at one time or another in the postwar history of Berlin.

Another blockade would have a more severe effect than the first blockade in 1948–1949. The city Senat has built up a stockpile of fuel and basic foodstuffs, but the stockpile could not sustain the city at current living standards through another eleven-month seige. Now the standard of living in West Berlin is much higher and the economy of the city is more closely integrated with the Federal Republic's. West Berlin also shares in the Common Market of Western Europe and must continue to attract capital and labor on a long-term basis.[17]

In the Berlin crisis of 1958–1962, the United States attempted to take advantage of the crisis and negotiate a written agreement with the Soviet Union on access to West Berlin. Unfortunately, the moment was not opportune because Soviet Premier Nikita Khrushchev was intent on redirecting the orientation of the city toward East Germany instead of westward.

The State Department made a little progress in the "tailgate crisis" of 1963. A flashback to 1961 is required to understand this mini-crisis. Rushing to West Berlin on August 19, 1961, in a show of force ordered by the White House, the commander of the United States Army battle group had accepted a Soviet request at the checkpoint to dismount his troops for a head count. Previously, American convoy commanders had refused this request to dismount and Soviet officers had made head counts with troops remaining in their trucks. This time, however, he complied to expedite passage. His action stuck as official practice between 1961 and 1963. In the autumn of 1963, the United States tried to restore the earlier no-dismount rule. The Soviets stopped all convoys, insisting on a head count by dismounting. As a practical matter, the tailgates of troop trucks were so high off the ground in 1963 that Soviet officers could not make a head count unless the troops dismounted.

Ambassador Llewellyn Thompson, who retired from his Moscow

17. Kurt Shell, "Berlin," *The Politics of Postwar Germany*, ed. Walter Stahl (New York: Frederick A. Praeger, 1963), p. 100. For a useful recent history of West Berlin's economic problems, see *Der Spiegel*, October 9, 1967, pp. 27-36. See also Berlin Senat, *Studien zur Lage und Entwicklung Westberlins* (*Studies on the Condition and Development of West Berlin*) Berlin, 1968.

post and returned to Washington in 1962, reached an agreement with Soviet Ambassador Anatoly Dobrynin in Washington. Thompson offered to dismount troops in convoys of thirty or more officers and men. Dobrynin did not object. No written agreement was reached, however.[18]

Generally, access interruptions since 1963 have been caused by East German reactions to West German parliamentary or electoral bodies using West Berlin as a site for meetings and conferences. East Germany objects to this practice as a violation of the "special status" of West Berlin, and treats West Berlin as an entity independent of the Federal Republic even though the Western powers do not concur. Moscow usually supports East Germany in letting objections be felt. In April 1965, for example, East German police closed the Berlin-Helmstedt *autobahn* to civilian traffic when the Bundestag—the West German lower house of parliament—met in West Berlin. Soviet aircraft produced sonic booms over the Kongress Halle, shattering glass and eardrums as the parliamentarians convened.[19] The Bundesversammlung, the convention for electing a Federal President, assembled in West Berlin in March, 1969. East Germany closed the *autobahn* again while Soviet tanks maneuvered in the background. But Moscow did not desire a crisis and encouraged Bonn to approach the East Germans to discuss restoring the Berlin wall pass agreements of 1963–1966 in exchange for relocating the election.[20] Talk of improving access arrangements appeared in the press.[21]

The incidents of 1963, 1965, 1969 and others occurred because of local actions in Berlin by the United States and West Germany to which East Germany felt compelled to reply. The Berlin crises of 1948–1949 or 1958–1962 did not begin this way. The best indicator of whether a great storm is brewing is Moscow's attitude toward Bonn. Berlin crises are Moscow's way of opposing Bonn's policies: in 1958 it feared nuclear weapons acquisition; in 1948 it opposed resurgence of German economic power. Berlin crises will recur as long as Moscow believes it has something to fear from Bonn.

18. Horst Mendershausen, *A View of U.S.-European Relations in 1964*, RM-4334, Rand Corporation, Santa Monica, California, November, 1964, pp. 8-9. Jean Edward Smith, "Erosion of a Principle," *The Reporter*, 29 (November 21, 1963), 32-37.

19. *The New York Times*, April 8, 1965, p. 1.

20. *Ibid.*, February 28, 1969, p. 1; March 1, 1969, p. 1.

21. *The Washington Post*, February 28, 1969, p. 1.

ACKNOWLEDGMENTS

THE BERLIN literature for the 1958–1962 crisis period—apart from the huge literature written about the closing days of the Second World War in 1945 and the Berlin blockade of 1948–1949—is sparse and scattered. The following works have been especially useful to me in examining the later Berlin crisis: Arnold L. Horelick and Myron Rush, *Strategic Power and Soviet Foreign Policy*; James L. Richardson, *Germany and the Atlantic Alliance: The Interaction of Strategy and Politics*; Jean Edward Smith, *The Defense of Berlin*; and Hans Speier, *Divided Berlin: The Anatomy of Soviet Political Blackmail*.

In Washington and in Europe, I interviewed participants in the Berlin crisis. I learned more about Berlin itself from Joachim Bölke, managing editor of *Der Tagesspiegel* in West Berlin, than from any other single source. Hans Wieck and Dirk Oncken in the West German Foreign Office improved my description of Bonn's foreign policy. French commentary on Bonn's foreign policy—elicited from French diplomats in Paris, Bonn, Berlin, and Washington—was sympathetic to Bonn while cautious about the stability of West German political life. From British politicians, diplomats, military officers, and academicians in London and Washington, I learned the depth of British frustrations about Bonn's veto in American foreign policy. John Ausland and Arthur Day skillfully interpreted Washington's policy in the Berlin crisis and assisted me in numerous other ways. General James H. Polk, formerly American Commandant in Berlin, and Brigadier General Dewitt C. Armstrong, III, generously gave their time to be interviewed about the military aspects of the crisis. Dean Acheson gave me a lucid interview and I thank him for his critique of both administrations' Berlin policy. There are other officials to whom I am grateful, but who shall have to remain anonymous.

I have relied on the Soviet press, particularly *Pravda* and *Izvestiia* and, to a limited extent, on the *Peking Review*, for analysis of Khrushchev's Berlin policy. Richard Löwenthal, Raymond Garthoff, David Dallin, Boris Nicolaevsky, Robert Conquest, Roman Kolkowicz, and Alexander George, through their works and—in the case of

Löwenthal and Garthoff—interviews as well, provided wise counsel on Soviet foreign policy. Herbert Marcuse's *Soviet Marxism: A Critical Analysis* proved a useful interpretation of Soviet policy. Abraham Halpern commented on Communist China's relationship with East Germany.

I must acknowledge my indebtedness to Paul Nitze and Henry Rowen for their assessment of the requirement for conventional military forces in the Berlin crisis. I am also indebted to Professor Hans Morgenthau of the University of Chicago, who generously provided resources for the research a book of this kind requires, and funds for research in Europe provided by the Rockefeller Foundation. Professor Morgenthau's office holds a magnificent file of eight newspapers for the period 1953–1960 from which I drew: *The Christian Science Monitor, Frankfurter Allgemeine Zeitung, Le Monde, The Manchester Guardian, The New York Herald Tribune, The New York Times, The Washington Post,* and the *Times* (London). John Ausland, Alexander George, William Harris, Paul Johnstone, Charles Burton Marshall, Robert Osgood, Jean Smith, Hans Speier, Robert Weinland, and Hans Wieck read and commented on portions of the manuscript. Glenn Snyder read the entire manuscript with generous and searching criticism. He shares in any merit the book may have.

I wish to thank the Dulles Oral History Project of the Princeton University Library for permission to read the transcripts of interviews relating to Secretary Dulles' views on Berlin, and *ORBIS* (Winter 1965) and the *Western Political Quarterly* (December 1965) for permission to reprint in revised form parts of Chapter 5 and 6 respectively. The following have also given permission: James MacGregor Burns for a passage in *John F. Kennedy: A Political Profile*, Harcourt, Brace, & World; Harper & Row, Publishers, Inc., for passages in John F. Kennedy, *A Strategy of Peace*, ed., Allan Nevins, and Geoffrey McDermott, *Berlin, Success of a Mission?*; Frank L. Howley for the passage in his *Berlin Command*, G. P. Putnam's Sons; Little, Brown and Company, Publishers, for a passage from Walter Lippmann, *The Communist World and Ours*; and Donald S. Zagoria for the quotation from *The Sino-Soviet Conflict, 1956–1961*.

My students at the University of Chicago and Lake Forest College, uninhibited critics of the work as it progressed, and Dean William

Dunn and Professor Robert Steamer of Lake Forest, who allowed me additional research time, helped very tangibly. Mrs. Robert Friedheim edited the final draft of the manuscript, Mrs. Gerald Decker, Mrs. Richard Weaver, Katie Humphries, Donna Choma, Sharon Thompson, Elaine Clark, and Mrs. David Perkins typed one or more drafts of the manuscript. David Kassing and John Rafuse assisted preparation of the manuscript, a courtesy extended to members of the professional staff at the Center for Naval Analyses. This book is dedicated to Nancy, my wife, who has shared the long process of research and writing, and offered editorial criticism from her own experience as newspaperwoman and teacher.

None of the persons mentioned here is responsible for errors that may appear in the volume, particularly persons interviewed. The responsibility is mine alone.

WASHINGTON, D.C.
December, 1970

PART I

The "Deadline Crisis"

CHAPTER 1

Khrushchev's Attack on Berlin and Bonn

As a rule, Berlin crises coincide with extensive Soviet diplomatic activity focusing on West Germany. Soviet diplomacy in Western Europe comes alive whenever the Federal Republic reaches a new stage of growth. Stalin imposed the Berlin blockade in 1948 after the three Western powers announced a decision on West German currency reform to promote economic recovery. When the United States was anxious to rearm West Germany during the Korean war, Soviet leaders again reacted sharply and proposed a peace treaty to freeze Germany in a state of permanent disarmament and neutrality. No Berlin crisis ensued because Western plans for incorporating a West German army into a European army failed.

Following the signature of the Paris protocols of 1954 by Bonn and the Western powers, Premier Nikolai Bulganin and party secretary Khrushchev promoted a "relaxation of tensions." The protocols allowed the Federal Republic to rearm with conventional weapons within the framework of the Western European Union and NATO.[1] The Soviets, attempting to reverse the effects of the protocols, proposed that the two Germanies should become disarmed neutral buffers rather than armed camps in forward areas.[2]

The provision in the Paris protocols recognizing Bonn's right to speak for all Germans was as unsettling for Moscow as West German

1. *Documents*, pp. 155–172.
2. David J. Dallin, *Soviet Foreign Policy After Stalin* (Philadelphia: J. B. Lippincott Company, 1961), pp. 274-285.

rearmament.[3] This combination of powers—rearmament and a voice for all Germans—alarmed Soviet leaders. War over Berlin is a nightmare for the West. But the prospect of a resurgent Germany, armed both with weapons and with claims against the East, is the Soviets' nightmare. The Kremlin leaders made a decision in 1955 to try to elicit from the West a denial of Bonn's all-German pretensions. They adopted a policy favoring recognition of two German states and took steps to implement it. They bestowed diplomatic recognition on East Germany and opened negotiations with Bonn to establish diplomatic relations with West Germany. In according sovereignty to East Germany, they granted it control of West German civilian access to Berlin.[4] They organized the Warsaw Pact as a legal means of keeping troops in the sovereign states of Eastern Europe.

In addition, the Soviet leaders proposed to abandon the occupation of Austria and agreed to an Austrian state treaty. They wanted Austria to serve as an example of a neutral, disarmed buffer in Central Europe. Austria illustrated what Germany could be like. Khrushchev and Bulganin pressed a package of European security proposals on the Western powers at the Geneva summit conference of 1955, with the Austrian model in mind.

Between 1955 and 1958, Soviet diplomacy sponsored or endorsed a number of plans for disengagement of the great powers from Germany requiring Bonn to leave NATO and East Germany to leave the Warsaw Pact. Khrushchev's objectives in the Berlin crisis of

3. In the Final Act of the Nine Power Conference held at London, September 28–October 3, 1954, the United States, Britain, and France declared that "they consider the Government of the Federal Republic as the only German Government freely and legitimately constituted and therefore entitled to speak for Germany as the representative of the German people in international affairs." In exchange for this declaration, Bonn pledged "never to have recourse to force to achieve the reunification of Germany or the modification of the present boundaries of the German Federal Republic. . . ." United States Department of State, *London and Paris Agreements, September–October 1954*, Publication 8659 (Washington: Government Printing Office, 1954), pp. 16-17.

4. In an exchange of letters between East German Foreign Minister Bolz and Soviet Deputy Foreign Minister Zorin on September 20, 1955, the two parties agreed that the East German state "exercises control over . . . the lines of communication between the German Federal Republic and West Berlin situated on GDR territory." They exempted Western military traffic: "the control of traffic of troops and material of the garrisons of France, England, and the United States stationed in West Berlin passing between the German Federal Republic and West Berlin, will temporarily be exercised by the command of Soviet troops in Germany, pending the conclusion of an appropriate agreement." *Documents*, p. 189.

1958–1962 were the 1955 policy goals. The Soviets never really wanted Germany to rearm. They controlled East German rearmament and had little to fear from it. But they regarded Bonn's rearmament with dread and foreboding. In their minds, Bonn's new army, the Bundeswehr, appeared as old German militarism dressed in American fatigues.

The depth of feeling about Germany retained by Soviet leaders was strikingly apparent in 1955 when they invited Chancellor Konrad Adenauer to Moscow to negotiate diplomatic relations with Bonn. As a condition for relations, Adenauer insisted on the release of German prisoners of war. This issue produced angry exchanges as the former enemies tortured each other with memories of the brutalities each had inflicted on the other in 1941–1945. Bulganin and Khrushchev raged about the slaughter of the Soviet population. Adenauer reminded them of atrocities the Red Army committed across Eastern and Central Europe. However, Adenauer took pains to distance himself from Hitler, saying: "I would have strangled Hitler with my own hands." Klaus Mehnert captured the spirit of the exchange:

> The main characters were not those present at the conference table in the Spiridonovka Palace, but the dead and wounded, the prisoners of war and those ravaged in the years 1941–45. They caused a sudden darkening of the bright conference room and filled the hearts and the lips of the men who were negotiating. In a German legend the ghosts of the men killed in the great battles of European history continued their fight for many years afterward; the contest on the battlefield was so violent that they could not find peace. Russian mythology contains similar legends. I was reminded of it again and again on that Saturday. The sufferings and emotions of the years 1941 through 1945 were still so much alive that even the wise, nearly eighty-year-old Chancellor, with his iron nerves, could not help being upset. It all probably had to be said once, because too much had been accumulated in the feelings of both peoples, and a valve had to be opened.[5]

5. Klaus Mehnert, *Osteuropa*, Stuttgart, December, 1955, p. 451, cited in Dallin, *op. cit.*, pp. 264-265; see also Wilhelm Backhaus, *Begegnung in Kreml: So würden die Gefengenen befreit* (Meeting at the Kremlin: Thus Were the Prisoners Liberated) (Berlin: Ullstein Verlag, 1955); Konrad Adenauer, *Erinnerungen, 1953–1955* (Memoirs) (Stuttgart: Deutsche Verlag-Anstalt, 1966), chapter 13.

Both sides purged themselves of pent-up emotions. Bonn agreed to restore relations and the Soviets to release German prisoners.

Even though relations were established in 1955, no territorial claims were settled. The Second World War still survives in the claims Bonn and Moscow have to the territories that lie between them. Bonn claims to speak for Germans in East Germany and has an interest in the Oder-Neisse territories—the former German provinces occupied by the Soviet Union and Poland at the end of the war. In 1954, Bonn renounced the use of force to achieve any eastern objectives and, as a practical matter, depends on NATO to defend West German territory. Bonn keeps its claims alive for bargaining purposes when, someday, a settlement can be reached. To Bonn, the claims have value in international law.[6]

To the Soviets, international legalists in their fashion, Bonn's claims must be formally and irrevocably withdrawn. The Soviet Union is as unhappy about the absence of a peace treaty deciding the territorial issues in its favor as the United States is about the absence of a written agreement regulating Berlin access. Moscow still wants the temporary border settlement in the Potsdam protocol of 1945 to be legally acknowledged by the Western powers. If they are willing, presumably Bonn would be compelled to acknowledge the Potsdam settlement as a permanent legal one.

In line with the 1955 policy decision to promote two Germanies —disarmed and neutral, recognized as such in international law— Premier Bulganin in December 1957 proposed a summit conference to discuss creation of a nuclear-free zone in Central Europe embracing West Germany, East Germany, Poland, and Czechoslovakia. President Eisenhower objected to this proposal because it did not address the division of Germany which the United States preferred to resolve first.[7] The Soviets pursued their proposal well into 1958, beginning in February with the offer of a foreign ministers' conference to prepare a summit agenda for considering creation of a nuclear-free zone, reduction in the numbers of foreign troops in Germany, and—

---

6. Wilhelm G. Grewe, " 'The Eastern Problem' in German Foreign Policy," 1959, Mimeograph. The Treaty of August 12, 1970 signed in Moscow by Chancellor Willy Brandt and Premier Alexei Kosygin holds these claims in reserve without abandoning them. The treaty is primarily a renunciation of force agreement. Cf. Federal Republic of Germany, Press and Information Office, The Treaty of August 12, 1970, Wiesbaden, 1970, p. 8.

7. *Documents*, p. 263.

an item unmentioned in Bulganin's December letter—conclusion of a German peace treaty. "Of course," the February aide memoire said, "the question of unification of the German Democratic Republic and Federal German Republic into one state . . . cannot be the subject of consideration at a forthcoming conference at the Summit." Secretary of State John Foster Dulles decided there was little point to another summit conference if the Soviets proposed to ignore the results of the last one in 1955 at Geneva. He argued that they had agreed at the 1955 summit that the great powers had a responsibility for the reunification of Germany.[8]

This unproductive dialogue continued through the spring of 1958. It ended abruptly in July, when crises in the Near East and Taiwan Straits seized the attention of Dulles and the Soviet leaders. A coup d'état in Baghdad removed Iraq from the Western camp, giving Eisenhower reason to feel he should send troops to Lebanon to stabilize the Near East. The Taiwan Straits crisis—Mao's bold attempt to isolate and subdue Chiang Kai-shek's garrisons on Quemoy and Matsu—followed on the heels of the Lebanon landing. In September, Moscow found time to inform the Western powers that it had received a diplomatic note from Pankow [9] proposing "the urgent creation" of a four-power commission to prepare a peace treaty and another commission composed of the two German governments to discuss reunification.[10] The State Department replied negatively. The German issue rested in a stalemate until November when Khrushchev, with the crisis in the Far East clearly terminated, turned back to the subject of a German peace treaty.

The Soviets persisted with Bulganin's proposal for a Central European nuclear-free zone because, again, they were reacting to a new stage in the evolution of the Federal Republic. They now

8. *Ibid.*, p. 285; Dulles made much of the following statement in the 1955 summit communiqué: "The Heads of Government, recognizing their common responsibility for the settlement of the German question and the reunification of Germany, have agreed that the settlement of the German question and the reunification of Germany by means of free elections shall be carried out in conformity with the national interests of the German people and the interests of European security." The preceding paragraph in the communiqué, on European security, was of much greater interest to Moscow.

9. The seat of the government in East Germany is located in Pankow, a borough of East Berlin.

10. George D. Embree (ed.), *The Soviet Union and the German Question,* September 1958–June 1961 (The Hague: Martinus Nijhoff, 1963), pp. 3-4.

perceived that West German rearmament would include access to nuclear weapons. In Bulganin's December 1957 letter, he referred to the United States plan to deploy intermediate-range nuclear weapons (IRBM's) in Western Europe. In November 1957, Secretary of Defense Neil McElroy announced to a NATO parliamentarians' conference that the United States wanted to establish IRBM sites in Europe and would consider granting allied control, not just of the launching vehicles, but of the warheads as well.[11] This proposal, with the implication of nuclear weapons in the hands of the Bundeswehr, the West German army, staggered the Soviets. Secretary Dulles, at a press conference, tried to be more explicit than McElroy, stating that the U.S. wanted "a very considerable measure of allied participation." He did not say that any allied power would have access to warheads.[12]

Bulganin expressed the Kremlin's fears openly when he wrote: "One likewise cannot fail to take into account, for example, the fact that the placing of nuclear weapons at the disposal of the Federal Republic of Germany may set in motion such forces in Europe and entail such consequences as even the NATO members may not contemplate."[13] The Soviets thus reacted to the awful possibilities they foresaw by proposing a summit conference to consider alternatives to the McElroy plan for NATO. Bulganin proposed a nuclear-free zone to prevent Bonn from acquiring direct or proximate access to nuclear weapons.

Bulganin's letter arrived in Washington on December 10, 1957. A few days later, the NATO foreign ministers held their annual meeting in Paris and agreed to the following plan: (1) bilateral agreements would be negotiated by the United States and interested allied governments for the deployment of IRBM's; (2) any decision actually to use the missiles would be a joint one, the United States retaining control of the warheads, the host ally control of the launching vehicles; and (3) nuclear warheads would be stockpiled in Europe under the custody of General Lauris Norstad, NATO supreme commander.

During 1958, Bonn urged the Eisenhower Administration to proceed in deploying nuclear weapons to West Germany in terms of the December 1957 NATO agreement ensuring American control of

---

11. *The New York Times*, November 16, 1957, p. 1.
12. *Ibid.*, November 20, 1957, p. 1.
13. *Documents*, p. 254.

warheads. In the same period, Moscow persisted with its alternative of regional disarmament. This struggle between Bonn and Moscow for influence over the direction of United States policy in Europe provided the immediate context for the Berlin crisis beginning in November. The crisis compelled the United States to pay attention to the alternatives Moscow outlined. Throughout the entire crisis over Berlin 1958–1962, the United States was caught between the rival demands of Bonn and Moscow. United States efforts to find some ground between the two for terminating the Berlin crisis and providing European security invariably got vetoed by Bonn or Moscow. The United States listened to Bonn as an ally, of course, but Khrushchev could always catch the ear of the President by reheating the crisis and threatening to blockade the exposed city.

The acute issue of nuclear weapons in Germany arose because of the Eisenhower Administration's decision in the autumn of 1957 to request the NATO Council for agreement to deploy them. But that decision, in turn, was a reaction to the spectacular space satellite launchings by the Soviet Union in late summer, 1957. The boosters necessary for the launchings implied that the Soviets had the capacity to develop missiles of intercontinental range (ICBM's). Bulganin, in his December letter, alluded to this factor: "It is also very obvious that all such activity [the U.S. plan for IRBM deployments in Europe] is taking place in an atmosphere of artificially created nervousness and fear with respect to the imaginary threat from the USSR and, in the effort to create such an atmosphere, particularly wide use is being made of references to the latest scientific and technical achievements of the Soviet Union." [14]

Perhaps if Khrushchev had not so obviously tried to blackmail British Prime Minister Anthony Eden and French Premier Guy Mollet in the 1956 Suez crisis—threatening their countries with utter destruction unless their troops withdrew from the Canal Zone—and, generally, to make political hay out of Soviet nuclear capabilities, the administration might not have felt compelled to move its available IRBM's to within range of the Soviet Union after the latest development in Soviet nuclear power.[15] The National Security Council reached the conclusion that the U.S. could survive the political

14. *Ibid.*, p. 252.
15. For an analysis of Khrushchev's behavior in the Suez crisis, see Hans Speier, "Soviet Atomic Blackmail and the North Atlantic Alliance," *World Politics*, 19 (April 1957), 307-328.

repercussions of an alleged "missile gap" favoring the Soviet Union by deploying missiles to Europe, much as Khrushchev decided in 1962 when he confronted a "missile gap" favoring the United States and deployed missiles to Cuba. In both instances, intermediate-range missiles were used as surrogate ICBM's, simply moved forward to cover the distance to target an ICBM could reach from greater distances.

Even in his letter to Eisenhower, Bulganin did not refrain from stressing that the new developments in Soviet nuclear power meant the territory of the United States would no longer be a sanctuary in the event of general war. He argued that forward deployment of United States missiles would not lessen the vulnerability of the United States itself. The administration, however, wanted to avoid a potential crisis of confidence in NATO resulting from doubts about the willingness of the United States to jeopardize itself in defending Western Europe. By sending missiles to Europe, the administration locked the United States into the defense of its allies much as NATO's dependence on the presence of American ground troops in West Germany had done earlier.

The development of long-range missiles by the Soviet Union and repeated use of this development by the Soviet leaders for political purposes created a chain of events. The Eisenhower Administration's reaction to the Soviets' newly acquired missile power produced, in turn, a protest from Bulganin that led eventually, as events tumbled from one quarter of the globe to another in 1958, to the Berlin crisis late in the year.

1. *A Trial Balloon*

The "deadline crisis" of 1958 began with the Soviet note of November 27, containing a deadline of six months before which, Moscow insisted, negotiations about the future of Berlin had to be productive. Before sending the note, Khrushchev floated a trial balloon carrying the major provisions to be included in the note.

Speaking at a Soviet-Polish Friendship Meeting in Moscow on November 10, he lectured the Western powers on the real results of the Potsdam protocol. This protocol between the United States, Britain, and the Soviet Union in August 1945 banned any substantial German rearmament and required an emphasis on "agriculture and peaceful domestic industries." [16] Khrushchev proudly noted that the Soviet Union had observed the measures of the protocol, to which the "anti-militarist, anti-fascist workers' state" of East Germany bore witness. By contrast, West Germany had taken a different path. Aided by the Western powers, he claimed, "militarism, far from having been eradicated, is rearing its head ever higher . . .," fascist generals and admirals are reconstructing the Wehrmacht—the Nazi army—and West German industry is redeveloping on a massive scale in the service of German militarism.

The Western allies, he suggested, had violated the protocol in all respects save one. The West retained its military presence in West Berlin because Western policy needed a source of subversion against the East German state—the Deutsche Demokratische Republik (DDR). Khrushchev said he saw no point in perpetuating the Western garrisons as a provision of the Potsdam protocol when the other provisions had been grossly violated. Therefore, he concluded:

> The time has obviously arrived for the signatories of the Potsdam Agreement to renounce the remnants of the occupation regime in Berlin and thereby make it possible to create a normal situation in the capital of the German Democratic Republic. The Soviet Union, for its part, would hand over to the sovereign German Democratic Republic the functions in Berlin that are still exercised by Soviet agencies.[17]

He apparently wished to convey the impression that the Soviet Union would withdraw unilaterally from the occupation agencies in which it still participated in Berlin. Eventually, in August 1962, the USSR disengaged selectively. It abolished the Soviet commandant's office in Karlshorst, a section of East Berlin, but retained an air control staff at the Berlin Air Safety Center and in other similar posts. The circumstances of the withdrawal in 1962, however, were very different from those in which he announced his intentions in 1958.

Secretary of State Dulles, at his next press conference, alluded to one curious point in Khrushchev's description of the Potsdam protocol. Khrushchev attributed the occupation of Berlin to the Potsdam protocol of 1945, when, in fact, the occupation derived from the

16. *Documents*, pp. 29-39.
17. *Ibid.*, p. 324.

occupation protocol of 1944.[18] The Potsdam protocol concerned the regulation of German political and economic life in the occupation zones well established by the time of the Potsdam Conference.[19] Dulles thought that Khrushchev's legal advisers simply made a mistake, and Khrushchev did acknowledge the correct origin later. Dulles may have diagnosed this curiosity accurately. Or Khrushchev may have attributed the origin of the occupation to the Potsdam protocol in order to overturn the remnants of the occupation regime more readily. Contending that the West had broken the Potsdam protocol by sponsoring the growth of the Federal Republic, he was at liberty to do the same, in this case, to terminate the occupation status of Berlin. This interpretation suggests that he deliberately rewrote history to favor his case. In any event, on November 10 he anticipated his later tactics in using the occupation issue and the status of Berlin as a lever for moving the Western powers to alter the status quo.

2. The Soviet Note of November 27, 1958

The Soviets dispatched a diplomatic note from Moscow addressed to the other three occupation powers in Berlin and to Bonn demanding a "solution" of the Berlin question in six months. The note constituted a bold and assertive move not altogether reflected in the press comment of the time.[20] The note offered a forecast of Soviet policy and action over the next four years. The Soviets probably did not expect the crisis to become as protracted as it did, but the claims they staked out for themselves in the note did not change, even though, periodically, they restated them in new form.[21]

A free city proposal was the central point of the note:

18. See *ibid.*, pp. 1-8.
19. See *ibid.*, pp. 29-39.
20. The press generally fastened on the deadline clause and interpreted it to mean that the Soviets had postponed any immediate action for six months. The *Times* (London) spoke of a "period of grace" and *The New York Times* reported a "sense of relief" in the British Foreign Office. *The Times* (London), November 28, 1958, p. 2; *The New York Times*, November 28, 1958, p. 12. The State Department was also reported "relieved at delay," *ibid.*, November 29, p. 1. These reactions were understandable in the context, however, because Soviet Ambassador Smirnov in Bonn previously had said the Soviets hoped to have the problem solved by Christmas.
21. For the text of the note, see *Documents*, pp. 348-363.

The Soviet Government on its part would consider it possible to solve the West Berlin question at the present time by the conversion of West Berlin into an independent political unit—a free city, without any state, including both existing German states, interfering in its life. Specifically it might be possible to agree that the territory of the free city be demilitarized and that no armed forces be contained therein. The free city, West Berlin, could have its own government and run its own economic, administrative, and other affairs.[22]

To achieve this solution, the Soviets proposed that the Soviet Union, the United States, Britain, France, the Federal Republic, and the DDR all offer guarantees for the free city status of West Berlin. The Soviets also invited the United Nations to approve the arrangement. West Berlin would be expected to negotiate with the DDR for access to West Germany.

For its part of the bargain, West Berlin would have to pledge not to permit "any hostile subversive activity" against the DDR. The Soviets acclaimed their solution to the Berlin question as a settlement which should be satisfactory to all parties. They offered to underwrite West Berlin's economy "by placing orders for industrial goods . . . and by regular deliveries on a commercial basis of the necessary quantities of raw materials and food stuffs. . . ." They suggested that West Berlin could prosper more under the new status than under the occupation regime.

Although the Soviet Union disclaimed any desire to annex West Berlin, it granted itself and the DDR a prominent place in the free city. As a former occupying power in all-Berlin—which virtually meant East Berlin—the Soviet Union proposed to join in the guarantees for West Berlin, an advance over its previous position. A desire to enhance Soviet influence over the population of West Berlin is also evident from its offer to underwrite the West Berlin economy, an opportunity previously unavailable. The most pointed aspects of the proposal were the provisions for demilitarizing the free city and for granting the DDR control of the access routes. All of these provisions made the proposal suspect because they would cause West Berlin to lose the means to sustain itself. Without independent military resources and communications, how could the Soviets speak of the city as "an independent political unit"? If the free city de-

22. *Ibid.*, p. 360.

pended on the continued suffrance of the Soviet Union and the DDR for its freedom, technically, the "free city" would be a misnomer.

As a legal agreement between the Western powers and the DDR, the pact guaranteeing the new status of West Berlin would bestow Western diplomatic recognition upon the DDR. The DDR's gain would be the Federal Republic's loss. Bonn could no longer act as the sole recognized representative of the German people as the Western powers, in the 1954 Paris protocols, stated it should be.

The deadline clause was contained in the following passage:

> The Soviet Government proposes to make no changes in the present procedure for military traffic of the USA, Great Britain, and France from West Berlin to the FRG for half a year. It regards such a period as fully sufficient to provide a sound basis for the solution of the questions connected with the change in Berlin's situation. . . .[23]

The Western powers had until May 27, 1959, to negotiate an agreement embodying the free city proposal. The Soviets said no other proposal would be acceptable.

To prod the Western powers in the desired direction, the note included a threat to act unilaterally and to disrupt the Berlin access routes:

> If the above-mentioned period is not utilized to reach an adequate agreement the Soviet Union will then carry out the planned measures through an agreement with the GDR. It is envisaged that the German Democratic Republic, like any other independent state must fully deal with questions concerning its space, i.e., exercise its sovereignty on land, on water, and in the air.[24]

And to stir up public opinion in Western countries, the note ended in a recitation of the horrors of war.

One section toward the end of the note illustrated how the Soviet Union used its new missile power for political purposes: "He who

---

23. *Documents*, p. 361; Hans Speier regarded this statement as an ultimatum. While subject to manipulation, he said, it was more direct and unequivocal than similar, but implied, Soviet ultimata in the Suez crisis of 1956 and the Taiwan Straits crisis of 1958. *Divided Berlin: The Anatomy of Soviet Blackmail* (New York: Frederick A. Praeger, 1961), pp. 31-32.

24. *Documents*, p. 361.

today speaks of non-recognition of the steps planned by the Soviet Union obviously would like to talk with the latter not in the language of reason and well-founded arguments but in the language of brute force, forgetting that the Soviet people are not affected by threats . . ." The Soviets aimed their warning at Dulles in particular—the alleged brinkman. Dulles was warned not to interfere as the Soviet Union, the injured party under the Potsdam protocol, pressed for redress of its grievances in Berlin:

> Methods of blackmail and reckless threats of force will be least of all appropriate in solving such a problem as the Berlin question. Such methods will not help solve a single question, but can only bring the situation to the danger point. But only madmen can go to the length of unleashing another world war over the preservation of privileges of occupiers in West Berlin. If such madmen should really appear, there is no doubt that strait jackets could be found for them . . . Any violation of the frontiers of the German Democratic Republic, Poland, or Czechoslovakia, any agressive action against any member state of the Warsaw treaty will be regarded by all its participants as an act of agression against them all and will immediately cause appropriate retaliation.[25]

This kind of language appeared in Khrushchev's correspondence with Eisenhower in both the Near East and Taiwan Straits crises. In the latter crisis, Eisenhower considered the intent of one of the letters so intimidating that he refused to accept it.[26]

Another aspect of the note is interesting for its psychology. The note portrayed the situation in Berlin as abnormal. Time had passed Berlin by, the note suggested, while the DDR developed and matured. It argued that the Western presence in West Berlin was an anachronism, sustained by incredible "feelings of hatred for communism." By contrast, it advertised the Soviet proposal, in tune with the times, as the ally of reason. In couching their argument in terms of a political psychology, the Soviet leaders expressed the aspect of their position that most troubled Dulles. Granting the West no rational ground for remaining in West Berlin, they conveyed the impression that the West could not be serious in holding onto its position there.

25. *Ibid.*, p. 362.
26. Morton H. Halperin (ed.), *Sino-Soviet Relations and Arms Control* (Cambridge: The MIT Press, 1967), p. 284.

It was as if the West would be bluffing if it declared the status of Berlin unalterable. Thus, Western decision-makers could not ignore the possibility that the Soviets were embarked upon an extraordinarily ambitious postwar confrontation to turn United States policy in Europe around and to point it in directions more compatible with Soviet long-range objectives. At a minimum, the Soviets were trying to undermine the legitimacy of the Berlin status quo.

On the evening of November 27, Chairman Khrushchev held a press conference on the subject of the note just released, an unprecedented practice for him. When asked why the Soviet government had selected this particular time to make its proposal, Khrushchev candidly stated that the Western powers had raised an "obstacle to the conclusion of a peace treaty . . . in their willingness to recognize realities of life"—two Germanies. His answer implied that the note had been sent because the Western powers had refused negotiations about a nuclear-free zone earlier in the year at the summit or any other level. Summing up his case, Khrushchev stated:

> One must proceed from the real facts. There is a divided Berlin where the occupation regime is still maintained. The war ended more than 13 years ago. Every normal person, I think, finds such a situation abnormal. It is necessary, therefore, to find a solution that will end this abnormality, because the present existence of the occupation regime serves no positive purpose at all.[27]

In reply to a question about the feasibility of negotiations if the Soviet proposal were the only one discussed, Khrushchev said there would be nothing to discuss if the United States "rejects as a whole the question posed in our document." However, he welcomed a move "to specify and discuss our proposals." In the context of the press conference which was free of the bluster and threats contained in the note, Khrushchev's answer appeared to indicate a certain flexibility. The very fact that he held a press conference for the purpose of entertaining questions on the note added to the appearance of flexibility. However, by holding a press conference on the same day Moscow released the note, he underlined the message of the note.

Khrushchev intimated on November 29 that the Soviet Union would take no unilateral action if the West were willing to *begin*

27. Embree, *op. cit.*, p. 42.

negotiations in six months.[28] This remark qualified the urgent terms of the note that "adequate agreement" had to *be achieved* within six months. On the day before Khrushchev dropped his hint of Soviet desires, a Soviet diplomat in East Berlin went even further than the Chairman in stating that Moscow would not be rigid about the six-month time limit.[29]

3. *Berlin as a Lever*

The initial United States reaction to the note ignored the narrowness of Soviet terms for negotiations. This reaction provided the Soviets with an opportunity to clarify their demands before the crisis was a month old. New York and Washington newspapers asserted that, contrary to what the Soviets said, the note was not directed at a Berlin solution as much as at negotiations on German reunification and European security. James Reston reported that the State Department viewed the Soviet proposal on Berlin as an opportunity to reopen larger issues of European security. Walter Lippman suggested the Soviets intended to employ the Berlin problem "as an instrument for raising the whole question of Germany." [30]

Replying on December 3 to these assertions, the Soviet government organ, *Izvestiia*, objected to the United States raising larger issues. Specifically, *Izvestiia* denied the possibility of treating German reunification as a subject of four-power negotiations and emphasized Berlin as the issue at hand. It commented on Reston's report by criticizing the State Department for "artificially stringing on some problems to others." [31]

Press comment in December 1958 reflected the reactions of Secretary Dulles and officials in the State Department. In expressing the view that the Soviet Union really wanted to consider a wider range of subjects than Berlin, the Department did not read the *Izvestiia* statement at face value. *The New York Times* reported the following

28. Khrushchev made his remark at an Albanian Embassy reception. The Soviet press did not report it. Speier, *Divided Berlin*, p. 11.

29. *The New York Times*, November 29, 1958, p. 1; in Pankow, Ulbricht appeared more rigid. In an interview with Sydney Gruson he stated that an allied airlift defying a Soviet transfer of traffic management to the DDR would constitute a military threat to the DDR. *The New York Times*, November 30, 1958, p. 1.

30. *The New York Times*, December 1, 1958; *The Herald Tribune*, December 2, 1958, p. 22.

31. *The New York Times*, December 4, 1958, p. 1.

statements attributed to "one Western diplomat": "What we are saying . . . is that we don't think the Russians meant what their note in fact said—namely, that if the Western powers did not agree to discuss making Berlin a demilitarized free city there was no topic left to talk on the Berlin question by the former occupation powers." The diplomat said that the West's ignoring passages in the note gave them "the benefit of whatever slight doubt there might be. All they need to do to keep in the clear is to keep quiet." [32]

At the time, the Soviets themselves did not make as much of a distinction between what they said and what they meant as the Department assumed. The Soviet note of November 27 contained much bluff and bluster. But the threat of unilateral action in the note served the specific policy task of moving the Western powers to consider the free city proposal. In the Berlin crisis, the Soviets generally said what they meant. In the note of November 27, they clearly stated the solution to the Berlin question they preferred: the free city proposal.[33]

The State Department treated Soviet diplomatic communications as mere propaganda. The Department freely substituted its own version of Soviet objectives for the objectives the Soviets actually had in mind. This practice of the Department allowed speculation about the "real intentions" hidden behind Soviet rhetoric and ignored the possibility that major Soviet documents, speeches, and diplomatic

32. *The New York Times*, January 1, 1959, p. 1; also December 3, 1958, p. 1.
33. Alexander George has described how Soviet and American approaches to risk calculation and risk acceptance differ. United States decision-makers control their risks by limiting their objectives. Soviet leaders, in contrast, accept far-reaching objectives and control their risks by limiting their means. George notes that Western decision-makers do not appreciate the distinction between the two approaches. "As for Western leaders and publics, their tendency to perceive and interpret Soviet risk-acceptance behavior erroneously from the standpoint of their own approach to risk calculation inclined them to make distorted judgments regarding Soviet intentions and the riskiness and significance of Soviet cold war initiatives. (One may note that, over time, Western leaders have perhaps come to understand better the Soviet approach to risk calculation and risk acceptance)." "The 'Operational Code': A Neglected Approach to the Study of Political Leaders and Decision-Making," *International Studies Quarterly*, 13 (June 1969), 215. George's analysis applies to the State Department's perception of Soviet behavior in the Berlin crisis. The Department did not believe that the far-reaching goals in the Soviets' free city proposal represented their intentions. They must be willing to settle for less, the Department assumed. In the Berlin crisis, Secretary Dulles substituted his own judgment of Soviet risk acceptance for the Soviets' preferred style of behavior, a style markedly different from Dulles'. This problem is discussed further in Chapter 2.

correspondence were quite carefully composed and intended to indicate Soviet official views.

Thus, the State Department perceived an implied willingness in the Soviet note to negotiate about Germany and European security, including Berlin. Since these broader questions were what the United States preferred to negotiate anyway, the Department, in effect, read its preferences into the note. Naturally, the Department wanted to negotiate on issues of greatest interest to the United States. The remarkable fact is that it believed it could negotiate on those issues in a heated atmosphere without misleading the Soviets to expect pressure tactics to produce concessions. If, however, the Department read the note at face value as a strictly Berlin proposal, as *Izvestiia* urged, a serious question remained whether the United States should be willing to enter negotiations under crisis conditions. Secretary Dulles had to decide whether or not to negotiate in the crisis and that decision rested on how he and the Department read the note.

In deference to the Western problem of note reading, it should be said that the Soviet position contained many elements, not all of which were revealed in the November 27 note. In their note, the Soviets used the Berlin proposal as the anchor of their position and the exclusive subject of the proposed negotiations. Yet they raised the "deadline crisis" to bring about negotiations for a nuclear-free zone to be embodied in a German peace treaty. It is important to observe that for them a Berlin settlement conditioned the broader negotiations in which they were interested. The Department accurately perceived that the Soviets were interested in discussing Germany and European security. But the Department discounted Moscow's insistence that unless Berlin were settled first the broader issues could not be satisfactorily discussed.

In the Soviet view the free city proposal operated as a pilot project for changing the status quo in Germany and Europe. Indeed, if the Western powers could accept the free city proposal as a model of change they would be psychologically prepared to accept the other "realities," as Moscow called them, of two Germanies and the forces favoring a nuclear-free zone. The Soviets, at any rate, had linked all the issues together.[34] Thus, the Soviets raised other issues in their Berlin proposal, but they raised them in a special way to favor their

---

34. The close and ingenious linkage between the free city proposal, diplomatic recognition of the DDR, and a nuclear-free zone is examined in detail in Chapter 3.

cause. The Soviets objected to the manner in which the United States approached negotiations and were quick to insist that Berlin should be the focus. Their deadline focused negotiations on Berlin because they directed the threat of unilateral action—conveyed by the deadline—against West Berlin.

Soviet reactions to the State Department's response to the note bear out this interpretation of the Soviet position. On December 12, in response to preliminary American statements about the note, Tass news service charged that the United States refused to assess soberly the situation emerging in Europe caused by the occupation regime in West Berlin. It rejected the State Department's attempt "to avoid" a Berlin solution by "speculation on the problem of German reunification" and, for the moment, stated that "the preparation and conclusion of a German peace treaty is another matter." [35]

On December 16, the NATO Ministerial Council issued a declaration expressing the decision of the Western powers to enter into broad negotiations. The declaration rebuffed Moscow's demand for narrow negotiations: "The Council considers that the Berlin question can only be settled in the framework of an agreement with the USSR on Germany as a whole. It recalls that the Western powers have repeatedly declared themselves ready to examine this problem as well as those of European security and disarmament." [36]

Soviet Foreign Minister Andrei Gromyko reacted on December 25 by saying that the Western powers had not "correctly understood the intentions of the Soviet Union." In so far as they were reading "hidden motives" into the Soviet position, they were mistaken. "But the Soviet government has nothing to conceal. In making its proposals on the Berlin question it is guided by the sole desire to put an end to the dangerous situation prevailing in West Berlin." [37] Gromyko referred to the NATO interest in linking a Berlin solution to German reunification as a "trick" for postponing a Berlin settlement.

4. *The Soviet Draft Peace Treaty*

On January 10, 1959, the Soviet Union presented a draft peace treaty for Germany to the Western powers, revealing their full

35. Embree, *op. cit.*, p. 53.
36. *Documents*, p. 365.
37. Embree, *op. cit.*, p. 76.

position. The accompanying note employed language similar to the Soviet note on Berlin of November 27, speaking of "that entirely abnormal situation" resulting from the delay in concluding a peace treaty with Germany and recognizing the DDR. The Kremlin proposed a peace conference for March 1959 in Warsaw or Prague to which both Germanies would be invited to sign the treaty "in the name of Germany."

By submitting a draft treaty so soon after the note of November 27, the Soviets maintained momentum for their campaign. The Western allies had just replied on December 21 to the earlier note and now faced another major document before the "deadline crisis" prompted by the first note had been resolved. More importantly, the note accompanying the draft treaty linked the treaty to a Berlin settlement:

> The Soviet Government expresses the hope that the Government of the United States of America will study with the necessary attention the proposals brought forward and also the attached draft of a peace treaty . . . *together with this* it would like to believe that the Government of the United States of America . . . will draw the necessary conclusions from the situation of the Berlin question . . . [my emphasis].[38]

The note and draft treaty of January 10 were part of the same effort expressed in the note of November 27. Much of the January 10 note, discussing a peace treaty, actually dealt with Berlin. In this note, the Soviets categorically rejected any four-power discussion of German reunification. The notes of November 27 and January 10 both argued for a Berlin settlement. The first note demanded a settlement directly; the second note demanded it as a prerequisite to a peace treaty. The November note proposed narrow negotiations on Berlin only; the January note made a bid for broad negotiations on the narrow basis of a prior Berlin solution.

The draft treaty itself revealed that Moscow intended the free city proposal to work as a model solution for Germany as a whole. The features of the new Germany were substantially identical to those of the free city.[39] The new Germany, like the new West Berlin, would be independent, demilitarized, and engaged in peaceful production. Moreover, the Soviets designed the peace treaty and the free city

38. *Documents*, p. 389.
39. For the text of the treaty proposal, see *ibid.*, pp. 389-401.

proposal to give them an effective veto in the deliberations leading to adoption. The preamble to the treaty indicates that one-third of the parties of the treaty would represent the Soviet position. Twenty-nine states, "as states which participated with their armed forces in the war against Germany," and Germany, "represented at the present time by the German Democratic Republic and the Federal Republic of Germany," would participate in the peace conference. By restricting the conference to the states which had fought against Germany rather than including all those which had declared war, and by placing the DDR on equal footing with the Federal Republic, one-third of the delegations could be relied upon to support the Soviet draft of a treaty or to veto any other version. In the note of November 27, an identical proportion—one-third—of the guarantors of the free city status of West Berlin would possess a veto.

The draft peace treaty omitted any provision for the reunification of Germany. This omission offered further evidence that the Soviet Union did not intend to discuss solutions of most interest to the Western powers, particularly the Federal Republic. In Article 22, the parties to the peace conference were to conclude a treaty with two Germanies. Reunification, if it occurred at all, would come about in the post-treaty period on the basis of "a rapprochement . . . between the German Democratic Republic and the Federal Republic of Germany." Article 23 specifically prohibited Bonn's version of reunification and Article 8 kept the demarcation line between the two Germanies in place. The treaty actually provided for three Germanies. The text incorporated the free city proposal which appeared as Article 25:

> Until the re-establishment of the unity of Germany and the creation of a unified German state, West Berlin will be in a position of a demilitarized free city on the basis of its own special statute.[40]

The draft treaty left the DDR relatively untouched. DDR sovereignty would be extended to all traffic on the Berlin access routes. By contrast, the provisions of the treaty made it clear that the Federal Republic would have to revert to Potsdam-like conditions in the post-treaty period. Bonn could not participate in any military alliance, e.g., NATO. It could not continue to ban the West German

40. *Ibid.*, p. 396.

Communist party or continue to allow anti-Soviet groups or parties in West Germany. It could not allow any foreign troops, military bases, or nuclear weapons on its territory. It would have a "peace economy." Khrushchev had argued on November 10 that these were criteria the DDR already had met or to which it could easily adapt. The government in Bonn regarded the draft treaty as a very harsh document.[41]

5. The Changing Status Quo

The draft peace treaty for Germany and the free city proposal for Berlin announced the Soviet Union's objectives in the Berlin crisis. Western leaders in 1958 could not be certain that Khrushchev really expected to achieve his objectives. They could only know that he intended to move them toward his objectives. And he certainly could not know how far he could move them. Probably he planned to probe and push where and when he could, depending on the evolution of the crisis, and to match his opportunities to his objectives.

Khrushchev perceived that in the case of Germany the status quo could be manipulated. His belief is illustrated by a statement he made on Germany in December 1957. He said, "On the basis of the status quo conditions could be created for the solution of the German problem." [42] In other words, he regarded the two Germanies as a given "basis" of things, but—more noteworthy—as a starting point from which he could proceed toward "created" conditions improving upon the place of the two Germanies in Europe.

After an interview with Khrushchev in October 1958, Walter Lippman described Khrushchev's view of the status quo:

> In his mind, the social and economic revolution now in progress in Russia, China, and elsewhere in Asia and Africa *is* the status quo and he wants us to recognize it as such. In his mind, opposition to this revolution is an attempt to change the status quo. Whereas we think of the status quo as the situation as it exists at the moment, he thinks of it as the process of revolutionary change which is in progress. He wants us to recognize the revolution not only as it is but as it is going to be [emphasis his].[43]

41. *The Christian Science Monitor*, January 13, 1959, p. 2.
42. Cited in David J. Dallin, *op. cit.*, p. 506.
43. *The Communist World and Ours* (Boston: Little, Brown and Co., 1959), p. 13.

Khrushchev's optimism and implied philosophy of history did not receive much recognition from Western analysts grappling with the implications of the "deadline crisis." Although most analysts agreed that he desired changes in the Berlin occupation regime, they did not as readily agree that he wanted changes in Germany at large. Some British analysts, for example, thought he intended only to consolidate the Soviet position in Central Europe to prevent any further uprisings, as had actually occurred in East Germany in 1953 and in Poland and Hungary in 1956. This opinion represented the traditional Western concept of the status quo, noted by Lippman, as a set of fixed conditions and did not acknowledge the dynamism Khrushchev attributed to the status quo as a process of historical change. The British and American press speculated that internal political and economic weaknesses of the DDR compelled the Soviet initiative.[44] By 1958, however, Premier Walter Ulbricht of the DDR had actually strengthened his internal position.[45] The static concepts inherent in the speculation did not fully account for the crisis.

J. M. Mackintosh, a British analyst, suspected that the Soviet Union was searching for ways to achieve long-term security. Gromyko confirmed this rationale, later, at the Geneva Conference of 1959. Mackintosh believed that the "deadline crisis" was caused by the Soviet reaction to the NATO agreement of the previous year for emplacing tactical nuclear weapons of the United States on the Continent. He regarded both the note of November 27 and the draft peace treaty as tactics in the campaign for a nuclear-free zone.[46] Richard Löwenthal, writing from Berlin, assessed the crisis in terms compatible with Khrushchev's perception of the status quo. He granted that Khrushchev's demands would consolidate the Soviet position in Central Europe. But he also stressed that whatever the intention, the proposal would severely hurt the West.[47] The Soviet

44. For a description of this "defensive theory," as he calls it, see John Mander, *Berlin, Hostage for the West* (Baltimore: Penguin Books, Inc., 1962), pp. 103-104. Cf. *The Herald Tribune*, December 2, 1958, p. 22, where Lippmann speaks of the Soviets' "dread of another Hungary."

45. Thomas A. Baylis, "The New Economic System," *Survey*, 61 (October 1966), 143.

46. J. M. Mackintosh, *Strategy and Tactics of Soviet Foreign Policy* (London: Oxford University Press, 1963), pp. 205-212, 214.

47. Richard Löwenthal, "The Impossible Defensive," *Encounter*, 17 (November 1961), pp. 22-23; see also Mander, *op. cit.*, pp. 107-109.

proposals, he suggested, would simultaneously strengthen the DDR and shatter the Federal Republic.

The working hypothesis of Khrushchev's Berlin policy used in this study is an adaptation of the Mackintosh and Löwenthal analyses written at the time. By 1958, any power which advocated fundamental changes in Germany confronted a highly structured situation which had developed and hardened over thirteen years. The issues still open for negotiation were now quite marginal. The DDR had developed in the East as an integral part of Moscow's European security zone, and the Federal Republic had developed in close relations with Western Europe and the United States. It was very late in the day to expect Bonn to submit to measures the Soviets proposed for reorienting the entire status quo.

In 1958, Khrushchev seemed unprepared to conclude that he could not make gains with crisis tactics. Given Bonn's alliance with Washington, he had to employ a low-risk strategy. But with the hubris he drew from the Soviet Union's achievement in missiles and rockets and the urgency he sensed for stopping or slowing the NATO program to arm West Germany with nuclear weapons, he was convinced he had to try.

6. The Role of the DDR

Pankow's relations with Moscow may help to explain some of the pressures on Khrushchev, pressures which affected the timing of several of his decisions throughout the whole conflict from 1958 until 1962. Ulbricht consolidated his own position within the East German Communist party in 1956 and 1957, using the economic and political disaster of 1953 to rationalize the elimination of his political opposition. He could not consolidate the rule of his party in East Germany until the Western powers legally recognized the regime. Ulbricht always felt more urgency than the Soviet leaders for resolving the Berlin question. West Berlin remained an acute embarrassment, if not denial, of DDR state sovereignty.[48]

48. Donald Zagoria observed: "Throughout the Berlin crisis, Ulbricht's speeches and threats have generally been more blatant than Khrushchev's. While this may be a calculated division of labor, it is also possible that Ulbricht seeks consciously to bring pressure on the Kremlin for a faster and fuller settlement of the crisis than the Russians would like to risk. There can be little doubt, at any rate, that Ulbricht plays his own game and that there are limits

Ulbricht served Khrushchev well during Khrushchev's struggle with Malenkov and Molotov in 1957. He probably convinced Khrushchev of the personal loyalty of the East German party. After the 1956 uprisings in Poland and Hungary, Moscow's and Pankow's international interests converged on the need for long-term stability in Eastern Europe. Ulbricht may have requested Khrushchev to support a drive for international recognition of the DDR. There is some evidence to suggest that Ulbricht made this kind of request earlier in 1958.[49]

On October 27, Ulbricht laid claim to West Berlin in a public address.[50] He referred to the city as originally "part of the Soviet zone of occupation," [51] ignoring the occupation protocol of 1944 and "Greater Berlin" as an area of joint four-power administration. As the heir of the Soviet Union in the Soviet zone, he implied that Pankow should exercise sovereignty over West Berlin and the access routes. Whether Ulbricht was more blunt than Khrushchev preferred is not known.

The pressure Ulbricht exerted on Khrushchev contained a Chinese dragon. Analysts differ about whether to date the origin of the Sino-

---

to the Soviet ability to force him into line." *The Sino-Soviet Conflict, 1956–1961* (New York: Atheneum, 1964), p. 396. Carola Stern agrees. For a brief history of Moscow-Pankow relations, see *Ulbricht, A Political Biography*, (New York: Frederick A. Praeger, 1965), chapters 5 and 6.

49. The State Department claimed to have information indicating that Ulbricht had petitioned Moscow to reopen the Berlin question. Eleanor Lansing Dulles, sister of Secretary Dulles and an official in the Department's German office, stated in a speech on February 21, 1959:

We know that Ulbricht went to Moscow, we know that he presented a complaint there. We know that as a result of this and various erroneous appraisals within the Kremlin made of the Western alliance . . . , that they thought the time came now to challenge what I call basic principles.

Contained in remarks of Representative Henry S. Reuss, *Congressional Record*, March 26, 1959 (mimeograph).

50. *The New York Times*, October 30, 1958, p. 4. He had been dropping hints and making assertions about West Berlin since 1956. Stern, *op. cit.*, pp. 185-186.

51. He made the same claim as the Soviet Military Governor prior to the Berlin blockade in 1948 and might have intended to revive fears of another blockade. For a discussion of Pankow's legal claims, see Peter Alfons Steiniger, "Rechts probleme der Entmilitarisierten Freien Stadt West Berlin," (Legal Problems of the Demilitarized Free City of West Berlin), *Probleme des Völkerrechts*, Band 2 (Berlin: Veb Deutscher Zentral Verlag, 1962).

Soviet dispute in 1958 or in 1959.[52] Zagoria argues that "an incipient Peking-Pankow axis" existed in both 1958 and 1959.[53] For example, East Germany expressed more sympathy than the Soviet Union for China's "Great Leap Forward" in that period.

Martin Esslin suggests that some aspects of Pankow's collectivization drive in 1960—"Socialist house communities," "workers meetings" at the end of the factory work day—seem to have been inspired by Chinese practices. High-level East German party and trade officials, including President Grotewohl, visited Peking in 1959 and 1960.[54]

If Zagoria and Esslin are correct, some guidelines for Ulbricht's Kremlin lobbying on Berlin can be discerned from Peking's stated position on international issues at the time. He probably did not espouse the Chinese position, but he may have been able to use it as an alternative appraisal of Moscow's foreign policy opportunities. On New Year's Day, Peking welcomed 1958 as a year of great advance: "Full Steam Ahead," "the east wind prevails over the west wind." [55] These slogans signaled the audacity with which Mao Tse-tung hoped to act that year, an audacity which strained the Sino-Soviet alliance, even if it did not break it, before year's end. Communist China, not a participant in the Near East and Berlin crises, optimistically appraised the opportunities for the Soviet Union in those crises and its own opportunities in the Taiwan Straits.[56]

The DDR as part of the Soviet camp could not lean very far toward endorsing the Communist Chinese appraisal of the international scene. Ulbricht seems to have admired the spirit of the Chinese revolution and perhaps took heart from the Chinese criticism of Khrushchev's general foreign policy as the criticism increased in volume and intensity in 1960, 1961, and 1962.[57] The growth of the Sino-Soviet dispute, which burst into public view during the prolonged Berlin crisis, may have enhanced Ulbricht's room for maneuver in Moscow.

52. Halperin, op. cit., chapter 10.
53. Zagoria, op. cit., p. 396.
54. Martin J. Esslin, "East Germany: Peking-Pankow Axis," The China Quarterly 3 (July–September 1960), pp. 85-88. The communiqué released by Grotewohl and Chinese Communist Foreign Minister Chen Yi on January 27, 1959, endorsing the Soviet peace treaty proposal appears in the Peking Review, February 3, 1959.
55. Zagoria, pp. 172-173.
56. Ibid., pp. 196-197; Peking Review, January 20, 1959, p. 20.
57. Cf. Esslin, op. cit., p. 84.

CHAPTER 2

Dulles' Flexibility

CONTRARY to the popular impression of Secretary Dulles as the coldest of the cold warriors, he responded with considerable flexibility to the "deadline crisis." He had to be flexible. First, the crisis offered the prospect of a direct confrontation between the United States and the Soviet Union. Soviet authorities could use East German troops in a buffer role on the ground routes, but only to a point or Moscow would lose control. The United States always insisted anyway that Soviet officers were responsible for actions of the East German police on the access routes.

Second, in Washington, a military judgment persisted—dating at least from 1948—that Berlin could not be defended. Dulles visited General Clay in the winter of 1949 during the airlift. General Howley, who in 1947 became American commandant in Berlin under General Clay, records that Dulles did not react enthusiastically to the airlift. Dulles believed that the airlift would prove insufficient and that the Soviets could win over the Berliners with offers of food.[1] Dulles may have retained his earlier attitude when he calculated his cautious response to the next Berlin crisis, ten years later, in 1958.

Third, a crisis in Berlin is never simply an American-Soviet affair. Both sides have allies and foreign parties they must consult. Poland and France, for example, have a direct interest in any settlement affecting the future of Germany. France and Britain are occupying powers in Berlin. Both Bonn and Pankow, of course, have high political stakes riding on the future of the city. Thus, Washington

1. Frank Howley, *op. cit.*, p. 224.

and Moscow are open to influence from many sources. Their policies are as bold as the least bold of their allies will allow. In the "deadline crisis" of 1958, Dulles tried to construct a consensus among the Western powers for negotiating with Moscow. Khrushchev, similarly, had to pull together his allies in Eastern Europe and he called Warsaw Pact meetings rather frequently in the crisis years. Little is known of his inter-ally negotiations during the crisis.

Fourth, Dulles' perception of Soviet intentions probably was the most significant factor in his flexibility. Dulles said he did not believe Khrushchev would press the crisis to the point of war. Nevertheless, he perceived Khrushchev to be more unpredictable and dangerous than Stalin, and wished to treat Khrushchev with a wider margin for error. To be certain of avoiding war with a power whose foremost official sometimes talked and gambled recklessly, Dulles quickly moved toward negotiations even though crisis conditions were not very promising for a settlement. He believed that any war in Europe would be a general war. He also perceived the Berlin crisis as an excellent opportunity to negotiate improved security for the Soviet Union in exchange for new safeguards guaranteeing the security of the Federal Republic and Berlin. He believed that Moscow had a severe security problem in Eastern Europe—demonstrated by the East German and Polish/Hungarian uprisings in 1953 and 1956 respectively—and had raised the Berlin crisis to resolve that problem. Just possibly, he thought, Moscow might consider measures to increase stability both in Eastern and Western Europe.

1. *The Berlin Policy of Secretary Dulles*

Before Premier Khrushchev's statement on November 10, 1958, the Washington press corps asked Secretary Dulles at his press conference on November 7 about his "allegedly adopting too rigid a position regarding possible talks with Russia on the German problem." Khrushchev had accused him of foot-dragging after Moscow proposed a summit conference in the Bulganin letter of December 10, 1957. In reply, Dulles did not deny his rigidity:

> The position of the United States so far remains as it has been historically for the last few years, and particularly as it was expressed in the joint communiqué which was issued as a result of the Geneva Summit Conference of 1955. We take the position

that the Four Powers, former occupying powers, have the responsibility to bring about the reunification of Germany. That was agreed to then by the Soviet Union. It was also agreed that Germany should be reunified in freedom by free elections. We hold to that.[2]

Obviously, free elections would allow the Federal Republic to absorb the DDR. The Soviets consistently rejected this proposal even though they seemed willing to consider it in 1955. Asked to comment on Ulbricht's claim to West Berlin, he replied: ". . . we are most solemnly committed to hold West Berlin, if need be by military force." [3]

Sixteen days after Khrushchev's November 10 statement about the Potsdam protocol, Dulles shifted his position. He was asked a prearranged question at a press conference and answered as follows:

Q. Mr. Secretary, what if, despite this responsibility, the Soviets go ahead and turn over to the East German authorities the check points on the Autobahn and control to the land, sea, and air routes? Now the question would arise; would we deal with the East German officials who would man the check points, for example, even as—

A. Well, we would certainly not deal with them in any way which involved our acceptance of the East German regime as a substitute for the Soviet Union in discharging the obligation of the Soviet Union and the responsibility of the Soviet Union.

Q. Does that mean that we might deal with them as agents of the Soviet Union?

A. *We might, yes. There are certain respects now in which minor functionaries of the so-called G.D.R. are being dealt with by both the Western Powers, the three allied powers, and also by the Federal Republic of Germany. It all depends upon the details of just how they act and how they function.* You can't exclude that to a minor degree because it is going on at the present time and has been. On the other hand, if the character of the activity is such as to indicate that to accept this would involve acceptance of a substitution of the G.D.R. for the present

2. *Documents*, p. 338.
3. *Ibid.*, p. 339.

obligation and responsibility of the Soviet Union, then that, I take it, we would not do.[4] [my emphasis]

In the press conference, Dulles repeated what he had said on November 7. Now, however, he acknowledged Khrushchev's threat of November 10 to invest the DDR with authority to manage traffic on the access routes. The "agent theory," as the State Department called it, enabled Dulles to remove the spike from Khrushchev's club. Let him replace Soviet officers with DDR police; the United States will accept the change, Dulles seemed to be saying. The "agent theory" was the first sign of Dulles' flexibility in the "deadline crisis."[5]

Dulles' remarks on November 26 can be explained by his estimate of the threat. He believed, as "a foregone conclusion," that the Soviets would accept the risks of transferring the functions of their traffic agencies to the DDR.[6] The State Department intended to request the United Nations Security Council to censure the Soviet Union when the transfer occurred. For military contingency planning, Dulles preferred to resort initially to another airlift rather than to challenge a blockade on the ground. If the Soviets withdrew from the Berlin Air Safety Center and threatened the continuation of flights, Dulles and the President believed the United States would probably have to "order military air transports and fighter aircraft into the corridors."[7] Dulles thought a military confrontation could be avoided if negotiating tactics were flexible enough.

On November 20, the National Security Council (NSC) heard Secretary Dulles' assessment of the crisis. If his later press conference remarks on November 26 were any indication of what he said at the NSC meeting, he perceived the issues that Khrushchev raised to be primarily of a political nature:

> Let me say, however, that nothing that has been said recently indicates there is any intention or desire on the part of either

4. *Ibid.*, p. 344. Prearranged questions are a State Department custom formally protecting the Secretary from blame. If his answer becomes controversial the Department can say that the question dictated the answer.

5. With each adjustment in his position, Dulles provoked an uproar in Bonn, partly because he did not give the West Germans prior notice of changes in his thinking. *The New York Times*, November 27, 1958, p. 19.

6. *Ibid.*, November 19, 1958, p. 1.

7. Eisenhower wrote later that his administration completed Berlin contingency planning as early as January 1954. See "My Views on Berlin," *Saturday Evening Post*, December 9, 1961, p. 19.

of [sic] the Soviet Union itself or the puppet regime, the G.D.R., to stop access to and from Berlin. The only issue that seems to have been raised is whether or not the Soviet Union can itself dispose of its responsibilities in the matter and turn them over to the G.D.R. . . . It would be a shift of responsibility and authority . . . and I think that, at least as far as it is exposed, the motivation at the present time would be not a purpose to drive us out of Berlin or to obstruct access to Berlin, but to try to compel an increased recognition and the according of increased stature to the G.D.R.[8]

Since the United States could not prevent the Soviet Union from transferring traffic management to the DDR, Dulles proposed that he bend to the extent necessary to accommodate Soviet pressure. He argued that a mere transfer of authority ought not to justify a war with the Soviet Union. For this reason, Dulles did not look for another blockade to occur immediately. Viewing Khrushchev's statement of November 10 as a demand for recognition of the DDR, Dulles changed his own position to prepare for a transfer of authority while holding the Soviets responsible for whatever they did. He certainly gave no indication of accepting Khrushchev's interpretation of the Potsdam protocol.

On November 21, Bonn signed a supplemental trade agreement[9] with Pankow, inadvertently confirming the Secretary's view that one could do business with the East Germans in strictly operational terms without granting them diplomatic recognition. Bonn drew a distinction between what the United States could do—as one of the four parties to the occupation protocol—and what Bonn had to do to support life in the Soviet zone. Pankow immediately took advantage of Dulles' "agent theory" as a sign of implied recognition.

In judging the crisis to be a political one, Dulles made a distinction between political and military factors which the Soviets themselves did not make at that time.[10] Moreover, the Soviet Union had no way "to compel an increased" recognition . . . to the DDR," as Dulles phrased the Soviets' intention, unless they exerted pressure on the access routes and expressed "a purpose to drive us out of Berlin or to obstruct access to Berlin . . ."

8. *Documents*, pp. 347-348.
9. *The Times* (London), November 22, 1958, p. 6.
10. Raymond L. Garthoff, *Soviet Military Doctrine* (Glencoe: The Free Press, 1953), chapter 3.

The note of November 27 challenged Dulles' assessment. The Soviet Union stated it would oppose any treatment of the East German police ignoring DDR sovereignty. By insisting on more than "a shift of responsibility and authority," the Soviets ruled out Dulles' "agent theory." They expressed a desire to abolish the Berlin occupation regime, including special routes of access. A few days earlier, Dulles had doubted that they had this objective. Their negotiating deadline effectively bound up the military aspects of the crisis with the political ones, again contrary to his expectation.

But Dulles did not change his mind about Soviet objectives. The State Department admitted the Soviet note did not appear to favor the Secretary's "agent theory." [11] It seemed more relieved that the transfer of authority over the access routes would not take place for six months. Again it desired to leave Moscow a way out when the deadline expired, although it doubted the crisis would reach military proportions. The note did compel Dulles to switch priorities. In a statement for the President, Dulles reacted sharply to Moscow's threat to change the occupation regime unilaterally and postponed any further discussion of his "agent theory." The administration wanted to give the population of West Berlin an urgently needed boost, now that Moscow threatened a new crisis.[12]

Dulles proved sensitive to the threatening tenor of the Soviets' note without, however, giving any indication of reassessing his own judgment of their objectives. As early as November 30, Dulles proposed to the President that the Western reply to the Soviet note should include an offer of negotiations.[13] At the NATO Ministerial Council meeting on December 15, Dulles recommended that he and his fellow NATO ministers negotiate a way out of the crisis.[14] He proposed the Western note of September 30, 1958, as a basis for preparing a reply to the Soviets. This note, representing the Western position of 1955, dis-

11. *The New York Times*, November 28, 1958, p. 1.
12. The Statement read: "The President reiterated our government's firm purpose that the United States will not enter into any new arrangement or embark on any course of conduct which would have the effect of abandoning the responsibilities which the United States, with Great Britain and France, has formally assumed for the freedom and security of the people of West Berlin." *Documents*, p. 364. In stating that "the United States will not enter into any new arrangement," Dulles momentarily de-emphasized the possibility of entering into operational relations with the East Germans.
13. *The New York Times*, December 1, 1958; p. 1; December 3, 1958, p. 1.
14. *Ibid., December* 17, 1958, p. 1 F.

cussed ways and means of achieving German unity.[15] In proposing that the last Western note be used as a basis for future negotiations, he seemed convinced the Soviets did not mean what they said in their November note, and that a real possibility existed for deflecting them from a collision course. If the alliance made a positive approach in favor of negotiations, he suggested it could avoid war and possibly derive political gains from the crisis. The allied declaration on Berlin of December 16 reflected Dulles' positive view.[16]

The initial United States response in the "deadline crisis" appeared in two documents. The first, a strictly legal rejoinder [17] by the State Department on December 20, tried to correct the distortions of the record which the Soviet note contained. The Department pressed at least one point to good advantage. It observed the contradiction between Khrushchev's assertion that the Western powers had voided the Potsdam protocol and had therefore released the Soviet Union from its obligation to the occupation protocol and his insistence that the Potsdam protocol itself had not been voided. If the two protocols were linked together, as he argued, the Potsdam protocol must have been voided along with the occupation protocol. The State Department concluded: "The position is, on its face, completely untenable."

Although Khrushchev held an untenable legal position, the position revealed again the one-sided objectives he had in the crisis. By reviving the Potsdam protocol, he could argue for demilitarizing the Federal Republic as the protocol had once required for all of Germany. By claiming the Western powers had nullified the occupation protocol, he could avoid having his argument for demilitarization apply to all of Germany, that is, to the DDR as well. In effect, he wanted Bonn to disarm without the DDR also disarming.

The second part of the Western reply to the Soviet note of November 27 came in notes from Washington, London, Paris, and Bonn on December 31.[18] The notes clearly bore Dulles' imprint. First, the allies accepted the Soviet proposal for negotiations with qualifications. Following Secretary Dulles' suggestion at the NATO Ministerial Council meeting, the notes quoted the Western note of September 30 containing a proposal for "free all-German elections." The December

15. *Documents*, p. 337.
16. *Ibid.*, pp. 364-365.
17. For the text, see *ibid.*, pp. 367-378.
18. *Ibid.*, pp. 378-381.

notes defined Berlin as "only one aspect, and not the essential one, of the German problem in its entirety." In rejecting the Soviet free city proposal, the allies indicated that any discussion of Berlin would have to be in a much broader context than the Soviet note allowed. They ignored Moscow's statement that unless they negotiated about the free city proposal no negotiations would be possible.

Second, the allies also ignored the deadline for changing Berlin's status within six months. The American note declared: "the United States could not embark on discussions with the Soviet Union upon these questions under menace or ultimatum; indeed, if that were intended, the United States would be obliged immediately to raise a protest in the strongest terms." The note gave the Soviets the benefit of the doubt: "It is assumed that the Soviet Government, like itself, is ready to enter the discussions in an atmosphere devoid of coercion or threats."

Third, the four allies proposed broad negotiations. Professing to find acceptable points in the Soviet note—for example, a willingness to discuss Germany and European security—the allies did not respond to the entirety of the Soviet note. Rather than replying at equal length to the long exposition of Soviet policy with which it had been presented in November, the allies shortened their reply to stress their interest in negotiations. They did not fully address the Soviet note. Instead, they replied with a counterproposal which took little account of the original note. The Soviet Union could therefore discount the allies' firm rejection of the free city proposal in light of their transparent desire to negotiate.

The Western notes were dispatched on December 31 before Soviet Deputy Premier Anastas Mikoyan left for Washington. At the December NATO meeting, Dulles announced that Mikoyan would visit the United States ostensibly for the purpose of stimulating East-West trade.[19] He expected Mikoyan to bear a Soviet reply to the Western notes in a continuing diplomatic dialogue.

On January 5, Mikoyan met Secretary Dulles and presented a memorandum outlining the forthcoming note of January 10 and draft treaty proposal. He was still in the United States when the note arrived and was therefore available for explaining it. When ques-

---

19. *The New York Times*, December 19, 1958, p. 1 H. Or as Mikoyan said, he was coming to the United States for a private "vacation trip." *The New York Times*, January 12, 1959, p. 1.

tioned before and after January 10, he stressed Moscow's willingness to negotiate. He said he was a reasonable man who sometimes "names a higher price than he expects to get for his goods." [20] But he did not suggest any substantive changes in the Soviet position and dwelled on the consequences of a nuclear war if the Western powers failed to negotiate.

Secretary Dulles apparently viewed the presence of Mikoyan in the United States and the note of January 10 as evidence of a serious Soviet interest in negotiations, all deadlines aside.[21] He did not read the peace treaty proposal at face value any more than he had the free city proposal. But he probably observed that the draft treaty covered broader issues than Berlin. Since Mikoyan urged negotiations strictly on Soviet terms and Dulles consistently recommended negotiations on Western terms, Dulles saw a possibility, therefore, that both parties could agree to negotiations *per se*.

At his press conference on January 13, Dulles took a definite step toward negotiations:

> Q. Mr. Secretary, is it our position that free elections are the only method of reuniting Germany? In other words, do we say, "No free elections, no reunification"?
>
> A. Well, we never have said that. The formula of reunification by free elections was the agreed formula. It seems to us to be a natural method. But I wouldn't say that it is the only method by which reunification could be accomplished.[22]

Dulles' statement on free elections loosened the rigidity of the free elections formula without abandoning it. He did not specify any other methods of reunification. He merely adopted a flexible posture which is all he claimed Mikoyan had done. Moreover, he desired flexibility because, as he understood it, Mikoyan had "made clear that there was no intention on the part of the Soviet Union to have their note treated as . . . an ultimatum with a fixed time limit." In other words, he thought Mikoyan had taken advantage of the December 31 note giving Moscow the benefit of the doubt. Thus, Dulles predicted that negotiations would take place: "There seems to be a sharp

20. *The Times* (London), January 10, 1959, p. 6.
21. *Ibid.*, January 12, 1959, p. 1.
22. *Documents*, p. 406. Again Bonn expressed shock at Dulles' remarks. *The New York Times*, January 14, 1959, p. 9.

difference of opinion as to what we talk about, but there is at least a common denominator, I think, in terms of a feeling that there should be discussions."

On his return to Moscow, Mikoyan suggested in a press conference that the six-month deadline could be extended if negotiations got under way. He said: "The main thing in our proposal is not the six-month deadline, but the proposal to have the talks"; and he added: "and to end the occupation status of West Berlin." [23] He expressed an interest in Secretary Dulles' statement pertaining to free elections, although he said, "it did not contain any constructive proposals."

The State Department immediately accepted Mikoyan's extension of the deadline as a concession and restated its own view that "negotiations would be useful." [24] It had the impression that the rejection of the Soviet deadline by the West had moved the Soviets to relent in their insistence for negotiations about Berlin alone. But, once again, Tass—in reporting Mikoyan's Moscow press conference— contradicted the Department's impression. The official news agency revised Mikoyan's statement to read: "If the talks take place in the spirit of a reciprocal desire to find a correct solution to the problem, and if we are convinced of good will on the part of the Western powers to negotiate with the object of ending the occupation regime in West Berlin, it would not be difficult, I believe, to extend the talks for two or three weeks, or even for two or three months." [25] The Soviets had not relented and Berlin remained the focus of Soviet objectives. When the Department thought the Soviets were relenting, the Soviets believed they were just beginning to score.

In his press conference of January 27, Dulles suggested how far the United States would go in negotiations. Dulles did not consider Soviet proposals of the early 1950's for a German confederation and, more recently, for a peace treaty with two Germanies to be useful solutions to the problem of German unity. They sealed the partition of Germany. When pressed to explain whether he could conceive of an acceptable form of confederation, he gave—surprisingly—the impression that he could:

> you can have a confederation which is, in fact, of very con-
> siderable progress toward reunification. . . . Now I don't like,

23. *The New York Times*, January 25, 1959, p. 1.
24. *Ibid.*
25. Embree, *op. cit.*, p. 103.

as I said, to use the word around which emotions revolve. But the matter of finding ways which, in fact, will promote re-unification is a matter which, I think, can be and should be studied as resourcefully as possible.[26]

With qualifications Dulles moved away from free elections—the 1955 formula—toward confederation leading to free elections as a method of creating unity in all parts of Germany. Having agreed on January 13 to negotiate with the Soviets, he then prepared on January 27 to negotiate with them on parallel subjects, in this case, the issues of a German confederation.

The subsequent course of the negotiations in 1959 revealed that Dulles had two proposals: a maximum proposal on German unity with safeguards for Soviet security and a minimum proposal—appearing later in 1959—for a Berlin settlement. Dulles wanted a *modus vivendi* on Berlin incorporating an access agreement in writing. Depending upon Moscow's price, a *modus vivendi* could be a gain for the Western powers, removing some of the uncertainties about the access routes.

From his experience in previous negotiating sessions with the Soviets, Dulles had little reason to be optimistic about a maximum or minimum settlement. On the other hand, he seemed convinced that the danger of war with which both sides had to contend provided a common basis on which a settlement might be constructed. In a statement to the House Foreign Affairs Committee on January 28, he said:

> Let us make perfectly clear that we are fully alive to the grave hazards in the present situation. Every reasonable and decent effort must be made to avoid needless provocations, to find a modus vivendi, and to reduce the danger of a war which under present conditions would involve a large measure of world-wide annihilation.[27]

Secretary Dulles' Berlin policy affirmed the feasibility of change in the status quo in Berlin and Germany, and he met the Soviets half way. But the emphasis on where change should occur first was not the same for Dulles and the Soviet leaders. Dulles preferred changes beginning in Germany as a whole resulting in changes for Berlin. Khrushchev and Mikoyan started from the other end of the problem,

26. *Documents*, p. 410.
27. *Ibid.*, p. 411.

demanding changes in Berlin as a requisite to larger changes in Germany. The two sides examined the status quo from very different perspectives. Confusion resulted when tactical shifts in the position of one were viewed through the perspective of the other. Confusion compounded when one considered a shift of the other a success in his own terms rather than in the terms and perspective of the other. Both favored change and therefore negotiations.

2. Dulles' Preference for Negotiations

The three instances of Dulles' flexibility—his "agent theory," his remarks on free elections, his movement toward discussion of a confederation—illustrate his intention to get negotiations started. Dulles did not simply reject Khrushchev's and Mikoyan's initiatives, but maneuvered to draw them onto more favorable ground for the United States. He acted in the spirit of conventional diplomacy which he believed was appropriate to the "deadline crisis" and which he was skilled in using.[28]

Dulles seemed confident his flexibility would pay off. He tried to persuade the Soviets to discuss German unity even though they said they had no interest in it. He did not consider the Soviets' fear of German unity and their campaign against West Berlin in a crisis atmosphere as sufficient obstacles to his diplomacy. Dulles also tended to ignore or to attribute little credibility to Soviet diplomatic notes.[29] He did not think all Soviet communications were propagandistic, necessarily, but most of them were for him unreliable indices of Soviet foreign policy.

Dulles had an explicit perception of Soviet policy which provided him with a substitute for face-value readings of diplomatic notes from Moscow. He prided himself on his knowledge of the Soviet Union.[30] An address Dulles delivered in the early days of the "deadline crisis" illustrates his thinking. On November 18, after Khrushchev's initial

28. The strengths and weaknesses of Dulles' diplomacy are perceptively described in Richard Gould-Adams, *The Time of Power: A Reappraisal of John Foster Dulles* (London; Weidenfield and Nicholson, 1962), especially chapters 1 and 16.

29. For an excellent discussion of this point and other aspects of Dulles' perception of the Soviet Union, see Ole R. Holsti, "Cognitive Dynamics and Images of the Enemy: Dulles and Russia," *Enemies in Politics*, David J. Finlay, Richard R. Fagen, and Ole R. Holsti, eds. (Chicago: Rand McNally and Co., 1967), p. 43 ff.

30. *Ibid.*, pp. 47-56.

pronouncement on Berlin, Dulles spoke to the National Council of Churches at its Cleveland conference on a changing world.[31] He directed himself to the "problem of change as seen by a Secretary of State."

Speaking about the Soviet Union, he said: "There is nothing 'inevitable' about communism except that it too is bound to change." He perceived six "forces" working for change in the Soviet Union. First, he argued that the Soviet emphasis on scientific education was incompatible with "enforced conformity of mind." As the Soviets penetrated outer space, they would also penetrate "the fallacies of Marxism." Second, the "growing demand for greater personal security" would have to be met by policy relaxation which, in turn, would allow "individualism" to assert itself all the more. Third, an increasing demand for consumer goods would operate in the same manner as the demand for personal security.

Fourth, he believed nationalism in Eastern Europe placed the Soviets in a dilemma: "The Soviet rulers must either grant more independence, and thus liberate forces which oppose the existing regimes, or else they must revert to the Stalinistic tactics of brutality, and face the increased likelihood of violent revolt. . . ." Fifth, he observed that a foreign policy of bluster and threat had brought the Soviets little results. They had resorted to a policy of professed friendship—peaceful coexistence—which the West had encouraged and through which, he thought, the Soviets would develop "a vested interest in respectability." Sixth, given the unpopularity of communism demonstrated, for example, by the refugee traffic through West Berlin, he argued that internal popular pressures which "will change the character of communist rule gain weight as that rule is denied external successes." He expected these six forces to liberalize the Soviet Union.

Dulles respected the technical and military power of the Soviets.[32] But he did not grant their regime real internal strength: "Dictatorships usually present a formidable exterior. They seem, on the outside, to be hard, glittering, and irresistible. Within they are full of rottenness." [33] In fact, he looked for the eventual ruin of the Com-

31. *The New York Times*, November 19, 1958, p. 6.
32. Holsti, *op. cit.*, pp. 272-273.
33. John Foster Dulles, *War or Peace* (New York: Macmillan and Co., 1950), p. 242.

munist Party of the Soviet Union (CPSU)[34] and correlated that event with further progress in world order: "I believe . . . that peace depends upon the growing internal difficulties of Soviet Communism and its inability to consolidate its present and prospective areas of conquest."[35] Dulles had no quarrel with the Soviet people. He looked to them and their demands for change as natural allies.

Dulles believed political change occurred through a dialectical process of demand, resistance, and new demand.[36] He thought that with appropriate encouragement this process would favor the West because Western communities, unlike dictatorships, allowed free expression of popular demands. He conceived of his diplomacy as an effort to guide the process of change through peaceful solutions of conflicts.[37] To encourage the Soviet Union to accept inevitable changes, he thought the United States should try to contain the Soviets externally, compelling them to confront their internal dilemmas. Once the Soviets turned inward, he believed they would be more willing to engage in "competitive efforts conducted by peaceful means, and not start a war that could consume us all."

For these several reasons—the changes occurring in the Soviet Union, the tenuous rule of the CPSU, and the general direction of history—Dulles did not treat Soviet official speech very seriously. He looked behind the speech—behind the November note, for example—to see what really motivated it. He professed to see a security motivation stimulated by internal contradictions. He probably regarded East Germany as a little USSR with the same internal problems, although more pronounced, than its sponsor-ally.[38]

34. For example, in 1956 in a statement to the Senate Foreign Relations Committee, Dulles described at great length the debilitating effects that—in his mind—Khrushchev's de-Stalinization campaign had produced in the Soviet Union. *The New York Times*, May 16, 1956, p. 8.

35. Dulles, *op. cit.*, p. 251.

36. He describes this process more fully in his earlier work, *War, Peace and Change* (New York: Harper and Brothers, 1939), pp. 164-169. His sister attributes his view of the dialectics of change to his "work with Bergson." Eleanor Lansing Dulles, *John Foster Dulles: The Last Year* (New York: Harcourt, Brace and World, Inc., 1963), p. 188.

37. In Beal's biography, Dulles is described as "having spent a lifetime evolving plans to channel the process of change to the ends of peace and human justice. . . ." John Robinson Beal, *John Foster Dulles* (New York: Harper and Brothers, 1957), p. 203; also chapter 2, p. 321. And according to Dulles himself, peaceful change is the highest value in political life. *War, Peace and Change*, p. 9.

38. *The Washington Post* reported that Dulles believed Soviet demands were

Dulles' perception of Moscow's political weaknesses gave him a certain optimism that the crisis could be exploited to the West's advantage. He judged that the Western powers could construct a powerful defense in the "deadline crisis" through political pressure on the internal dilemmas of the Soviet regime in Eastern Europe. Dulles urged that great pressure be placed on Moscow, but he believed that the pressure should be exerted by political rather than military means because of the danger of general war any Berlin crisis raised acutely. He warned Khrushchev that the United States possessed the will and capacity to defend West Berlin. But he devoted his efforts to reducing tensions, and the United States carefully refrained from using available forces in a warning demonstration.

He much preferred to deploy the "armies" of world public opinion. World opinion was a moral and legal concept Dulles used to justify the settlement of disputes within the bounds of international law. He believed that the CPSU, for example, would "pay attention to other people's sense of right and justice. That is always of interest, even to despots." [39] He also believed that power of world opinion explained the influence he perceived 'individualism" and "nationalism" exerting in the Soviet Union and Eastern Europe. He associated the concept with his earlier interest in a policy of "liberation," essentially a propaganda offensive beamed at the populations of Eastern Europe.[40]

In the Berlin crisis, Dulles was aware of the propaganda value of his Berlin policy and tried to deflect Soviet propaganda from drumming on the theme of imminent war and to expose Moscow's proposals as vindictive and oppressive to the German people. He vigorously rejected the Soviet case for holding down "a great people like the Germans." He set two propaganda requirements for the United States position in the "deadline crisis": (1) that the history of Western occupation in Berlin be restated to counter the Soviet version of it, and (2) that the Western alliance assume a positive negotiating position, offering counterproposals on the future of Berlin and Germany to place Moscow on the defensive.

On January 7, 1959, the State Department released a document entitled "The Soviet Note on Berlin: An Analysis," which contrasted

---

motivated by fears of an East German uprising. *The Washington Post*, December 21, 1958, p. 1.

39. Dulles, *War or Peace*, p. 164.

40. *Ibid.*, pp. 9, 164-169.

Soviet allegations in the note of November 27 with the record of Western occupation. According to the Soviet note, for example, the Western powers "are ruling the roost in West Berlin, turning it into a kind of state within a state and using it as a center from which to pursue subversive activity against the GDR, the Soviet Union, and other parties to the Warsaw Treaty." The State Department, clearly appealing to public opinion, responded by stating:

> It is clear that the USSR, the United Kingdom and the United States agreed that there should be a rebirth of free political parties and the reestablishment of essential political freedom in Germany as a whole including the free flow of information and publications. . . . These principles were never practiced inside the Soviet Zone of Germany. . . . It was this direct Soviet action that led to the popularity and the significance of Western newspapers and radio stations . . . in Berlin and in East Germany.[41]

The Department blamed the Soviets for obstructing the provisions of the Potsdam protocol allowing "the free flow of information." This case presumably accorded with German public opinion, the prime audience in the crisis.

Dulles' second propaganda requirement was to assume a positive negotiating position. In the period immediately following the Soviet note of November 27, he seemed anxious to present a constructive response. He studied the Soviet position for ways to match it for novelty or to strike parallels with it. For example, Dulles readily agreed with Khrushchev about the "abnormal" condition of a Germany divided for thirteen years. In his experimentation with Berlin access, free elections, and confederation, he prepared to offer proposals for change equally attractive to those of the Soviet notes. In effect, he tried to deprive the Soviet leaders of political influence in Western Europe and America with their subtle but popular argument that the time had come to recognize the "reality" of two Germanies. His diplomacy had to demonstrate flexibility when elements of British opinion, for example, favored change.

---

41. The United States Department of State, *The Soviet Note on Berlin: An Analysis*, Publication 6757, January 1959, p. 13.

3. *The Risks in Negotiation*

In opting for a strategy of negotiations in the "deadline crisis," Dulles incurred two risks. First, his preference for negotiations could mislead Khrushchev to believe that the United States would accept some of his proposals, particularly an improvement of relations with the DDR. Dulles' relatively forthcoming attitude was the kind of gain Khrushchev wanted and expected from pressure tactics. Khrushchev also preferred negotiations as a method of producing desired changes. A decision not to negotiate or to delay would have signaled a more difficult United States attitude. He would have had to consider that his drive to overturn the Berlin occupation regime had little effect on the United States.

Dulles thought he could prevent miscalculation by moving swiftly to open negotiations. Negotiations, he believed, would clarify intentions on both sides. In principle, negotiations should clarify matters. But Soviet leaders were looking for the kind of responsiveness Dulles displayed as evidence that he recognized their growing nuclear power. And when they saw that he reacted flexibly to the pressures of a crisis they were tempted to conclude that he recognized and feared their strength.

The Soviet leaders at the time were prone to miscalculation because they were no more inclined to accept diplomatic correspondence at face value than Secretary Dulles was. It should be noted that Khrushchev distinguished between "progressive elements" in the United States favoring détente with the Soviet Union and "reactionary forces" striving to bring the two powers close to war.[42] He perceived a struggle in the Eisenhower administration over the formulation of policy similar to the struggles in the Kremlin. He observed, however, that the initial American response favored negotiations. Dulles hedged on the agenda, insisting that European security and German unity take the place of the Soviet proposed peace treaty. But with further encouragement from the Soviet Union, perhaps Khrushchev thought, the hand of the pro-détente faction in the administration would be strengthened. Then a discussion of the treaty could begin in earnest. If Khrushchev ignored what Dulles said and judged him by his actions—his willingness to negotiate—he probably felt en-

42. See, for example, his speech on the U-2 incident. *The New York Times*, May 6, 1960, p. 7.

couraged. Dulles' position contained ambiguity, but perhaps Khrushchev did not expect a perfectly clear response, given his assumption of a struggle of factions within the administration.

Dulles provided the Soviets with ample information they could misconstrue. In his idea that East German agents could represent the Soviet Union on the Berlin access routes he made a gesture toward Soviet proposals. Similarly, in his move away from free elections and his move toward confederation—away from the solution favored by Bonn and toward a solution often advanced by Pankow—he probably raised Soviet expectations. He did not wander far from the 1955 formula, but—most noteworthy—he demonstrated a willingness to negotiate and to alter the old formula.

Dulles incurred a second risk by stressing negotiations to the neglect of a fall-back position. He did not speak with any urgency for a military strategy: a plan for using conventional forces to defend the access routes and West Berlin. As mentioned earlier, persistent military judgment originating in the Berlin blockade of 1948–1949 held that Berlin could not be defended on the ground.[43] And, as always, military options were in short supply for defending an enclave like West Berlin.

These factors aside, however, General Maxwell Taylor, Army Chief of Staff, tried to develop a conventional forces strategy for Berlin in November 1958 and later.[44] For example, when *The Herald Tribune* reported that Dulles believed the Soviets would transfer traffic management to the DDR, rumors circulated in Washington that the administration would resist this kind of move by forcing armed convoys or armed trains through East German obstacles on the Berlin-Helmstedt *autobahn*.[45] The Army reportedly prepared contingency plans to implement this option, if necessary. One plan called for the graduated application of force: (1) armed truck convoys would be sent up the *autobahn*, and (2) if East German police barred these convoys from entering or leaving the *autobahn*, another con-

---

43. At the time of the Berlin blockade, General Clay and Ambassador Robert Murphy urged the use of force on the Berlin-Helmstedt *autobahn* so the Soviet Union would be compelled to recognize Western rights of access. Failure to do so, they thought, would make the Western position more precarious than ever. They were overruled by the National Security Council which preferred an airlift. Davison, *op. cit.*, pp. 126-127.

44. *The New York Times*, November 13, 1958, p. 1.

45. *The Herald Tribune*, November 21, 1958, p. 1.

voy escorted by infantry and tanks would be sent "to test Soviet intentions." [46]

After the Soviet note of November 27 arrived in Washington, the commander, United States Army, Europe, stated publicly that he would not accept any "infringement" of ground access to Berlin.[47] At the December NATO Ministerial Council Meeting, General Norstad, Supreme Allied Commander Europe, requested the Council to accelerate planned increases in allied divisions, nuclear-armed battalions, and integrated air defense forces.[48]

Joseph Alsop, in his column of December 19, explained the Army's emphasis on ground countermeasures in contingency planning. He reported that the U.S. could no longer rely completely on an airlift to break a blockade. Alsop wrote: "Radar jamming is the development that blocks the escape by airlift from the Berlin impasse. . . . Sometime ago, powerful Soviet radar jamming mechanisms were installed at four sites surrounding Berlin." [49] Alsop criticized the lack of a decision at the NATO meeting to assemble and organize appropriate ground forces for an *autobahn* probe.[50]

NATO itself continued to rely on a military strategy favoring the first use of nuclear weapons to deter Soviet aggression. Since 1953, the Eisenhower Administration had decelerated increases in United States ground forces deriving from requirements for the Korean War and had approved actual reductions. In the address in which he stated the massive retaliation policy for deterring general war, Secretary Dulles referred to NATO discussions in which he said: "The U.S. put forward a new concept, now known as that of the 'long haul' that meant a steady development of defensive strength at a rate which will preserve and not exhaust the economic strength of our allies and ourselves. This would be reinforced by the striking power of a strategic air force. . . ." [51] In NATO's version of the massive retaliation policy, the alliance powers planned nuclear retaliation for

46. *The New York Times*, November 25, 1959, p. 12.
47. *Ibid.*, December 1, 1958, p. 1.
48. *Ibid.*, December 18, 1958, p. 16.
49. *The Washington Post*, December 19, 1958, p. 13.
50. He hailed the appointment of Deputy Under Secretary of State Robert Murphy to serve as the United States representative in interallied contingency planning sessions as an encouraging sign. As in 1948, Murphy favored ground countermeasures rather than an airlift to relieve West Berlin. *The Herald Tribune*, January 19, 1959, p. 16.
51. *The New York Times*, January 13, 1954, p. 2.

any Soviet incursions into NATO territories.[52] With the advent of "battlefield" nuclear weapons in the late 1950's, Dulles toyed with the idea of limited nuclear war,[53] but he never urged any change in retaliatory strategy.

General Norstad proposed in 1957 that NATO develop a force of thirty divisions on the Central European front. He suggested the primary purpose of this force should be to enable NATO to control a small Soviet incursion without initial resort to nuclear weapons or to compel the Soviets to invade in great strength, requiring a NATO nuclear response clearly as a measure of last resort.[54] Norstad's proposal received considerable public discussion, some of which even suggested that "a 30-division force on the line might be able to cope with a massive conventional assault without calling down reprisal." [55] The communiqué of the NATO December meeting did not acknowledge the Norstad proposal. Drawing upon this proposal and the Army's plan for ground resistance on the *autobahn*, the Kennedy Administration eventually constructed a conventional military strategy to defend West Berlin.

The fact remains that in January 1959 Dulles did not possess the plans and organized conventional forces for a military strategy in the "deadline crisis." The United States retained an airlift capability and fighter aircraft in West Germany or within reach of West Germany and, perhaps, enough ground forces which could be spared for an armed or escorted *autobahn* convoy, but no authorized conventional strategy for using them. Dulles had a fragmentary fallback position at best. Although the 1954 policy was modified, Dulles still depended upon that policy and corresponding strategic nuclear forces of massive retaliation alone to sustain the presence of the United States in Berlin.[56]

52. According to Roger Hilsman: "Present NATO policy does not allow for a conventional response to even a limited aggression. And this policy means exactly what it says, principally because the means for any other policy are not available." "The Developing Strategic Context," *NATO and American Security*, Klaus Knorr, ed. (Princeton: Princeton University Press, 1959), p. 36.

53. Dulles, "Challenge and Response in United States Policy," *Foreign Affairs*, 36 (October 1957), 25-43.

54. Robert E. Osgood, *NATO, The Entangling Alliance* (Chicago: University of Chicago Press, 1962), pp. 160-165.

55. Roger Hilsman, "On NATO Strategy," in Arnold Wolfers (ed.), *Alliance Policy in the Cold War* (Baltimore: Johns Hopkins Press, 1959), p. 173.

56. Reston reported that Dulles would consent, if necessary, to an armed convoy in another Berlin blockade. *The New York Times*, February 10, 1959,

The absence of a known and authorized fallback position other than general war offered further evidence to encourage Khrushchev to believe that the United States would have to accommodate his proposals. The Soviets' position included an assessment of the balance of nuclear power. Khrushchev believed an era of nuclear parity had arrived. He thought each side merely had to demonstrate, as in the Sputnik launchings of 1957, a capability for producing a long-range offensive delivery system. Given a stand-off at the nuclear level, the Red Army had—in Khrushchev's mind—a preponderant influence in Europe. He seemed convinced that the time had arrived when he could reverse any United States threat of retaliation into a factor paralyzing Western diplomacy. He expected Soviet nuclear power to produce a handsome political payoff by the Western powers, in a way yet to be evolved, accepting some form of the Soviet proposals. To deflate his expectations, the United States would have had to demonstrate the military capacity to remain in West Berlin without reliance on a starting strategy which simply and horribly called down a nuclear war on Berlin, on all of Europe, and possibly on the United States itself.

4. *Acheson's Alternative*

Speaking for the Democratic Advisory Council, a shadow-cabinet of sorts, former Secretary of State Dean Acheson deplored the lack of conventional military preparedness in the "deadline crisis." [57] For this reason, he scored the Eisenhower Administration's optimism about the outcome of the crisis. Acheson regarded Berlin as the "linch-pin" of the entire Western position in Europe. The loss of Berlin would be so great a blow to the Atlantic alliance, he argued, that the United States might very well find its influence confined to

---

p. 4. A policy for ground action was compatible with the massive retaliation policy, however, if undertaken with the idea that the action would succeed because the Soviets were not likely to risk massive retaliation by opposing it. In this sense, a ground probe would serve merely as an adjunct to the threat of massive retaliation and probably would not be intended as a very substantial non-nuclear action. This conclusion seems particularly evident since the policy of massive retaliation and Berlin contingency planning were both completed in 1954 and were undoubtedly related in the series of papers the National Security Council produced that year. Eisenhower, *op. cit.*, p. 19.

57. Acheson, "Wishing Won't Hold Berlin," *Saturday Evening Post*, March 7, 1959, p. 86.

the Western Hemisphere. The Soviets, in his mind, forced the issue to learn how the United States would react. He diagnosed the crisis as a contest of wills and he proposed a reaction appropriate to the contest. He said: ". . . the Soviets must be convinced that we are genuinely determined to keep traffic to Berlin open, at whatever risk, rather than abandon the people of Berlin and permit the whole Western position to crumble." [58]

He proposed reducing reliance on massive retaliation because the U.S. no longer had a nuclear monopoly. Instead, he favored an initial and extended non-nuclear response for Berlin contingencies: "the only visible alternative is to use Western conventional power to remove obstacles to traffic to and from Berlin, both on land and in the air." He urged "a building-up of NATO power in Europe, an increase in American troop strength and a return of British and French divisions to the continent, possibly Turkish and Italian reinforcements, and a strengthening of NATO's tactical air force." Also, he argued for a mobilization of Army strength and a "crash" ICBM program to close an anticipated missile gap.

Acheson suggested that these actions would raise risks for the Soviets to ponder because "the West would have disclosed the will to resist." These measures—Acheson's argument aside for the moment —would have been spectacularly offensive to Khrushchev's prestige, making it more difficult for him to back away. A contest of wills is peculiarly difficult for a great power to refuse.

General Taylor supported Acheson's call for non-nuclear military options, although not necessarily all of Acheson's measures. Taylor also announced that General Norstad had requested supplemental forces for the "deadline crisis" and that he, Taylor, had seconded the request.[59] In another context, he said that in the event of an engagement between Soviet and United States troops: "I would expect that at such a time common sense would apply and I could well visualize a considerable preliminary phase before the fateful decision to pass to general war were taken." [60]

58. *Ibid.*

59. *The New York Times*, March 15, 1959, p. 1; *The Washington Post*, March 15, 1959, p. 1.

60. *The Christian Science Monitor*, March 20, 1959, p. 16. In his later book, Taylor recommended a substitute policy for massive retaliation which he called "The Strategy of Flexible Response." He complained that the Eisenhower policy inhibited Berlin contingency planning. *The Uncertain Trumpet* (New York: Harper and Brothers, 1960), pp. 6, 8. The Kennedy Administration, in 1961, used Taylor's phrasing, "flexible response," to describe its own military policy.

Most importantly, Acheson and Taylor proposed forces needed for the fallback position missing from Dulles' brief. Some of Acheson's proposals probably exceeded what was needed. He candidly admitted nuclear war could result from the course he recommended. He believed that the Soviets would reverse themselves when confronted with an obvious will to resist. He stressed the military aspects of the crisis because he saw little chance for successful negotiations if the Soviet Union insisted it would negotiate only on its own terms. He thought negotiations on arms limitations in Europe could be useful if the Soviets would consent to troop reductions. In any event, he thought it would be most unwise to put off a confrontation. The risks would be greater for all parties the longer the issue remained unresolved. He particularly feared the effects on Bonn of a prolonged crisis.

The administration ignored its critics. The President implied that even if Congress appropriated increases for conventional forces, he would not expend the appropriations.[61] The administration's defense of its policies indicated that it lacked military options. On February 18, President Eisenhower declared at a press conference that the Soviets would be responsible for war over Berlin. He also said, "We are not saying that we are going to shoot our way into Berlin." [62] This statement did not explain how the Soviets would realize that they were responsible for a nuclear war, particularly if the United States would have to initiate one because it refused to shoot its way into Berlin with conventional forces. He did not say, for example, that the Soviet Union should be aware that the United States would initiate appropriate military action if Moscow interrupted access to Berlin.

On February 25, in response to a question from the press on the subject of Berlin contingency planning, the President stated that "plans" existed for defending Berlin, implying the existence of alternatives to massive retaliation.[63] But he reiterated on March 12: "We are certainly not going to fight a ground war in Europe. What good would it do to send a few more thousand or indeed even a few divisions of troops to Europe?" Presumably, massive retaliation remained the only significant possibility. The President balked at this conclusion in the following exchange:

61. *The New York Times*, March 12, 1959, p. 12.
62. *Ibid.*, February 19, 1959, p. 1.
63. *Ibid.*, February 26, 1959, p. 12.

Q. Is the United States prepared to use nuclear weapons if necessary to defend free Berlin?

A. Well, I don't know how you could free anything with nuclear weapons. I can say this: the United States, and its Allies, have announced their firm intention of preserving their rights and responsibilities with respect to Berlin. If any threat, or any push in the direction of real hostilities is going to occur, it's going to occur from the side of the Soviets.

Now if that would become reality, and I don't believe that anyone would be senseless enough to push that to the point of reality, then there will be the time to decide exactly what the Allies would in turn, expect to do.[64]

In other words, the President admitted that a nuclear defense of Berlin would be self-defeating. Yet, when asked if he envisaged an intermediate response to a Berlin contingency, he answered: "No. I think we might as well understand that—might well all of us understand this: I didn't say that nuclear war is a complete impossibility. I said it couldn't, as I see it, free anything. Destruction is not a good police force."

The administration continued to rely on a massive retaliation policy in the "deadline crisis," nonetheless acknowledging the contradiction that destruction caused by massive retaliation "is not a good police force." [65] The contradiction is, of course, inherent in defending West Berlin and is the source of the nightmare associated with the risks of war in a Berlin crisis. Conventional military options can alleviate —they do not remove—the contradiction. With saber-rattling, the Soviet Union can always make the problem scary. If the President did not believe the Soviets would be "senseless enough" to "push in the direction of real hostilities," they could confound his thinking by acting close to the brink. In 1958, they were prepared to press the administration quite far on Berlin to extract concessions on Bonn's access to nuclear weapons. But without the local forces to at least raise the nuclear threshold and maneuver the Soviets into some hard choices of their own, the administration had no way to even alleviate

64. *Ibid.*, March 13, 1959, p. 12.
65. By March 8, Secretary of Defense McElroy had rejected the Army's proposal for increasing conventional forces. He said it would be very difficult to restrict a military contingency in Berlin to "limited war" proportions. *The Christian Science Monitor*, March 9, 1959, p. 9.

the harshness of the contradiction posed by a rational defense of Berlin.

5. Dulles' Travels

Thus armed or disarmed without a fallback defense of Berlin, Dulles proceeded in late January and early February to prepare for East-West negotiations. Before these negotiations could begin, he had to fashion an agreed Western position. Soon after Mikoyan departed Washington, Secretary Dulles announced he would be visiting London, Paris, and Bonn. Acknowledged differences persisted among the Atlantic allies on the content and timing of negotiations. Dulles had to contend with a wide range of approaches to the "deadline crisis." At one end of the spectrum, Prime Minister Harold Macmillan proposed tactics of even greater flexibility than Dulles and favored a relatively early conference with the Soviets. He shared Dulles' premise that the Soviet Union initiated the crisis to obtain security guarantees. At the other end were the French, who looked askance at diplomatic flexibility and favored a later conference, after the May 27 deadline expired. They did not share Dulles' views about Soviet motives. Chancellor Adenauer, while appearing more flexible than President Charles de Gaulle, actually preferred the French position or something harder.[66] Dulles found himself in the middle of this range of opinion.

In London, Dulles discovered that the British wanted an East-West conference by late April or early May in Geneva.[67] In addition, Macmillan wanted to take diplomatic initiatives himself. Nineteen fifty-nine was an election year. The day before Dulles arrived, the London press reported that Macmillan would visit the Soviet Union to hold bilateral discussions on Berlin and other issues with Khrushchev.[68] Dulles believed that Macmillan's move probably would antagonize de Gaulle and Adenauer. In London, Macmillan confirmed that Khrushchev, at Macmillan's suggestion, had consented to bilateral discussions. Dulles apparently did not raise strong objections.

Now it seemed a little more urgent that they reach a meeting of minds on what, exactly, should be negotiated. Together, they ex-

---

66. *The New York Times*, February 1, 1959, p. 1.
67. *The Herald Tribune*, February 2, 1959, p. 2; *The New York Times*, February 4, 1959, p. 3.
68. *The Times* (London), February 3, 1959, p. 10.

plored possible security measures which might be conceded to the Soviets in exchange for concessions loosening Moscow's hold on Germany. Dulles did not have the same longstanding passion for limiting arms that Macmillan did. Dulles earlier opposed any suggestion that the Western powers should withdraw from Central Europe—a suggestion which figured explicitly in British plans for limiting nuclear and non-nuclear forces on both sides in Central Europe. He still flatly opposed disengagement in 1959. However, his consideration with Macmillan of a possible exchange of concessions over Berlin drew him—interestingly enough—into a serious exploration of British proposals that he had previously rejected.

Macmillan and Dulles agreed to an early foreign ministers' conference. Macmillan seemed amenable to an "agent" arrangement with the East Germans for Berlin access. Dulles heard Macmillan's opposition to any plans for ground countermeasures as they discussed interallied contingency planning.[69] In spite of the technical difficulties, the British preferred an airlift because, they argued, it was to the West's advantage to force the Soviets into a position where they would have to take responsibility for the first shot.

After his consultation with Dulles, Macmillan officially announced he would visit the Soviet Union for the purpose of exploring "what our policies and actions should be." [70] Actually, he wanted to test Khrushchev's reaction to Western assurances of European security, including: (1) British proposals—dating back to the Geneva Conference of 1955—for the creation of a "bigger state" embracing West Germany and a neutral East Germany; (2) suggestions for precautions against surprise attack on the central front; and (3) a partial reduction and limited withdrawal of Soviet and Western forces in a zone incorporating Central Europe. Macmillan insisted he did not and could not plan to negotiate anything. He simply wished to explore the Soviet proposals, he said, and to outline Western ones.

Paris did not react favorably to Macmillan's Moscow visit. The French deplored his timing. De Gaulle predicted that the Soviets would think the Western powers were eager to negotiate within the deadline period.[71] He opposed an East-West conference before May

69. *The New York Times*, February 11, 1959, p. 1.
70. *Ibid.*, February 6, 1959.
71. *Ibid.*, February 5, 1959, p. 3.

27, arguing that negotiations in the context of Soviet threats would jeopardize the occupation regime in Berlin. De Gaulle also informed Dulles that France held to the 1955 free elections formula for German unity without much confidence that the Soviets would accept that formula now. De Gaulle expressed reluctance in promoting changes in the status quo and opposed the so-called "agent theory." Agreeing with the British, he preferred an airlift to a ground probe for contingency planning.

In Bonn, Dulles and Adenauer reached a general accommodation. They did not attempt to build specific joint positions. Although unfavorable to flexible diplomatic tactics, Adenauer agreed anyway to negotiations with the Soviets before May 27. He had reservations about the proposals for European security which Dulles and Macmillan contemplated. He decided not to obstruct Dulles' efforts because, in any event, the future of the Federal Republic lay with the alliance. Adenauer deferred to Dulles, leaving the United States free to probe the Soviet proposals without having to specify beforehand the type of settlement to be reached.[72] Dulles and Adenauer agreed to a "no concessions without counterconcessions" formula.[73] On the military aspect of Berlin access, the West Germans also agreed with the British that an airlift would be the least dangerous course.[74] They rejected Dulles' "agent" proposal.

While none of his allies changed position, Dulles, on returning to Washington, expressed satisfaction: "We are willing to talk with the Soviets in a sincere effort to reach agreements." [75] Thus the alliance moved toward negotiations before May 27. The French opposed negotiations and consented only because they did not, at this point, want to be diplomatically isolated. The British desired early negotiations and led the way toward them. Dulles rested, satisfied he had brought the alliance to the point where it accepted early negotiations. The specific terms of negotiations remained controversial and undetermined. If negotiations failed, he said: "We are in general agreement as to the procedures we shall follow if physical means are

72. Charles Wighton, *Adenauer—Democratic Dictator* (London: Frederick Muller, Limited, 1963), pp. 273-274.

73. *The Times* (London), February 9, 1959, p. 8.

74. Bonn preferred an airlift anyway to avoid total interruption of civilian traffic to West Berlin.

75. *Documents*, p. 413.

invoked to interfere with our rights in this respect." Presumably, this statement meant the allies would rely on an airlift if the Soviets blocked ground access.

On February 16, the Western powers replied to the Soviet note of January 10. On the basis of an unqualified right to remain in Berlin, they proposed a four-power foreign ministers' conference to discuss the entire German problem "in all its aspects and implications." [76] Unexpectedly, they offered the Soviets a concession: "German advisors should be invited to the conference and should be consulted." This gesture acknowledged Moscow's case that the Germans themselves should be responsible for achieving unity between them—without granting the full Soviet position that two Germanies existed and should be diplomatically recognized.

6. *Macmillan's Initiative and the End of the "Deadline Crisis"*

In the late winter of 1959, Britain acted as chief spokesman of the Western powers. A few days before the note of February 16 appeared, Secretary Dulles was hospitalized with the illness which led to his death later in May. Until April, when Under Secretary Christian Herter succeeded Dulles, the leadership of the alliance passed to Macmillan. Like Dulles, he believed the "deadline crisis" to be a political one not requiring unusual military preparations.[77] He hoped, like Dulles, that Moscow's interest in avoiding war could be used to formulate a new, written Berlin *modus vivendi*.

Macmillan's initiative—his visits to Moscow, Paris, Bonn, and Washington in the winter of 1959—should be examined in the context of the arms limitations schemes given wide currency in Britain after 1955. At least four plans had gained popularity in London. The Eden plan, presented by Prime Minister Sir Anthony Eden at the 1955 Geneva summit conference, included a proposal for demilitarizing an area of Central Europe, provided this limitation of forces included a system of inspection. The Rapacki plan, drawn up by Polish Foreign Minister Adam Rapacki in 1957, featured a nuclear-free zone to embrace the Federal Republic, the DDR, Poland, and

76. *Ibid.*, p. 414; they left the date of the conference open to placate the French.

77. On November 21, Macmillan stated: "I have the very strong impression this is a diplomatic rather than a real move by the Russians." *The New York Times*, November 22, 1958, p. 1.

Czechoslovakia. In 1958, Rapacki amended his plan to include a reduction of conventional forces in the zone.

In 1957, Hugh Gaitskell, Chairman of the British Labour Party—and his colleague, Denis Healey—offered an even broader set of proposals. These encompassed the unification of Germany, the withdrawal of foreign forces, and the inspection of local force levels not only in Central Europe, but in Hungary, Rumania, and Bulgaria as well. The same year, George Kennan, in British Broadcasting Corporation home lectures, proposed withdrawing American and Soviet troops to their own soil, unifying and demilitarizing Germany—all in the context of a European security system guaranteed by the great powers. The authors of these several plans intended to make German unity palatable to the Soviet Union and, therefore, end the division of Europe.[78]

Khrushchev endorsed Eden's plan for a demilitarized area and Rapacki's for a ban on nuclear weapons in a zone principally featuring the territories of Bonn and the DDR. Khrushchev's notion of arms limitations tended to discriminate against Bonn, as evidenced in the Soviet draft treaty proposal.

Dulles, with Acheson's support, opposed each of the arms proposals, especially Kennan's. They believed that unless changes in the status quo were carefully phased and circumscribed a worse situation than currently existed could be produced. They argued, for example, that a withdrawal of American and Soviet troops each to their own soil would give the Red Army an advantage of proximity to Central Europe while United States forces remained at a greater relative distance. Leaving Bonn to fend for itself without even the authority to raise an army would make the Federal Republic an open target for the Soviet Union. Kennan acknowledged this argument when he later amended his plan to allow for twelve German divisions, once the Western powers withdrew.

Dulles and Acheson were not altogether opposed to controlled arms limitations in Europe. They insisted, however, that the Eastern side had to reciprocate Western reductions and that some agency be allowed to inspect the Eastern side to verify reciprocation. They agreed with Kennan that German unity would be highly desirable. They looked to the Soviet Union to indicate a reciprocal desire.

---

78. See Osgood, *op. cit.*, pp. 309-310. For a comprehensive analysis of the disengagement debate, see his chapter 10.

Otherwise, they perceived no alternative to "the basic thesis of Adenauer," as Dulles described it, that the most practical solution for preventing a resurgence of German nationalism was "to tie Germany in"—to integrate the Federal Republic into Western Europe through the developing institutions of NATO, the Western European Union, the European Economic Community, the European Atomic Energy Agency, and others. One weakness, of course, in Dulles' and Acheson's argument was Berlin's exposure in the Eastern camp, a point Dulles felt acutely during the "deadline crisis."

The disengagement debate swirled about Macmillan in his tour of capitals because he drew upon the plans so controversial at the time in his approach to the Berlin crisis. Much of the heat in his arguments with Adenauer, de Gaulle, and Eisenhower over Berlin can be traced to his interest in arms limitations, particularly his interest in the Eden plan or revised versions of it.

On his departure for Moscow, Macmillan sounded a theme of arms limitations: "All the same, in these atomic days, each side has a tremendous interest in peace. I would call it almost a vested interest, and we therefore must in that spirit somehow find agreement." [79] Arriving in Moscow, he engrossed himself in discussions with Khrushchev, listening to a great extent, asserting himself where he considered the Soviets mistaken about Western policies toward Germany. The Berlin discussions did not prove productive; the trade discussions did. The first round proved inconclusive.

On the fourth day of Macmillan's visit, Khrushchev interrupted the bilateral discussions to deliver a re-election speech. Starting from Macmillan's premise that war had to be avoided, he drew quite different conclusions. If war were absurd, then, he insisted, the DDR could not be overturned through outmoded Western schemes of German unification.[80] He continued to propose a summit meeting instead of the foreign ministers' conference proposed by the Western powers. Khrushchev spoke disparagingly about Bonn's influence in the Western alliance and about the Geneva nuclear test ban negotiations, both subjects in his presumably confidential discussions with Macmillan. And Khrushchev addressed Macmillan from his election platform, offering him "a treaty of friendship and non-aggression" for a twenty- or fifty-year period. He did not mention this offer during the private discussions.

79. *The Times* (London), February 23, 1959, p. 6.
80. Embree, *op. cit.*, p. 111.

Khrushchev's thunderbolts "stunned" Macmillan, who felt insulted and contemplated returning immediately to London.[81] He decided instead to press Khrushchev to clarify his charges. Publicly, the British delegation put as good a light on Khrushchev's speech as possible. In the second round with Khrushchev in private, Macmillan warned him that unless the Soviets consented to negotiations—as proposed in the note of February 16—the Western powers would feel compelled to move quickly toward preparing extraordinary measures to defend West Berlin.[82] At this point in the visit, Macmillan's initiative had completely failed.

On February 28, before a third round, the Soviets turned amiable again. Mikoyan joined the British delegation on tour in Leningrad, inviting Foreign Secretary Selwyn Lloyd to a meeting with Gromyko. The next day Mikoyan identified the Soviet policy of peaceful coexistence with the "wise" old British phrase: "Live and let live." [83] With more confidence that he was being heard, Macmillan replied: "I have been struck by the universal approval with which I have met during the short tour of your country when I have said that we both have a common interest in peace."

Although the stage was set for the third round, the Soviets decided to relay a diplomatic note in reply to the Western note of February 16. Their note deflated the third round as effectively as Khrushchev's speech soured the second. In their note of March 2, the Soviets finally agreed to a foreign ministers' conference—on the terms they had originally proposed in their note of November 27—to consider their free city proposal and a peace treaty. In consenting to talk, they removed the six-month deadline of May 27, proposing an April conference lasting not more than "two or three months." [84] They urged, however, that a foreign ministers' conference should prepare the way for a summit conference with a broad agenda. This note terminated the so-called "deadline crisis." Khrushchev did not achieve negotiations at the level he preferred, but he did succeed in achieving negotiations on the future of Berlin.

Khrushchev let Macmillan examine the note before he sent it. He did not discuss it with him. A British counterproposal to the Soviet suggestion for a nonaggression pact proved to be the only tangible

81. *The New York Times*, February 25, 1959, p. 1; March 25, 1959, p. 1.
82. *The Times* (London), February 28, 1959, p. 6.
83. *The New York Times*, March 2, 1959, p. 1.
84. Embree, *op. cit.*, p. 226.

product of the third round, although other arms limitations measures were discussed. The conversation must have been awkward, since the Soviets had again pre-empted the diplomatic exchange through their latest note. Twice during the British visit, they spoke to the world at large, first rejecting a foreign ministers' conference, then accepting one. Both statements tended to ignore the bilateral Anglo-Soviet discussion in progress. Macmillan was twice insulted for his efforts.[85] The Tories glossed over the insults later with election slogans that Macmillan had resolved the "deadline crisis."

The Anglo-Soviet communiqué at the conclusion of Macmillan's visit asserted the dubious claim that "the free interchange of views and ideas which has taken place has created a better understanding of the respective attitudes of the two governments and has thereby made a useful contribution to the forthcoming international discussions in a wider circle." [86] The passage arousing most interest abroad, inserted by the British, referred to the usefulness of further study of "the possibilities of increasing security by some method of limitation of forces and weapons, both conventional and nuclear, in an agreed area of Europe, coupled with an appropriate system of inspection."

Khrushchev's chicanery during the visit discouraged any conclusion that Macmillan broke the deadlock over the level—summit or foreign ministers'—that negotiations would initially assume. However, the visit certainly indicated to Khrushchev that sentiment existed in the Atlantic alliance for early negotiations and for exploring alternatives to the status quo in Central Europe and probably in Berlin as well. The most that can be said about Macmillan's visit, ironically, is that it probably further encouraged Khrushchev's expectations previously aroused by Dulles' flexibility.

Macmillan returned to London with a peace platform on which to electioneer. But across the Channel, he faced angry neighbors.[87] He upset de Gaulle and Adenauer with the communiqué reference to "some method of limitation of forces and weapons . . . in an agreed

---

85. Emrys Hughes wrote an amusing and critical account of Macmillan's journey to Moscow from an accompanying Labour M.P.'s perspective, *Pilgrims' Progress in Russia* (London: Housman's Publishers, 1959).

86. *The New York Times*, March 4, 1959, p. 3.

87. Adenauer and de Gaulle commiserated in Paris, March 4, about Macmillan's initiative. It rankled Adenauer for months to come that Macmillan had even gone to Moscow at this juncture. *Ibid.*, March 5, 1959, p. 1.

area of Europe. . . ." They understood from what Dulles had said earlier that incentives would be offered the Soviets only in exchange for steps toward the 1955 free elections formula. The communiqué did not state that any progress had been made on the German problem to justify the statement on security measures. They suspected Macmillan had found the Soviets adamantly against German unity and had turned to arms limitations as a substitute for progress on the essentials.[88] Adenauer believed that Macmillan had made concessions without counterconcessions.

Macmillan and Foreign Secretary Lloyd went to Paris and Bonn in March to mend fences. They clarified the security measures they had in mind. No disengagement, they said, but a "thinning out" of troops and nuclear weapons more accurately described their thinking.[89] Specifically Macmillan proposed a "controlled limitation of forces" within a Central European zone.[90] The British intended to improve the status quo, reducing the tension associated with the armed division of Europe. To Adenauer, the improvement Macmillan suggested appeared too one-sided. Bonn did not want changes in the military side of the status quo until a settlement of the political side— involving the division of Germany, the future of Berlin, and other issues—seemed possible. Macmillan, in practice, did not support Bonn's Eastern interests. Not very sincerely, Macmillan suggested

88. *The Times* (London), March 5, 1959, p. 8; *The New York Times*, March 6, 1959, p. 3; one should keep in mind the general distrust that Adenauer and de Gaulle had for the British in this period because of Britain's opposition to and attempted obstruction of the formation of the Common Market. Roscoe Drummond and Gaston Coblenz, *Duel at the Brink: John Foster Dulles' Command of American Power* (New York: Doubleday and Co., Inc., 1960), p. 59; more generally consult Dorothy Pickles, *The Uneasy Entente: French Foreign Policy and Franco-British Misunderstandings* (London: Oxford University Press, 1966) ; D. C. Watt, *Britain Looks to Germany* (London: Oswald Wolff, 1965).

89. *The New York Times*, March 11, 1959, p. 3.

90. *Ibid.*, March 13, 1959, p. 1. Macmillan did not always explain whether he proposed a "freeze" on forces in Central Europe or a "thinning out," a different but, related possibility. At the 1955 Geneva foreign ministers' conference following the summit of that year, he put forward on Prime Minister Eden's behalf a proposal similar to his own in 1959. *Documents*, pp. 194-195. Macmillan discussed plans both for a "freeze" and a "thinning out," the "freeze" to precede the "thinning out" in a process of reducing tension. Since progress really lay with the latter, he placed his emphasis there. Eugene Hinterhoff, *Disengagement* (London: Stevens and Sons, Limited, 1959), p. 263; cf. pp. 180, 260-264, 275-276.

that his proposal would advance the cause of German unity. Adenauer, equally insincere, refused to accept a reciprocal reduction of forces unless accompanied by a general disarmament agreement.[91]

De Gaulle backed Adenauer, insisting on a linkage between German free elections and arms limitations.[92] France, like Britain, did not have any enthusiasm for Bonn's Eastern interests. De Gaulle and Adenauer apparently reached an understanding—how explicit one can only speculate—that if Adenauer supported de Gaulle on Common Market policies, de Gaulle would support Adenauer on Berlin and other Eastern issues.[93]

Macmillan expected greater support from Eisenhower than he got from either Adenauer or de Gaulle, or for that matter, from Khrushchev. To make headway with Eisenhower, Macmillan had to persuade the President that the 1955 German free elections formula could be advanced through arms limitations. He argued that the reduction of tension in Central Europe through arms limitations would create an opportunity for Bonn to take the initiative itself and work to overcome the division of Germany. Eisenhower, still leaning on the 1955 formula, said he would consider only an inspected arms "freeze" and, then, only if it would not change the local balance of power in Central Europe, discriminate against Bonn, or damage NATO's military posture.[94]

Macmillan also argued for a summit conference. Eisenhower, after spurning Bulganin's offer for over a year, now shared this interest. He changed his mind because Khrushchev consented, in the Soviet note of March 2, to a prior foreign ministers' conference.[95] Eisenhower insisted, as Dulles did, that the prior conference would have to be a productive one, although he did not specify how productive. Adenauer and de Gaulle were beginning to change their minds about a summit meeting because of the wider agenda suggested in the Soviet note.

Macmillan also impressed the President with the following argu-

91. *The New York Times*, March 14, 1959, p. 1.

92. *The Christian Science Monitor*, March 11, 1959, p. 2.

93. Edgar S. Furniss, Jr., "France under de Gaulle," *Headline Series*, January–February, 1960, p. 49; see also Alfred Grosser, *French Foreign Policy under de Gaulle*, trans. Lois Ames Pattison (Boston: Little, Brown and Company, 1967), pp. 66-67.

94. *The New York Times*, March 23, 1959, p. 1.

95. *Ibid.*, March 18, 1959, p. 1.

ment: consent now, in March, to a summit rather than in some greater crisis where Khrushchev could confine the choice to either a military confrontation or concessions—both undesirable options. Proceeding from Dulles' flexibility to the point of developing proposals for a negotiated settlement of Berlin and related issues, Macmillan pressed his allies to move toward a summit to avoid a worse crisis than they had already experienced since November.

7. The "Inflexibles"

While Macmillan led the way to the summit, President de Gaulle, as a prospective conferee, objected to the British agenda. Specifically, he categorically opposed Macmillan's arms measures for arms limitations. In the first of his semiannual Elysée monologues with the press on March 25, he intimated that if the Soviets worried about their own security, they might follow France's example and put away "the memory of trials suffered" at German hands.[96] He remained unconvinced that Moscow had no alternative to its current German policy. "We shall thus support nothing which would be such as to lead the German people to despair or to compromise its peaceful future. . . ." In French foreign policy, the DDR—"this arbitrary construction"—would in no case be treated as an equal of Bonn.

He sketched the solution to the German problem that he believed all parties should accept. It had to allow for an "entirely free" Germany. It had to have two provisions: (1) the present frontiers should remain and (2) the Germans should "move toward integrating themselves one day in a contractual organization of all Europe for cooperation, liberty, and peace." "A contractual organization of all Europe" would include the Soviet Union or, at least, European Russia. How precisely an all-European organization would be constructed could only be glimpsed in the kind of structures being developed for Western European cooperation. In other words, German unity should be part of a general European settlement. Admittedly, this solution did not seem possible at the moment, and no other was acceptable. "Awaiting the time when this ideal can be achieved," he recommended that the Germans "multiply between themselves links and relationships in all practical fields." But de Gaulle went on, rather unexpectedly, to endorse the Oder-Neisse

96. For his complete text, see *ibid.*, March 26, 1959, p. 8.

line as a frontier between Poland and Germany and to urge Germans on both sides of the dividing line to cooperate where they could. Clearly, he had limits to his support for Bonn's Eastern policy.[97]

De Gaulle opposed Dulles' and Macmillan's flexibility. His opposition did not mean that he opposed all negotiations or that he opposed the agenda they suggested. He regretted their tactics and their timing. He preferred not to offer to negotiate at a time when the Soviet Union tried to intimidate the Western powers in a Berlin crisis.[98] He felt vindicated in his views when he observed Khrushchev's rude treatment of Macmillan in Moscow. He finally agreed to negotiate only when the Soviet Union relinquished its six-month deadline in the note of March 2.

Although Bonn did not have a legal role in the Berlin occupation regime, the Adenauer cabinet worried terribly about the outcome of the "deadline crisis." Contrary to some British and American opinion at the time, Bonn seriously wanted to retain an option for Germany with Berlin as the capital of a restored state because the legitimacy of the Federal Republic as the representative of all Germans was at stake. Adenauer perceived dangers for the Federal Republic in changing the status quo that his allies scarcely considered. They were much less sensitive than he to the risks incurred in any negotiations on the status of Berlin. He did not consider the Soviet draft peace treaty a mere expression of Soviet fears for their security. He saw it as very radical surgery for his own country's political life and limb. Indeed, if West Germany became part of a nuclear-free zone, its sovereignty, legitimacy, and entire foreign policy would be affected, not just its military policy.

The fate of the regime in Bonn is closely tied to the fate of West Berlin. Through a system of special subsidies, Bonn remained largely responsible for the standard of living in West Berlin. The Federal Government obligated itself to maintain a sufficient level of Deutschmarks for circulation in West Berlin, to promote markets abroad for West Berlin products, to include West Berlin in the

97. Bonn had unsettled territorial claims against Poland. Thus, Bonn was upset and Moscow pleased that de Gaulle endorsed the Oder-Neisse frontier. Some West German officials have since suggested that he later retracted this endorsement in an address to a joint session of the United States Congress in 1960, but this conclusion is not apparent from a reading of the address. See *The New York Times*, April 26, 1960, p. 18.

98. *The Washington Post*, February 10, 1959, p. 9.

Federal social insurance programs, to extend credits to Berlin industry, and to allow tax concessions for Berliners. These measures stimulate purchasing power in the city, more purchasing power than the city could command simply on the basis of goods sold.[99]

The Federal Government and the West Berlin Senat by practice and by law treat West Berlin as a land or state within the Federal Republic. The United States, Britain, and France, as occupying powers, continue as the ultimate legal authority in West Berlin. They acknowledge and support the economic, political, and legal connections of the city to West Germany, defining the viability of the city as a vital interest of their own.[100]

The Soviets' free city proposal would have severed the network of connections between West Germany and West Berlin. Not surprisingly, Bonn directed efforts in the "deadline crisis" to deflecting prospective negotiations away from Berlin, toward general disarmament and other unlikely projects. As soon as he received the Soviet note of November 27, Adenauer proposed to his allies—in a rather obvious diversionary tactic—that the note should be exploited to convene a four-power conference on Germany.[101]

Adenauer's critics—Lippmann and others—argued that the interzonal trade agreements between Bonn and Pankow contradicted his rigid opposition to a peace treaty and to diplomatic relations with Pankow.[102] On November 22, 1958, for example, Bonn reached a supplemental trade agreement with Pankow on the exchange of Ruhr coal for East German brown coal and wheat.[103] Many similar agreements operated between Bonn and Pankow relating to transportation, health, and postal services.[104]

99. Franz Kluge, "The Economic Viability of Berlin," *Berlin—Pivot of German Destiny*, trans. and ed. Charles B. Robson (Chapel Hill: The University of North Carolina Press, 1960), pp. 146-148; see also Bruce L. R. Smith, "The Governance of Berlin, *International Conciliation*, Number 525, November 1959.

100. For a discussion of the legal aspects of the Berlin question, see Roland J. Stanger (ed.), *West Berlin: The Legal Context* (Columbus; Ohio State University Press, 1966).

101. *The New York Times*, December 3, 1958, p. 3.

102. Lippmann in *The Herald Tribune*, January 8, 1959, p. 16.

103. *The Times* (London), November 23, 1958, p. 6.

104. The trade agreements were negotiated by the Agency for Interzonal Trade in Berlin, representing Bonn, and the East German Ministry for Internal German and Foreign Trade. Federal railway officials met with East German Reichban officials on a regular basis. Postal, inland waterways, and health authorities met irregularly. *Ibid.*, November 20, 1958, p. 10.

In 1961, interzonal trade represented 11 percent of the DDR's total foreign trade. It was an important 11 percent, composed of finished or semifinished products, special steels and machinery in short supply in East Germany. Interzonal trade represented about 2 percent of the Federal Republic's foreign trade. The terms and restraints on interzonal trade were, to a large extent, Bonn's conditions for Pankow's commercial access to West Germany.[105] Since the trade continues to be of relatively greater importance to the East German economy than to the West German, Bonn entered into trade agreements with Pankow as a rough *quid pro quo* for uninterrupted access to West Berlin.[106] Theoretically, this understanding—sometimes more tacit than explicit—should enable the economy of West Berlin to be less sensitive to potential blockade threats. In practice, cancellation has proven to be a rather clumsy tool for influencing Pankow's actions in Berlin crises. The trade agreements are a complex and unique relationship between West Berlin and Pankow regulated by Bonn. The agreements exhibit a mutual dependency by West Berlin and Pankow on the West German economy.[107]

On political grounds, Bonn could make a reasonable case for maintaining commercial relations with Pankow without diplomatic relations. Bonn regarded the trade agreements as understandings between "peoples" and "currency areas" rather than governments. In Bonn's view, nondiplomatic relations with the DDR enhanced the political influence of Bonn in East Germany in two respects: (1) it made a portion of the East German economy dependent on Bonn

105. The two parties used the Deutschmark-West rather than the Deutschmark-East. Bonn could curtail the trade by refusing export permits to West German firms, if a serious trade imbalance occurred. Horst Mendershausen, *Interzonal Trade in Germany, Part I: The Trade and the Contractual Relations*, RM-3686-PR, The Rand Corporation, Santa Monica, California, July, 1963, pp. 15-29.

106. The "Berlin clause" in the agreements operated to the effect that any interference by Pankow of commercial traffic to West Berlin would result in an immediate cancellation of the complete agreement by Bonn. Mendershausen, *Interzonal Trade in Germany, Part II: Interaction with Early Berlin Conflicts*, RM-3686-PR (Part II), The Rand Corporation, Santa Monica, California, November, 1963, p. 38. Since the mid-1960's a specific Berlin clause is no longer used in the trade agreements.

107. Mendershausen considers interzonal trade a subject economists are wary of because of its political and esoteric character. He describes it as "silent" or "hostile trade" between "fictional partners." Officially, it is trade between "currency areas." Mendershausen, *Interzonal Trade in Germany, Part I*, pp. 12-15.

and (2) it contributed to the standard of living of the East German population. Commercial relations did not constitute an accommodation with the DDR. Rather they gave substance to Bonn's claim of being representative for the whole German people. Bonn treated Pankow not as a foreign power but as an "authority" illegally administering the affairs of 17,000,000 Germans.

For these reasons, Adenauer opposed Dulles' accommodation to East German administration of the access routes.[108] Adenauer believed that short-term conveniences for access would endanger long-term security for Berlin. East German access controls would also irretrievably damage Bonn's legitimacy and foreign policy. Adenauer firmly believed that if his allies, as occupying powers, engaged in operational relations with the DDR, they would, in effect, abandon their commitment embodied in the 1954 Paris protocols to recognize Bonn alone as spokesman for Germany. Adenauer perceived the readiness of the United States to engage in operational relations with the DDR as a disturbing measure of Washington's reluctance to continue earlier policies toward Germany. He regarded Dulles' suggestion for a German confederation in the same light. While Bonn consented to study possible forms of confederation to find an acceptable version incorporating free elections, it generally treated confederation as antithetical to its own policy and interests.[109]

Bonn feared isolation from its allies, particularly the United States, as the greatest single danger in the Berlin crisis. For the Soviets, Bonn's diplomatic isolation was the key to success. Moscow pressed hard throughout the period to shake the United States' confidence in Bonn. Adenauer felt constrained to strike a balance between supporting and restraining his allies. He had to go along to avoid isolation. He had to oppose them, carefully, when he believed they ignored Bonn's concerns. Dulles' and Macmillan's campaign to negotiate a way out of the "deadline crisis" placed great strains on their relations with Adenauer. And the negotiations which followed became extraordinarily awkward for him. He had to lobby vigorously for Bonn's place among presumed friends, not always successfully.

108. *The New York Times*, November 23, 1958, p. 1.

109. *The Herald Tribune*, January 21, 1969, p. 8; see Adenauer's memoirs of this period, *Erinnerungen, 1955–1959* (Stuttgart: Deutsche Verlag-Anstalt, 1967), chapter 14.

8. *The Decision to Negotiate*

The Western powers agreed to negotiate, but the agreement was a composite mix of perceptions. Dulles and Macmillan wanted negotiations with the Soviet Union in order to avoid war and to exert political counterpressures on Moscow. They considered Soviet proposals in the "deadline crisis" to be negotiable. Acheson and the Eisenhower Administration's domestic critics perceived risks in a negotiating strategy—a strategy they believed inappropriate to the crisis. De Gaulle agreed with Acheson that the threatening tenor of Soviet demands precluded useful negotiations. De Gaulle finally agreed to negotiate after the Soviets retracted their deadline in March and consented to a foreign ministers' conference to be followed by a summit conference with a wide agenda. He probably felt the wider the agenda the more readily he could steer the negotiations away from the issues most sensitive to Adenauer and himself, or veto any incipient settlements which seemed undesirable. Adenauer shared this view.

The Western decision to negotiate combined the option Dulles and Macmillan urged—to conduct serious negotiations—with the option de Gaulle and Adenauer preferred—to conduct no negotiations or very broad negotiations. The decision to negotiate, therefore, contained latent contradictions. This kind of decision could rather easily come undone in practice, as eventually happened. The decision held through the Paris summit conference in the spring of 1960. After that time, the Western powers could no longer agree on negotiation as an appropriate strategy. For the moment, the United States and Britain had the chance to test their hypothesis that Moscow initiated the crisis because of a security interest in consolidating its Eastern European empire.

The Western powers miscalculated in their early decision to negotiate. They underestimated Moscow's fears of West German rearmament and failed to communicate that they were really unwilling to concede what the Soviets desired. Acheson's option, a military demonstration, might have avoided early confusion, although it contained significant risks. It had the benefit of warning Khrushchev not to expect a political payoff from the crisis, but it risked producing an exchange of provocations. He would have been more informed of the hazards in his policy, even though he probably would have pressed on to remove all doubt.

PART II

Berlin Negotiations and the U-2 Incident

CHAPTER 3

Geneva I:
Negotiations under Duress

AT GENEVA in May 1959, the Western allies tested Dulles' and Macmillan's negotiation strategy in response to Khrushchev's Berlin project. This strategy proved unproductive and, in fact, decidedly counterproductive. Soviet Foreign Minister Gromyko—with threats in hand and Khrushchev voluble in the background—drove his Western colleagues from one corner to another, disposing of all their proposals. When the Western ministers had exhausted their supply of proposals, they asked for a recess. Since Dulles had not prepared a fallback position for the contingency when negotiations failed and Moscow persisted, his successor had to construct one *ad hoc*. Herter and Eisenhower decided to relieve the impasse in Geneva by resorting to bilateral summit diplomacy between Eisenhower and Khrushchev. Eisenhower invited Khrushchev to the United States and Herter flew back to Geneva for a final round, awaiting Khrushchev's reply. In that round, Gromyko led the Western ministers into discussing recognition of the DDR. At this point, they perceived two bleak choices: either to continue a discussion in which the risks seemed to be increasing or to risk a greater crisis leading to war if the conference ended in failure. Khrushchev spared them the choice when he decided to accept Eisenhower's invitation. Soviet diplomacy successfully eroded Eisenhower's insistence that a productive foreign ministers' conference had to precede a summit conference.

Two aspects of the Geneva Conference are of general interest. First, in the course of the conference the Western ministers succeeded in drawing from Gromyko—in one of his more candid moments—a statement of what Moscow's objectives really were. He said it wanted to disarm Bonn. Second, the record of the conference provides material for a study in some detail of Soviet negotiating behavior.

1. *The Diplomatic Game at Geneva: Quarrels within the Western Team*

Before the Geneva Conference, Khrushchev put the Western foreign ministers on notice that he eventually wanted a summit conference and that he expected them to "cut the Gordian knot," opening the way. He dropped a few ideas for them to consider. He admitted, for the first time, that the Western powers had a legal basis for occupying Berlin. But their rights would have to expire with a peace treaty. He suggested that the United Nations might find a role in the settlement.[1]

All parties agreed on May 11 as opening day at Geneva. The Western foreign ministers, with Herter acting for Dulles, met several times in Paris before that date to argue out detailed proposals. On April 4, they approved a working outline of a package plan with two parallel sets of measures. One set provided for German unity to develop in three stages beginning with the integration of divided Berlin, proceeding to the development of commercial and political relations between the DDR and the Federal Republic, and culminating in a peace treaty with a new, integrated German state. The other set linked progress in arms limitations to progress in each stage of political integration in Germany. Its provisions included force reductions in a zone of Central Europe, prevention of surprise attack, and a general nuclear test ban. Arms limitations and political settlements would move together in a lock-step procedure. The Western plan contained provisions representing the range of opinion within the alliance. To be sure, it incorporated British proposals for a Berlin settlement and zonal arms limitations. French and West German views could be detected, as well, because German unity and comprehensive disarmament appeared in the ultimate stage. The

1. Embree, *op. cit.*, p. 146.

American delegation seemed more concerned to have the alliance speak in unison.

Unfortunately, the Western plan did not present a united front to Moscow. Allied divergencies were all too obvious. Considered as a whole, the plan appeared to favor Bonn because it provided for German unity. Considered in its parts, the plan seemed to be a British product with a Berlin settlement accompanied by arms limitations. The plan struck an observer as both unyielding and conciliatory.

The British, dissatisfied and grumpy in April, did not consider the plan to be conciliatory enough. What was the purpose of East-West negotiations, they asked, unless the West offered to make concessions in exchange for Soviet concessions? Macmillan's efforts at coalition diplomacy in February and March had not produced discernible results by early April. Nevertheless, the British position of April 1959 eventually won the day in allied circles in spite of Bonn's opposition, although not until later in the Geneva Conference. The Macmillan government played the role of broker between the United States and the Soviet Union, assuming a catalytic function in the conference. The parts of the final Western plan which were British in origin increasingly attracted attention.

Basically, the British argued that if a relaxation of tensions could be negotiated, the internal economic contradictions in the Soviet Union would be aggravated, for example, the contradiction between producing arms and raising the standard of living.[2] This argument assumed, without demonstrating, a correlation between a relaxed foreign policy and a relaxed internal policy. One could argue with equal force to demonstrate a correlation between a relaxed foreign policy and a tight internal policy or between a tight foreign policy and a relaxed internal policy. The British argument really implied an assumption about the nature of the Soviet regime, specifically, that the regime had to answer to the consumer population, somewhat as a British prime minister had to answer to the working population of Britain. How the British perceived the Soviet regime determined their choice of correlations. True, Britain could not endure a heavy arms budget coupled with domestic austerity because of international

2. Lippmann in *The Herald Tribune*, April 8, 1959, p. 1.

trade and payments deficits and the political strength of the trade union movement. Simply to project Britain's problem as Russia's, however, took little account of the differences between the two economies.

The British contended that the Western powers were in an embarrassing position if the old occupation agreements, resting on the right of conquest, constituted their only legal defense for remaining in West Berlin. Theoretically, as a party to the German surrender and as the conqueror of Berlin in 1945, Moscow could lay claim to West Berlin by right of conquest.[3] As a practical matter, they were not impressed with the security of Western access to Berlin. To improve the legal and military position of the alliance in West Berlin, they proposed a new statute for all-Berlin to internationalize the city. The statute contained explicit, new safeguards for security of the access routes and the Western military garrisons. The three Western powers would remain guarantors of West Berlin. The British believed that a new statute called for some manner of relations, as a matter of course, between East and West Berlin and between Pankow and Bonn. They thought the United Nations might wish to maintain a "presence" in the city until Berlin could be restored as the capital of Germany. The British proposal amounted to a separate settlement for Berlin, tacitly setting German unity aside.[4]

Walter Lippmann concurred in the British proposal and offered a rationale for it. He said:

> My conviction is that the future of West Berlin must be protected not by standing pat, but on insisting that West Berlin needs and is entitled to have a new status. When Mr. K tells us that the present status of Berlin is obsolete, it is a mistake for the West to act as if any departure from the status quo would be a defeat and surrender. It might be an improvement. At present the status quo is from our point of view extremely unsatisfactory. The right answer to Mr. K is to propose that we negotiate a new charter or statute in which West Berlin is guaranteed an ordered future by the presence of Western troops acting under international auspices.[5]

3. Lippmann, *ibid.*
4. *The New York Times*, April 8, 1959, p. 1.
5. *The Herald Tribune*, April 8, 1959, p. 1.

The British did not know whether the Soviets would be receptive to a new statute erected on the basis of the old occupation regime. They felt encouraged by Khrushchev's comments accommodating the West's military presence or the United Nations in West Berlin. The British based their case for the internationalization of Berlin on the "reality" of two Germanies, diplomatically recognized or not. They suggested that the Soviet Union might accept a Berlin settlement if the allies offered the incentive of new security arrangements in Central Europe to accompany it. They contemplated a *modus vivendi* developing from a realistic consensus on all sides that German unity could not be readily achieved and that Berlin should be treated as a special problem.

The British proposal outraged Bonn. The West German ambassador in Washington, Dr. Wilhelm Grewe, challenged their assumption that German unity had to be ruled out, that new relations between Pankow and Bonn were required. He reminded the British that the Western powers had pledged in the Paris protocols of 1954 to support Bonn's policies in Germany.[6] Berlin was a special problem, he admitted, not because of a vain German hope for unifying a divided city, but because the Soviet Union chose to generate a crisis over the city. He flatly opposed a new statute for West Berlin. In negotiating a statute, he thought the West would be conceding the negotiability of the occupation regime. Once negotiated, he argued, Berlin's status would rest on a contractual basis Soviet leaders could ignore at will. By contrast, he proposed that an alternate legal concept applied—the right of belligerent occupation, distinguished from the right of conquest, which avoided legal dependence on the Soviet Union for the Western presence in Berlin. A United Nations "presence," a presence deriving from "shifting majorities" in the U.N. General Assembly, would offer little security for the city. To Bonn's satisfaction, the French lined up squarely behind Grewe.

Lippmann replied to Grewe as follows:

> This is a strange argument. Why does a new statute or treaty about Berlin have to make any such preposterous concession to the Soviet Union? Why cannot the new statute or treaty recognize and reaffirm the right of the Western Allies to be

6. *News from the German Embassy*, April 15, 1969.

present in Berlin? To argue that "every new treaty arrangement" can only surrender our rights in Berlin, that no new treaty arrangement can fortify our rights, is not a legal or political proposition. It is a political neurosis engendered by profound self-distrust.

Lippmann rigorously criticized Bonn because he believed that Adenauer's policies generally had little support in Europe. He thought the United States should no longer allow Adenauer a veto over American foreign policy. West Berlin ought to be defended in a way which had the "assent and approval of the whole society of nations." [7]

The State Department tried to mediate the quarrel, agreeing with the British that the Soviet position should be explored in depth and with Bonn that possibilities for a settlement probably remained sharply limited.[8] A diplomatic working party in London eventually thrashed out a negotiating position which narrowed, without resolving, the differences between Britain and Bonn.[9] On April 30, in Paris, the four foreign ministers, with Herter now Secretary of State, set their seal of approval on the final plan.

One tactical question remained: whether the Western plan should be presented in a package or in separate proposals. As a package, Soviet rejection of any one part would be tantamount to rejection of the entire plan and negotiations would quickly terminate. If, however, the allies presented the plan as a set of interrelated, albeit separate proposals, Soviet rejection of one proposal would concentrate negotiations on the others with, perhaps, greater prospect of success. Understandably, the Soviets would be interested in separating the allied proposal on Berlin from the other proposals.[10]

Each foreign minister favored a package to the extent that each favored or disfavored a separate Berlin settlement. The British disavowed the package. Bonn and the French preferred it. Herter proposed a compromise: present the plan initially as a package and leave open the question of how to proceed if the Soviets rejected the plan as

---

7. *The Herald Tribune*, April 22, 1959, p. 22.
8. *The New York Times*, April 11, 1959, p. 1.
9. *Ibid.*, April 23, 1959, p. 1.
10. *The New York Times*, May 1, 1959, p. 3; as Lippmann described it: "the object of the negotiations will be a *modus vivendi* which, while it recognizes that there is in fact a partition of Germany, keeps alive the right and the hope of an eventual reunion." *The Herald Tribune*, May 5, 1959, p. 22.

a whole. The others accepted this arrangement.[11] In effect, the ministers agreed to renew the debate among themselves in the middle of the conference.

During the period of the allied discussions of the Western plan, two military incidents occurred bringing two notes of protest from the Soviet Union.[12] On March 27, American transport aircraft flew above the customary 10,000-foot level for Berlin air corridor traffic. The State Department stated that the particular kind of aircraft involved operated most efficiently above 10,000 feet. The aircraft, the Lockheed Hercules C-130 transport, had a capacity for carrying twenty tons of cargo.[13] Actually, the Pentagon wanted to test Soviet reactions to the possibility of an airlift using aircraft that could double the supply tonnage to the garrisons and population of West Berlin. The flight also demonstrated that an airlift from French bases could be used in another blockade.

Soviet fighter aircraft buzzed the transport in the corridors. This action, in turn, provided the administration with an opportunity prior to a blockade to state: "the United States never has recognized and does not recognize any limitation to the right to fly at any altitude in the corridors." [14] The administration made its point in a unilateral test without acquiring the consent of the British or other allies, who considered the test provocative. The Soviets objected that the United States wanted to wreck the Geneva Conference. On April 15, the Pentagon repeated the test with a transport flying at 20,000 feet from northwest France to Berlin.

The tests served to indicate that the United States probably would resort to an airlift, if necessary. But the result of the flights proved ambiguous. The fact that American aircraft were not destroyed in the air on one or two occasions did not provide conclusive evidence of the feasibility of an airlift using C-130's.

2. The Diplomatic Game at Geneva: The West Opens

The Geneva Conference of 1959 was an exhausting, grinding series of sessions that never ended with an opponent that never relented.

11. *The New York Times*, May 1, 1959, p. 1. The Soviets, aware of this allied opening strategy, could, of course, simply oppose it and wait for the package to be untied.

12. *Documents*, pp. 444-445; *The New York Times*, April 30, 1959, p. 5.

13. *The New York Times*, April 2, 1959, p. 1.

14. *Documents*, p. 445.

It extended from May 11 until August 5, a total of sixty-five working days and nights, excluding the late June-early July recess. It involved a hard-fought contest before full galleries of the international press. Two strategies of negotiation clashed. Since both sides preferred negotiations, the clash did not lead to war, but it did not produce a settlement either. The proposals of each side got fully aired, but even gestures for compromise, as matters stood at the end, were incompatible.

The conferees, including two German delegations seated at two side tables,[15] consumed the first two weeks discussing the Western plan and the Soviet draft treaty. Herter presented the Western plan on May 14. The plan contained four stages of evolving agreement, beginning in Stage I with a Berlin settlement integrating the two parts of the divided city, leading in Stage II to the creation of a "mixed German Committee" for drafting an electoral law to carry the German people through a transition period, moving into free elections for an all-German government in Stage III, and culminating in a peace treaty, in Stage IV, between the German state and the United Nations powers of the Second World War.[16]

One feature became unexpectedly important later in the conference —the "mixed German Committee." The committee would consist of twenty-five representatives designated by Bonn and ten by Pankow. A requirement that decisions be taken by a three-fourths majority of the members guaranteed Pankow a veto. Following Dulles' flexibility on the confederation approach to unifying Germany, the United States apparently persuaded Adenauer to allow the mixed committee, a form of confederation, to initiate a process of integration leading to free elections. Herter continued to stress, as Dulles had in 1955, that free elections were the only legitimate basis of a new German government. Now, in 1959, the United States conceded that free elections could be deferred, that the Germans themselves should be responsible for drafting an electoral law and supervising elections, and that the DDR should have a veto throughout the process.

Parallel to the political measures, the plan incorporated—in each of

15. Each German delegation addressed the conference only with unanimous four-power consent.

16. The United States Department of State, *Foreign Ministers Meeting, May–August, 1959*, Geneva, Publication 6882, September 1959, p. 19 (hereafter referred to as *Foreign Ministers Meeting*), pp. 55-60.

the four stages—steps toward general disarmament. Stage II, for example, included Macmillan's proposals for reducing force levels, removing nuclear weapons, preventing surprise attack, and banning third-power possession of nuclear weapons in a zone of Central Europe. Dulles' idea of combining a restored Germany and security guarantees for the Soviet Union could clearly be discerned in the plan.

Speaking from Moscow on May 16, Khrushchev categorically rejected the Western plan. He intervened frequently during the conference. Gordon Craig commented that Khrushchev's interventions revealed his general attitude about negotiations. He did not regard negotiations as a reciprocal matter. He wanted Soviet proposals accepted, either freely or under compulsion.[17] For example, speaking in Tirana, Albania, on May 31, he condemned the "no concessions without counter-concessions" principle. There should be no petty bargaining at Geneva, he said: "We do not have to make any concessions because our proposals have not been made for bargaining." He implied he could not make substantive concessions because he could not compromise about West German "militarism"—read: West German access to nuclear weapons. Most of his speech was an attack on Bonn.

Gromyko submitted his draft treaty on May 15. He did not lose any time in suggesting ways of untying the Western package to get at the British proposals on Berlin he had been reading about in the Western press. On May 19, he started the conference moving in informal channels, giving British Foreign Secretary Lloyd three choices—at lunch—for a Berlin settlement. Lloyd could choose any one he liked: (1) simply withdraw the Western garrisons from Berlin; (2) keep the Western garrisons but add a Soviet one in West Berlin; (3) replace the Western garrisons with neutral United Nations contingents. Lloyd rejected all three, although somewhat encouraged by Gromyko's informality.

May 18 marked the advent of a separate conference on Berlin. James Reston called it "the conference of the villas" because it consisted of a series of luncheon and dinner exchanges at the respective residences of the foreign ministers. He described the daily conference

---

17. "Techniques of Negotiation," *Russian Foreign Policy, Essays in Historical Perspective*, ed. Ivo J. Lederer (New Haven: Yale University Press, 1962), p. 369.

of the three Western ministers and West German Foreign Minister Heinrich Von Brentano in the morning before the four-power meetings as a third Geneva conference.[18]

After May 18, two Geneva conferences proceeded simultaneously, distinguished by the degree of formality and by the substance of discussions. The plenary conference focused on the plan and the draft treaty. The private conference pursued a Berlin settlement at the margin of the great dispute over the future of Germany. This procedure endured until the plenary conference turned to Berlin on May 26.

Just before Herter consented to untie the Western package and discuss Berlin, he demanded that Gromyko specify why the Soviets would not even treat the plan seriously:

> Why is it may we again ask, that the Soviet Union is today brusquely rejecting a Western Peace Plan carefully tailored to meet concerns expressed by the Soviet Union respecting the Western proposals of 1955? Why does the Soviet Union now insist that German reunification be carried out only by the German Federal Republic and the so-called German Democratic Republic? Why has the Soviet Union rejected any linkage between German reunification and European security when it insisted upon such linkage in 1955, with Mr. Khrushchev in the forefront of that insistence? [19]

Herter openly speculated that the answer to his question involved a change in Moscow's perception of its security requirements. He assumed, at least for the sake of argument, that in 1955 the Soviets favored German unity providing it occurred in the context of mutually agreed security guarantees. Now, he thought the Soviets had convinced themselves that their security required a permanently partitioned Germany.

Gromyko denied that the Soviet positions of 1955 and 1959 differed. Both positions left German unity to the Germans. He admitted that previous Soviet proposals contained plans for an all-German government, but he insisted that these proposals had been made in vain:

> They would not listen to these arguments in Bonn at the time, just as they will not listen to them today, if we are to judge by

18. *The New York Times*, May 20, 1959, p. 17.
19. *Foreign Ministers Meeting*, pp. 139-140.

the policy which the Government of the Federal Republic of Germany is pursuing, a policy which is alien to the interests of peace.[20]

Gromyko blamed West German "militarism' 'and "revanchism" for the alleged change in Soviet policy in Germany.

Interestingly, he said the Soviets did not object to "some of the ideas" on European security in the Western plan. He objected to the linkage between these ideas and German unity. He thought the Big Four could make progress on European security issues even while Bonn continued to oppose Moscow on strictly German issues. Thus, he admitted that the Soviet draft treaty had considerable implications for Soviet security. By the end of the second week, Gromyko had clarified the nature of Soviet objectives and the reasons for deadlock in the discussion of the Western plan.

On May 25, Gromyko stated the substance of the Soviet position:

> No one is entitled to expect of us that we should consign to oblivion the stern fact that both the first and the second world wars, which were started by the German militarists, took away the lives of millions of our people. For this reason it is futile to expect that we will allow ourselves to be persuaded that the question of a peace treaty with Germany—in other words, of guarantees of her peaceful development—is a sort of minor question, which can be solved or not solved, which can be discussed today or postponed indefinitely. It is natural that we cannot budge one step where the interests of the Soviet Union are concerned, and we shall defend these interests with the utmost consistency and insistence.[21]

Here, he candidly stated that the Soviet Union intended that its proposed peace treaty would improve its security through the "peaceful development" of Germany. But he was not completely candid. He did not also say that in the name of Soviet security, the treaty would severely damage the West German state.[22]

20. *Ibid.*, p. 150.
21. *Ibid.*, pp. 184-185.
22. DDR Foreign Minister Lothar Bolz echoed Gromyko on this point: "The crucial issue, if tension in Germany is to be reduced and peace in Europe guaranteed, is to prevent the development of German militarism and its equipment with rockets and nuclear weapons. A peace treaty must not by-pass this crucial issue." *Ibid.*, p. 576.

In a note prior to the Geneva Conference, Moscow called attention to the Eisenhower Administration's accelerated implementation of the NATO agreement of December 1957. The agreement with Bonn, the note stated, violated the Potsdam protocol and jeopardized the success of the forthcoming conference.[23] Washington responded arguing that, if the Soviet Union continued to introduce modern weapons into its armed forces, NATO would have to do the same.[24] In another context on May 21, Gromyko assailed "those dangerous steps being taken on the part of Western Germany in the matter of war preparations."[25] Later on May 23, the Soviets sent another note threatening "extremely dangerous consequences" if the United States armed Bonn with nuclear weapons. They charged that to equip Bonn with these weapons represented a threat to Soviet security.[26] The State Department, in reply, accused Moscow of misrepresenting the NATO agreement because the United States—in the terms of the agreement—retained control of the warheads.[27]

3. *The Diplomatic Game at Geneva: Gromyko on the Allied Wicket*

French Foreign Minister Maurice Couve de Murville casually described the Western ministers' decision to untie their package plan as follows:

> I think that the discussion has not been useless, but we have now arrived at a point where we must recognize that our positions have not, for the moment, come closer together. That is why a few days ago we asked Mr. Gromyko what we were going to do now, and Mr. Gromyko replied very simply, "Well, let us talk about the Berlin question."[28]

Neither German representative received an invitation to the private sessions. In the third week of the conference, when the Western ministers proposed a discussion of Berlin without the direct participation of the Germans, they took the first step toward the Berlin *modus vivendi* they were seeking. By agreeing to a Berlin discussion on

23. *Documents*, pp. 446-448.
24. *Ibid.*, p. 455.
25. *Foreign Ministers Meeting*, pp. 139-140.
26. *Documents*, pp. 495-497.
27. *Ibid.*, p. 497.
28. *Foreign Ministers Meeting*, p. 231.

May 26, the ministers did not intend to mislead Gromyko, even though they must have anticipated that he would focus the ensuing discussion on West Berlin and would ignore their questions about East Berlin. Nevertheless, this decision probably encouraged Khrushchev to believe that his pressure tactics had produced first a public conference on Germany and now a secret one on Berlin.

At this point, all the ministers, including Gromyko, flew to Washington. May 27—the date of the original six-month deadline set by the Soviet Union in the note of November 27—ironically found the foreign ministers, including Gromyko, at the graveside of John Foster Dulles. The next day they reviewed the state of their deliberations with President Eisenhower. The President insisted on a "measure of progress" to justify a summit meeting. One particular measure interested him: he still wanted a retraction of the deadline and the threat of unilateral action contained in the Soviet note of November 27. If this could be achieved, he thought that a summit conference would be held without a crisis atmosphere and the Western powers would not be negotiating under duress. He considered a preliminary agreement not to change the status quo in Berlin, except by quadripartite consent, another measure of progress.[29] In other words, the United States could agree to a summit conference on Berlin if the Soviet Union did not try to alter the Berlin status quo before, during, or after the conference. This condition, of course, would deprive the Soviets of their leverage for extracting concessions.

The ministers held their initial secret session on Berlin enroute from Washington to Geneva in Secretary Herter's plane on May 28. On May 29, in the second session, Gromyko reiterated the three bleak choices for changing the Berlin status quo he had proposed to Lloyd on May 18. The three Western ministers refused Gromyko's choices, but they said they were willing to concede changes in certain characteristics of the occupation regime, such as the dissemination of propaganda and the operation of intelligence agencies in West Berlin. At the May 26 open session, before the Dulles funeral, Herter had already discussed an interim Berlin settlement and had offered a greater concession: to negotiate changes in the level of garrison forces. He also invited the Soviets to negotiate a new agreement for the security of the access routes.[30] The American delegation hoped

29. *The New York Times*, May 30, 1959, p. 1.
30. *Foreign Ministers Meeting*, pp. 207-209.

that a settlement would issue from this concession and this invitation.

Gromyko replied to Herter's proposal on May 30. Although he rejected it, he suggested the creation of an international commission to oversee the free city status of West Berlin, an idea the allies later adapted to their proposals. Gromyko proposed that the four occupation powers and East Germany be represented on the commission.[31]

The Western ministers pressed Gromyko to explain precisely in which ways Moscow considered the status of Berlin provocative. In effect, they asked him the price of a settlement. How could 10,000 Western troops in the midst of twenty-two Soviet divisions contribute to tension, they asked. The Western delegations, in the fourth week of the conference, directed their efforts toward easing Gromyko's expressed concern about a threat to Soviet security emanating from Berlin. On June 2, Gromyko said he welcomed the Western attitude. He raised the hopes of his counterparts suggesting that a Berlin settlement and recognition of the DDR were "two different matters." And he admitted that Western troops were not in West Berlin illegally; their presence was simply outdated.[32] These statements implicitly withdrew the threats in the note of November 27.

Either in response to Gromyko's unusual statement or as a means of drawing him out, on June 3 the Western ministers explicitly proposed to him that if he would guarantee free access to Berlin, they would consent to a ceiling on the force levels of their garrisons in the city. Gromyko undoubtedly knew that they wanted to improve free access to Berlin for civilian traffic—the economic lifeline of the city—when they also proposed a commission of the four powers, Bonn, and Pankow to manage the access routes.[33]

The British lead is apparent in the Western proposal on June 3. In fact, they urged their allies to go further and propose an agreement guaranteeing Western rights in Berlin supplemented by a protocol defining the implementation of access rights more precisely than in

---

31. *Ibid.*, pp. 214-225.
32. *Ibid.*, pp. 234-243.
33. *The New York Times*, June 4, 1959, p. 1. For Bonn and Pankow, the West had in mind roles equivalent to their advisory roles at the Geneva Conference. The commission suggested here emerged again in 1962 in the Western proposal for a Berlin International Access Authority with a membership including the four powers, the Federal Republic, the DDR, West Berlin, and East Berlin.

any of the wartime documents. They also urged a reduction of garrison troops from 11,000 to 8,500 or 7,500.

On June 10, Gromyko responded, on new instructions from Khrushchev who had been discussing with Ulbricht the unsatisfactory state of affairs at Geneva. Gromyko restored the earlier Soviet deadline threats, deflating the hopes he had raised on June 2. He declared:

> The USSR, taking into account the position of the Western Powers, is prepared not to insist on the immediate and complete abolition of the occupation regime in West Berlin. The Soviet Government could agree to the provisional maintenance of certain occupation rights of the Western Powers in West Berlin, but on condition that such a situation would exist only for a strictly limited period, namely one year.[34]

He also said that the Soviet Union expected Bonn and Pankow to create a mixed German committee consisting of an equally divided membership within one year. The committee would be charged with the task of developing intra-German relations and preparing a peace treaty.

He went further to identify the kind of interim settlement Moscow would accept. It had to contain the following elements: (1) a reduction of the Western garrisons to "token contingents"; (2) a stop to West Berlin propaganda; (3) a ban on nuclear weapons in the Western sectors. Western access to Berlin would be guaranteed, he said, if the ministers assented to this proposal. This settlement would bestow diplomatic recognition upon the DDR as a signatory to the four-power protocol fixing the "provisional status of West Berlin."

If the West did not accept his proposal, Gromyko said, the Soviet Union would not "confirm its agreement to the continuation of the regime in West Berlin." If the West accepted the proposal, but, in the interim period, the mixed committee did not advance toward a treaty, "Then, the Soviet Union . . . will be compelled to sign a peace treaty with the German Democratic Republic," he warned. Agreed or not agreed, West Berlin's lease would expire and Gromyko served notice of eviction. His proposal incorporated two threats: (1) either renew the lease on new terms or the Soviet Union would act unilaterally; (2) once renewed on those terms, either submit to

---

34. *Foreign Ministers Meeting*, p. 261.

DDR management or, again, the Soviet Union would increase the risks of war through unilateral action.

Herter vigorously rejected the proposal. He said he saw no need drastically to reduce Western troops, since Soviet troops already outnumbered them in the vicinity of Berlin. He objected that Gromyko proposed curtailing propaganda and subversion from West Berlin, without also curtailing it from East Berlin. He could agree to a nuclear ban for Berlin as a separate item in an otherwise unacceptable package. More important, he considered the time limit another deadline implying a threat to West Berlin. Herter identified the Soviet proposal as "the same element of duress that was contained in the Soviet note of November 27, 1958, which we and our allies flatly rejected." He asked the Soviet Union to reconsider.[35]

After this explosion on June 10, the Conference deteriorated rapidly. Lloyd spoke for his colleagues in saying that "the wheel seems to have come full circle and after five weeks or so we find ourselves back at the beginning." Adenauer chimed in from Bonn, urging a recess because he did not like the concessions in the June 3 Western proposal. The final Western proposal, submitted June 16, went still further than previous ones. It omitted an express statement of Western occupation rights because Gromyko had suggested during the second week of the Berlin discussions that a new Berlin agreement could be written without mentioning occupation rights. This understanding satisfied both sides in the second week. Gromyko subsequently retracted this suggestion. The Western ministers adopted the June 16 proposal to advance the prospect of an agreement.[36]

It is worth noting that in the three weeks of discussion on Berlin each successive Western proposal became increasingly candid and specific. Beginning with the rather ambiguous discussion of May 26, amplified by the proposal of June 3, the Western ministers finally on June 16 submitted the kind of terms for which they were actually willing to settle. They went as far toward the Soviet position as they felt they could, enduring the renewal of threats in the Soviet proposal of June 10.

The private sessions with Gromyko since May 26 must have become increasingly frank as the Western ministers urged Gromyko to state his price and informed him what they considered a fair price.

35. *Ibid.*, pp. 267-271.
36. *Ibid.*, pp. 312-313.

Unfortunately, Soviet press releases at the conference indicated that Gromyko meant what Khrushchev had been saying on the sidelines. The Soviets, Khrushchev implied, could not bargain about West German access to nuclear weapons. Gromyko seemed to be holding steady while his confrères took initiatives to ease the conflict. The difficulty remained that, for the Soviets, the Western powers did not enjoy a credible position as long as no fallback strategy appeared.

The Kremlin evidently did not wish to reach a settlement at this point, because Gromyko rejected the June 16 proposal. The Western ministers decided to recess the conference for three weeks and Gromyko consented. The two sides departed, bickering about who should be blamed for the failure of the conference.

4. *The Diplomatic Game at Geneva: A Long Shot on a New Play*

After six weeks of discussion, the participating governments took stock of what had happened. They had to make fresh decisions. The only item they could all agree on was a ban on nuclear weapons in West Berlin which, as Lloyd said later, was a "ridiculous" suggestion anyway.

Once the conference recessed, considerable uncertainty existed about how it could be revived in time for the next round. This question involved the larger question of what would happen after Geneva. Several choices were available to prevent the situation from deteriorating. The United States, in particular, had to decide whether to (1) continue to focus somehow on Berlin at the risk of having to make further concessions to achieve agreement; (2) raise the discussion to the summit level; or (3) resort to extra-conference tactics, military or otherwise. The first alternative could backfire. The second could not easily be rationalized because the requisite progress toward a Berlin settlement Eisenhower demanded had not been accomplished. The administration believed that the third alternative would risk the war the conference had been called to avoid.

Whether the administration favored the first choice depended on its view of the second and third. If it chose not to refuse a summit conference without a measure of progress, it might opt for the first alternative with less fear of a collapse at Geneva. Similarly, if it decided upon military preparations, it had less to fear from the first option. In other words, failure in the first need not rule out resorting to the second or third.

The administration adopted a combination of the first and second approaches in early July, although it did not announce its decision until early August. It decided to continue discussions on Berlin and, simultaneously, to explore Soviet receptivity to an exchange of visits—without conditions—between Eisenhower and Khrushchev. The administration fell upon the possibility of a halfway house—the bilateral summit—between the foreign ministers' conference and a four-power summit. Macmillan had established the precedent.

Before the foreign ministers returned to Geneva, Soviet Deputy Premier Frol Kozlov appeared in New York to open the Soviet Exhibition of Science, Technology, and Culture. Deputy Under Secretary of State Murphy approached Kozlov with Eisenhower's invitation at Idlewild airport just as Kozlov emplaned for Moscow on July 11.[37]

By combining the first and second alternatives, the administration found a way to revive the conference or to continue negotiations if the conference failed. The decision to combine options gave Herter greater room for maneuver because he would not have his back to the wall, having to fear a collapse of the conference and a subsequent deterioration in East-West relations. By the same token, the combination could also deflate Herter's efforts by depriving the Soviets of any incentive to produce a Berlin agreement. The administration did not make the invitation to Khrushchev contingent on progress at Geneva.

According to Eisenhower, he did not intend to omit his standard insistence on a measure of progress. In his memoirs, he wrote that Murphy misunderstood him to mean the invitation should be unqualified. Eisenhower blamed himself for failing to make his intention clear to the State Department. He did not welcome an extended tour of the United States by Khrushchev, who was responsible for an unproductive foreign ministers' conference. But for all practical purposes, Khrushchev received the decision as Murphy conveyed it.[38] The administration's action at this juncture had the effect of indicat-

---

37. Reston, *The New York Times*, October 8, 1959, p. 11. Murphy later confirmed he had contacted Kozlov, but his explanation did not seem adequate. The United States proposed an exchange of visits, he said, to allow Eisenhower a chance to visit the Soviet Union and make a favorable impact on the Soviet people. Robert Murphy, *Diplomat among Warriors* (New York: Doubleday and Co., Inc., 1964), p. 478. Murphy says nothing about the administrations' desire to keep the negotiations alive.

38. Dwight D. Eisenhower, *The White House Years, Waging Peace 1956–1960* (New York: Doubleday and Company, Inc. 1965), pp. 405-408, 411-412.

ing before the Geneva Conference concluded that the original purpose of the conference no longer obtained, despite the administration's
long-standing proscription against an unprepared summit. This action
probably fueled Soviet miscalculation.

By late June, two signs had already appeared that the Geneva Conference would be replaced by some other forum to sustain the negotiations track. The first indication was a dissociation by the United
States of the foreign ministers' conference from a prospective four-
power summit. In his press conference of June 17, President Eisenhower stated that lack of progress on Berlin did not necessarily mean
no summit could take place at all. If a Berlin discussion stalled, a
summit could consider other matters of importance. He noted that
another conference in Geneva had been negotiating a nuclear test ban
and that progress had been achieved unmarred by threats. France,
however, had not participated in the test ban negotiations and would
therefore be excluded from a summit on that subject. Herter and
Couve de Murville apparently had discussed this problem when they
were in Geneva.[39] And at his press conference, Eisenhower expressed
an interest in meeting with de Gaulle.[40]

The British had long favored dissociating progress toward a Berlin
settlement from a summit. They believed that a failure of the foreign
ministers to agree on Berlin made a summit all the more urgent.[41]
Macmillan skirted the lack of progress issue by declaring on June 23
that the Geneva Conference had made progress through the mutual
clarification of views justifying a summit. Gromyko echoed this
sentiment on June 28. Khrushchev, of course, had been urging a
summit since 1957.[42] Thus, the administration's bilateral approach
to Moscow occurred in an "atmosphere" of favorable sentiment for
a summit meeting.

The second indication of the administration's preference for continuing negotiations was its disinclination to aggravate the local
situation in Berlin. For example, the American embassy in Bonn
recommended evacuation of Western dependents in Berlin. The
administration, to avoid alarming the Berliners, did not authorize
evacuation. It increased the readiness of divisions in Europe quietly

39. *The New York Times,* June 16, 1959, p. 8.
40. *Ibid.,* June 18, 1959, p. 1.
41. *Ibid.,* June 21, 1959, p. 1.
42. At the Twenty-First Party Congress in January 1959, Khrushchev
obliquely invited himself to the United States. *Current Soviet Policies, III,* ed.
Leo Gruliow (New York: Columbia University Press, 1960), p. 203.

rather than noisily.[43] Inter-allied contingency planning also proceeded quietly.

In late June, the administration's foes on defense spending roundly criticized its whole approach to the crisis. The Democratic Advisory Council, headed by Acheson, issued a pamphlet entitled, "The Military Forces We Need and How to Get Them."[44] In the pamphlet, the Council berated the administration for not taking measures to increase nuclear weapons production to overcome a possible "missile gap" in 1960–1962 and for not increasing NATO conventional forces for limited war. Acheson declared on June 30 that the administration ignored a shift in the world balance of power caused by Soviet weapons developments.[45] In Congress, the Army's chance of a man-power increase dwindled.[46] The lack of a renewed defense effort indicated that the administration preferred or continued to have hopes for results from negotiations and that it considered current force levels adequate support.

The administration made its choice to continue the Berlin discussions in Geneva supplemented by a bid for a bilateral summit. Discussion in the press raised the question of how long the administration should persist with the conference as a timely reminder to the administration that risks remained in proceeding with negotiations unsupported by obvious and noisy military preparations. Some critics believed that the Soviets remained intransigent in Geneva because they did not consider Eisenhower's April defense declarations seriously. Alsop reported the reaction of a "neutral European diplomat" to the administration's approach:

> But if your President really means what he says, in God's name why does he not act as though he meant it. In the Kremlin, they judge by acts, not words. They may misunderstand. And then there will be a real danger of war that can destroy us all.[47]

43. Alsop reported that military convoys were now heavily armed on the *autobann* and NATO aircraft were deploying out of France into West Germany. *The Herald Tribune*, July 12, 1959, p. II-1.

44. *Democratic Programs for Action*, No. 4, June 1959, pp. 4-5, 7-9. Arthur Krock disagreed with the council's conclusions, but, for once he and Lippmann agreed that the pamphlet merited serious attention. *The New York Times*, June 26, 1959, p. 24.

45. *Ibid.*, July 1, 1959, p. 2.

46. *Ibid.*, June 25, 1959, p. 11.

47. *The Herald Tribune*, June 15, 1959, p. 14.

Averell Harriman interviewed Khrushchev on June 23. In the interview, Khrushchev said that the Geneva Conference must be reconvened on the basis of the free city proposal. Otherwise, he would sign a separate treaty with the DDR and would lend military support to Pankow for control of the Berlin access routes. Harriman quoted Khrushchev as shouting: "If you send in tanks, they will burn, and make no mistake about it. If you want war, you can have it, but remember it will be your war. Our rockets will fly automatically." [48] The West had to face facts, Khrushchev said, and the central fact was a change in the balance of power favoring the Soviet Union. Khrushchev impressed Harriman with his confidence and arrogance: "he appears to be so confident of his strength that he is determined to force a solution of the problem." [49] Harriman thought Soviet miscalculation was a real possibility: "It would be a grave mistake to believe it is all bluff. The present situation is dangerous, for the Russian Premier might well overplay his hand." Harriman—splitting with Acheson—agreed with the administration's negotiations strategy. He suggested that Khrushchev should be invited to view American strength at first hand by a visit to the United States because he also found him relying on faulty information about the American economy. President Eisenhower at his press conference of July 8 objected to Khrushchev's crude threats. Eisenhower described the Western position in Berlin as an "unmovable stone." The pattern of Western concessions at Geneva probably did not communicate Eisenhower's firmness.

5. *The Diplomatic Game at Geneva: The Soviets Take the Game*

The second part of the Geneva Conference opened on July 13 with Couve de Murville raising an issue in public session. He said he had noticed that Gromyko's proposal of June 10 seemed to link the German problem with Berlin. In his proposal, Gromyko had said that Moscow expected Bonn and Pankow, in a mixed committee, to develop relations between themselves and to prepare a peace treaty during the interim period of the Berlin settlement that he had proposed. Gromyko offered to clarify the matter. The interim status of West Berlin would be *conditioned*, he said, on the work of the mixed com-

48. *The New York Times*, July 8, 1959, p. 3.
49. *Ibid.*, July 3, 1959, p. 1.

mittee. The failure of the committee would bring the four foreign ministers back into conference. He confirmed that the Soviet Union had meant to link the two problems, Berlin and a peace treaty, in a temporary Berlin settlement.

This question of the linkage between the two problems dominated the second part of the conference. On July 15, Couve de Murville interrogated Gromyko further. He reminded Gromyko that the first two weeks of the conference had been consumed by an unproductive discussion of the German problem. Why then "add difficulties to difficulties, to link together problems which are nevertheless quite distinct, in short . . . to jeopardize the whole negotiation." This plea sounded very much like Gromyko's criticism of the Western plan. Couve de Murville did not object to a discussion on Germany, but, he said, this discussion would be a digression from the effort toward an interim Berlin settlement—the conference's principal task since May 26. He did not see how it would be possible to consider the two subjects simultaneously.[50]

Under questioning from Lloyd, Gromyko declared: "We have repeatedly tried to explain to our colleagues in the negotiations that there is a logical link between the question of West Berlin and the question of an all-German committee and its works, and that this link is by no means artificial." He denied his approach was a new one, saying both questions had long been associated in the conference. Gromyko did not intend to discuss German free elections or other aspects of the Western plan. He placed the allied ministers in an awkward position because they could not discuss a mixed committee without also discussing free elections, and that discussion had already proven fruitless.

Gromyko's tactic in the July conference was a clever trap. At first, he seemed to be leading his counterparts in circles, returning to discuss the German problem after his proposals at the end of the first part of the conference had fixed attention on an interim settlement for Berlin. On the contrary, his maneuver was not so pointless. When the allied ministers turned to Berlin on May 26, they consented to play Gromyko on their wicket, knowing the discussion would focus on West Berlin, not East Berlin. Gromyko pressed them hard for several weeks, focused attention on their position in Berlin, and got

50. *Foreign Ministers Meeting*, pp. 404-408.

them to respond with concessions to obtain an interim settlement. On July 15, Gromyko began to push the allies further in the direction he wished to see them go. He revealed that his Berlin proposals led straight into recognition of the DDR. The Soviets struck upon a very compact mode in which to relate their Berlin proposals to their draft treaty without raising the issue of German unity. Gromyko's latest play illustrated how skillfully the Soviets used Berlin as a lever to compel interest in a peace treaty.

As Lloyd pointed out, Gromyko's proposals incorporated an interchangeable threat mechanism—failure in the mixed committee would threaten West Berlin and the deadline threat to West Berlin would apply pressure on the committee.[51] They also illustrated the inadvertent effects of the diplomacy of the Western powers. Gromyko used the West's own desire for an interim settlement to move it toward a peace treaty. The Western powers could have an interim settlement, if they liked. But the mixed committee device would also start them down the track toward a treaty between the two Germanies.

The conference returned to secret sessions on July 17. In that forum, Gromyko refused a discussion on Berlin in favor of one on the mixed committee. He raised the price of agreement. Over Couve de Murville's mild objection, Lloyd and Herter, with West German Foreign Minister Von Brentano's consent, revived parts of the Western plan and followed Gromyko into a discussion of Germany.

It is not clear why they decided to follow Gromyko at this point. They surely could not have expected any substantive results in favor of the Western plan. Judging by the sessions of the next few days, they wanted to learn the content of Gromyko's instructions for the second round. They did not follow him very far because he did not proceed very far.

On July 20, Herter began a discussion of the mixed committee. First, he emphasized that the Soviet proposal wrenched the original Western proposal for a mixed committee out of the context of Stage II of the Western plan and related it to Berlin in a way which completely distorted it. Second, he offered an alternative: let the Geneva Conference, as currently constituted, (four-power participants and German advisers), become a permanent conference, perhaps at a lower level than the foreign ministers, to consider the "extension and

51. *Ibid.*, pp. 444-449.

development of contacts between the two parts of Germany." By this method, the four powers would retain responsibility and also encourage contacts between Bonn and Pankow.[52]

Gromyko said he could think of alternatives to a mixed committee, but none involved four-power responsibility. On July 22, Gromyko eased the deadlock a little. He backed off and said he would be willing to participate in "a parallel exchange of views" concerning an interim Berlin settlement. To assuage the West's anxiety about interim negotiations, he made the following declaration: "During the period of validity of an interim agreement on West Berlin, and during the negotiations to be held at a meeting of the Governments participating in the Geneva conference, for the purpose of reviewing the question of West Berlin, the Soviet Union will take no unilateral action." [53]

In reply or exasperation, Herter spoke his mind. He described Gromyko's tactics as a "strategy of duress." Moscow had used this strategy three times to date: first, in the note of November 27, 1958, giving the West six months to discuss the free city proposal or evacuate West Berlin; second, on June 10, demanding the West accept a mixed committee for settling the German problem or face further pressure in West Berlin; and third, on July 13, implying that unless the mixed committee settled the German problem by the time an interim Berlin settlement expired, West Berlin would once again be exposed to intimidation. Herter regarded the linkage of the Berlin and German questions by the Soviet Union as "an ingenious device whereby it clearly hopes to apply pressure on the Western Allies eventually to accept changes injurious to their rights and interests in respect of either Berlin or Germany—or preferably both." He rebuked Gromyko for the declaration Gromyko had just made. It offered assurance of no unilateral action only during the period of an interim settlement, not after that period elapsed.

Herter concluded by saying:

> In effect, what the Soviet Union is proposing to do is to hold for ransom a whole city—two million human beings. And the Soviet Union even suggests that we should become its un-witting accomplice in this deal by agreeing to the very arrangements which would make this possible.

52. *Ibid.*, pp. 439-444.
53. *Ibid.*, p. 463.

This is, in brief, why the Soviet Union proposes that the questions of the all-German committee and of any interim agreement on Berlin be inextricably linked.

This in brief also is why the Western Powers reject this linkage.[54]

Vice President Nixon arrived in Moscow on July 23 authorized to complain about the impasse in Geneva. On his arrival, he said that he feared if problems went unresolved they might lead to an increasingly dangerous impasse.[55] He urged Khrushchev not to let the Geneva Conference end in failure. Their own discussion did not fare much better than Herter's and Gromyko's.[56]

On July 30, Nixon began to prepare public opinion for the prospective bilateral summit conference between Eisenhower and Khrushchev. Of his own visit to Moscow, he said, "I hope that this may be one of the first steps, which will be followed by others, increasing the contacts between the leaders and people of our two countries." [57] On August 2, he stated explicitly that Khrushchev should be invited to Washington.[58]

After Eisenhower's announcement on August 3 of the forthcoming bilateral summit, the Geneva Conference entered an anticlimactic phase. On August 4, the four ministers agreed to recess the conference again rather than to terminate it and issued, on August 5, a vague rather than specific communiqué: [59]

A frank and comprehensive discussion took place on the Berlin question.

The positions of both sides on certain points became closer. The discussions which have taken place will be useful for the further negotiations which are necessary in order to reach an agreement.

The date and place for the resumption of the work of the conference will be settled through diplomatic channels.[60]

54. *Ibid.*, p. 465.
55. *The New York Times*, July 29, 1959, p. 2.
56. *Ibid.*, July 25, 1959, p. 1; July 28, 1959, p. 1.
57. *Ibid.*, July 31, 1959, p. 1.
58. *Ibid.*, August 3, 1959, p. 8. Khrushchev probably had already accepted the invitation. Nixon's visit to Moscow amounted to a dress rehearsal for the Chairman's visit to Washington.
59. *Ibid.*, August 5, 1959, p. 1.
60. *Foreign Ministers Meeting*, p. 512.

Theoretically, the conference could be resumed to discuss the results of the bilateral summit. No power wished to assume blame for the inconclusive nature of the conference, although another conference like the Geneva conclave would not appear for some time. In 1961, when Khrushchev tried to reinvigorate Berlin negotiations, all parties seemed wary of entering into an endless formal proceeding.

In the Geneva Conference, the honors for diplomatic footwork went to Gromyko. In the first weeks of the conference, he outsat his colleagues until their efforts collapsed. The four allies entered negotiations to explore the opportunities for a grand settlement combining German unity and European security and possibly a *modus vivendi* for Berlin. They left Geneva, as Lloyd said, content merely to have kept diplomacy alive and to have avoided a deterioration in relations. But in the process, Gromyko cut away much of the small margin for bargaining the allies had in negotiating about the Berlin occupation regime. No further discussion of German unity would ensue. Future discussions of European security would be much less grandiose. Concessions on the allied position in Berlin were on record and could be the point at which negotiations would begin the next time. In the diplomatic game, the allies lost and lost badly. If Gromyko judged the allies by their actions, he must have been delighted to see them relent and follow his initiative all the way through the conference. The Geneva Conference increased Soviet momentum in the crisis, contrary to the claims of the Western ministers that their diplomacy had prevented the crisis from worsening.

CHAPTER 4

The Failure of Dulles' Strategy

THE GENEVA Conference of foreign ministers failed. Chiefs of state then became foreign ministers. From August 1959 to May 1960, more summits occurred than at any other time since the Second World War. All of the summits before May served as a prelude to the grand summit in Paris, and Macmillan planned that summit as the first in a series. Dulles' policy of peace through negotiation produced a spate of diplomatic activism. But the U-2 incident disrupted the Paris Conference and shattered the negotiations track. Khrushchev switched over to military posturing and encouraged Ulbricht in late 1960 to work away at *de facto* changes in Berlin. Pankow unilaterally assumed selective management of traffic patterns in the city. Bonn tried unsuccessfully to oppose this action. Failing to achieve Western consent for their free city proposal, the Soviets demonstrated that they would support limited attempts by Pankow to achieve their objectives through pressures creating conditions for the isolation of West Berlin. In the vacuum left from the failure of summit diplomacy, the Eisenhower Administration faced a deterioration of the local status quo in Berlin.

1. *Eisenhower's Latent Interest in Summitry*

At background dinners with the press in early August 1959, Eisenhower talked about his hopes and plans for the summit with Khrushchev. The President said he could understand Soviet fears of a united Germany, although he did not think Berlin should be a great problem for the Soviets. He proposed to offer them security guarantees to assuage their fears of the Germans—much as the Western plan at Geneva had tried to do. Finally, he said he wanted to improve Soviet-American relations in the time that remained to him in office.[1]

To prepare for Khrushchev's visit, Eisenhower and Herter conferred with Adenauer, Macmillan, and de Gaulle in Europe. Eisenhower had to go to Europe because de Gaulle and Adenauer looked askance at the invitation to Khrushchev. Eisenhower assured Adenauer that the United States would not make debilitating concessions to Khrushchev.[2] In his conversations with de Gaulle, Eisenhower restored his condition for a measure of progress toward a Berlin settlement to justify a four-power summit.[3] Eisenhower's hopes for Soviet concessions now lay with the bilateral summit, since the foreign ministers' conference had failed to produce any. Macmillan correctly pointed out that, if Eisenhower still insisted that Khrushchev remove all elements of duress in the crisis, the principle had already been breached by the Geneva Conference. Gromyko had invoked and reinvoked deadline threats to Berlin, yet the negotiations had continued. Macmillan argued that a series of four-power summits should be planned, saying that he much preferred to keep on talking than to let the conflict get out of hand.[4]

2. *Khrushchev's Vision of a Two-Power Settlement*

On the eve of his visit, Khrushchev wrote an article for *Foreign Affairs*.[5] He implied that he had decided to visit the United States in order to point out to Americans the unreality of their current foreign policy. He wanted to explain the necessity of a *détente* between the United States and the Soviet Union and to remove misunderstandings about the Berlin crisis.

Khrushchev argued that *détente* should include a repudiation of war and an obligation by each power not to interfere in the affairs

1. These were Max Freedman's and Roscoe Drummond's recollections of Eisenhower's views. *The Manchester Guardian*, August 13, 1959, p. 3; *The Herald Tribune*, August 7, 1959, p. 10.
2. *Ibid.*, August 28, 1959, p. 1.
3. *The New York Times*, August 9, 1959, p. I-1.
4. *Ibid.*, September 4, 1959, p. 1.
5. Nikita S. Khrushchev, "On Peaceful Coexistence," *Foreign Affairs*, 38 (October 1959), 1-18.

of the other. In effect, he tried to persuade the United States to accept nuclear parity, recognize the DDR, leave West Berlin a free city, and alter its commitment to Bonn. If the United States accepted these policies, the result actually would be a diplomatic revolution—an *entente,* not simply a *détente,* between the two long-standing enemies of the cold war era.

Harrison Salisbury thought Khrushchev wanted two-power world rule.[6] Salisbury assumed that Soviet objectives in the Berlin crisis were security oriented in strictly defensive terms. Granted that assumption, two-power rule could result from an *entente.* If, however, Soviet security requirements had destructive implications for the West, particularly for Bonn, one-power rule in Europe might result through the progressive elimination of American influence. Of course, either a two-power or a one-power world would be unpalatable to France or China. De Gaulle had already accused the United States and Soviet Union of dividing the world between them at Yalta.

Khrushchev could not hope to create Soviet-American "cooperation" in one visit. An *entente* lay somewhere at the end of many visits, summits, and negotiations. In New York, Los Angeles, San Francisco, Des Moines, Pittsburgh, and Washington, Khrushchev expounded the merits of the broad scheme he envisioned.

Detailed discussions with Eisenhower began at Camp David on September 25. Two days later, Eisenhower and Khrushchev concurred in a communiqué on the following points.

1. On disarmament, they agreed it dwarfed every other problem.
2. On Germany, they held "an exchange of views."
3. On Berlin, "an understanding was reached, subject to the approval of the other parties directly concerned, that negotiations would be reopened with a view to achieving a solution which would be in accordance with the interests of all concerned. . . ."
4. On trade, they held "useful conversations."
5. On cultural exchanges, "substantial progress was made" with an expectation of future agreements.
6. On relations in general, they agreed to settle disputes "not by application of force but by peaceful means through negotiations."

6. *The New York Times,* September 15, 1959, p. 1.

7. On a visit for Eisenhower to Russia, they agreed that a spring date would be arranged.[7]

The third point attracted most attention because Eisenhower apparently had succeeded in reaching "an understanding" with Khrushchev. The hopes stirred by the bilateral summit seemed to be justified, although the communiqué stated: "The talks were not undertaken to negotiate issues."

Khrushchev read the joint communiqué to the press in Washington, after racing down from Camp David behind schedule. Questioned about the reference in the communiqué to Berlin, Khrushchev spoke vaguely. He hinted that a summit conference could not be called until the other heads of government consented. After a television address to the American people in which he once more urged *détente*, Khrushchev emplaned for Moscow. In Moscow, he declared he had convinced the President that Soviet proposals on Berlin and a draft treaty had been misunderstood.

Eisenhower clarified the Camp David communiqué at his September 28 press conference. He announced a diplomatic procedure or formula for breaking the impasse in Berlin negotiations:

> "And over and above this, we agreed, in addition to what we said, the communiqué said, that these negotiations should not be prolonged indefinitely but there could be no fixed time limit on them." [8]

Eisenhower conceded to Khrushchev that negotiations should not be prolonged indefinitely. Khrushchev, in turn, conceded to Eisenhower that negotiations ought not to labor under a fixed time limit. Eisenhower emphasized that Khrushchev gave him oral assurances the Soviet Union did not intend to threaten West Berlin. He requested Khrushchev to repeat Soviet assurances for the record. Khrushchev agreed that if Eisenhower would announce the formula on September 28, he would announce—from Moscow—his agreement to Eisenhower's statement.

Eisenhower accepted the Camp David formula as a sufficient measure of progress to advance toward a four-power summit: "The

7. *Khrushchev in America* (New York: Crosscurrents Press, 1960), pp. 189-190.

8. *The New York Times*, September 29, 1959, p. 16.

conditions I have set so far, so far as I am concerned, I mean the conversations have . . . removed many of the objections that I have heretofore held. . . ." [9] If his allies concurred, a date for the summit could be quickly set. Eisenhower proposed postponing his visit to Russia until after the summit.

As a strictly procedural device, the Camp David formula preserved the negotiations track for both parties.[10] No negotiations on the substance of the Berlin crisis occurred at Camp David. But the original Soviet notes in the "deadline crisis" had so connected substance with procedure—the free city proposal, for example, with a deadline for negotiating it—that the formula could be readily misconstrued by each side. Eisenhower, unfortunately, interpreted the formula optimistically:

> There is no fixed . . . time on this. No one is under duress, no one is under any kind of threat and as a matter of fact, he stated emphatically that never had he any intention to give anything that was to be interpreted as duress or compulsion.[11]

And he used language confusing the substance of the matter as well:

> Q. Mr. President, when we move into these new negotiations on Berlin, could you tell us whether we will be guided by the same standards and principles that we had before, namely, that any solution must guarantee Allied rights there, and protect the freedom of the West Berliners?
>
> A. I can't guarantee anything of this kind for the simple reason I don't know what kind of a solution may finally prove acceptable, as I say, but you must start out with this. The situation is abnormal. It was brought about by a truce, a military truce, after the end of the war, an armistice, and it put strangely a few—or a number of free people in a very awkward position. Now, we've got to find a system that will be really acceptable to all the people in that region, including those most concerned, the West Berliners.[12]

9. *Ibid.*
10. In a report to Congress on the Camp David meeting, Herter said nothing had changed except that now further conferences could be held without a factor of duress intervening. *The Herald Tribune*, October 2, 1959, p. 1.
11. *The New York Times*, September 29, 1959, p. 16.
12. *Ibid.*

Eisenhower accepted Khrushchev's terminology in speaking of Berlin's situation as "abnormal," causing a flutter of speculation in the press corps. Within an hour of the President's remarks, the White House explained that the President did not mean to say he could not "guarantee allied rights" and "the freedom of the West Berliners." He intended to say that he could not predict the detailed provisions of a Berlin settlement.

The confusion could be attributed to the formula itself. The formula provided that negotiations would not be indefinitely prolonged. If they did become protracted, however, the factor of duress Eisenhower disavowed presumably still remained. Since the formula also provided that negotiations would not be held under a fixed time limit, the factor of duress did not remain! Meaning all things to all men, the formula loosely satisfied both parties. Eisenhower and Khrushchev were still divided on matters of substance, a fact the Camp David formula simply omitted.

The ambiguity of the formula allowed Khrushchev to misconstrue Eisenhower's intent just as Eisenhower had interpreted Khrushchev's too optimistically. The Soviets probably agreed to postpone their threat to the Berlin occupation regime because they regarded postponement as a means to a favorable negotiation. Further, they did not abandon pressure tactics. They merely held them in reserve because the formula ruled out indefinite negotiations. Duress remained implicit in the terms of the formula. In this peculiar sense, Eisenhower had not refused to negotiate a settlement under duress, and the Soviets could expect that they might yet win a basic change in the status of Berlin.

On September 29, Khrushchev responded to Eisenhower's announcement:

> We have indeed agreed that the negotiations on the Berlin issue should be resumed and that no time limit should be fixed for them but that they should not be protracted indefinitely.

and he added:

> The Soviet Government would like to express again the confidence that all parties concerned would strive for the question of West Berlin to be settled without delay and in accordance

with the interests of easing tension in Germany and in Europe, the interests of consolidating peace.[13]

His first statement corroborated the procedural agreement with Eisenhower. His second statement indicated that he had not changed his substantive position. Assuming that he would not have consented to the procedural agreement if it contradicted his substantive position, he must have regarded the Camp David formula as a step forward.

When Khrushchev affirmed the Camp David formula, he did it in a strange way. On September 29, Tass news service released a summary of Eisenhower's press conference curiously omitting Eisenhower's explanation of the Camp David formula.[14] Tass released Khrushchev's statement affirming the formula in a separate interview with the Chairman.[15]

The New York Times suggested that Tass censored Eisenhower's words because Khrushchev believed Eisenhower had gone too far in interpreting the formula and wanted to have his own interpretation on the record.[16] This explanation seems inadequate because Khrushchev's method of affirming the Camp David formula probably related to his insistence that he return to Moscow before he publicly affirmed the "understanding" Eisenhower and he had reached. By returning to Moscow, Khrushchev could control his own media more effectively, and he must have wanted to control the announcement because the formula had to be manipulated to have any impact at all. First, he took credit at home for the formula by censoring Eisenhower's announcement of it. Then, he had to think about how to make something of the formula in the next few months in order to produce a settlement at the four-power summit.

After Camp David, Soviet media expressed great concern about retaining the "atmosphere" or "spirit" of Camp David. Khrushchev's success depended upon it because the "spirit" of Camp David constituted nothing more than a mechanism for reviving the Berlin negotiations. One of the greatest gambles of Khrushchev's career—and he had gambled and won many times previously in his rise to power—was his attempt to transform the procedural agreement at Camp David

13. *Ibid.*, September 30, 1959, p. 1.
14. *Ibid.*, p. 3.
15. *Ibid.*
16. *Ibid.*

into a substantive one at a four-power summit. He played the role
of a wizard, trying to make a "spirit" into a body, something out of
nothing. Like any respectable wizard, he kept his secrets to himself
in the following exchange with the press in Washington after the
Camp David meeting:

> Q. When President Eisenhower asked you for assurances that
> Western rights in West Berlin would continue to be respected,
> what was your answer?
>
> A. We exchanged views with the President on many questions,
> and I think there is no need for a public report on anything.
> We have already said a great deal. We shall meet again, talk
> again, and after that shall once again say what we consider it
> necessary to say. How inquisitive you are! Have patience; we
> shall tell you—when the time comes, we'll tell you everything.[17]

Actually, he had nothing to tell because they had decided nothing.
The discussion had not been as substantive as the reporter's question
implied. Eisenhower and he had agreed merely to keep talking, as
Macmillan had urged. A settlement depended entirely on future
developments.[18]

The Camp David summit did not dispel the Berlin crisis but it did
place Khrushchev and Eisenhower in tenuous positions. They committed themselves to negotiate a settlement and Eisenhower agreed
to visit the Soviet Union after the grand summit in Europe. In the
period from Camp David to the Paris Conference, the United States
and the Soviet Union strove to preserve an atmosphere of *détente* in
order to reach a Berlin settlement. The two powers tacitly agreed,
in effect, to woo their allies to accept *détente*. Their agreement did
not quite fit Harrison Salisbury's version of a two-power world. But
an initial two-power accord could lead to a four-power Berlin settlement, if all the other powers concerned followed the lead of the United
States and the Soviet Union. In that event, and as Salisbury expected,
the two powers not only would have a great influence on the content
of the settlement but on the future of the other powers as well, since
any Berlin settlement would have far-reaching implications for Europe
as a whole.

17. Embree, *op. cit.*, p. 192.
18. Hans Speier suggested Khrushchev spoke as though real *détente* had been
achieved in order to create a self-fulfilling prophecy. *Op. cit.*, p. 61.

3. *Third-Power Intervention*

No sooner had Eisenhower and Khrushchev agreed to work for *détente* than their allies objected and the two became increasingly harassed by internal and external opposition. Some critics objected that they were not approaching *détente* in the right way; others flatly opposed the whole project. The world of two powers began to disappear simultaneously as the possibility of it emerged. Eisenhower and Khrushchev held to their course in the eight months which elapsed between their bilateral summit at Camp David and the summit in Paris. Eisenhower persisted, as he said, to improve Soviet-American relations before he left office, and Khrushchev to settle the "German problem." [19] They both desired a broad settlement in Europe of the issues outstanding since the Second World War, a war in which each had figured prominently.

Khrushchev flew to Peking to persuade Mao Tse-tung that *détente* would serve Peking's interests. Macmillan congratulated Eisenhower on his achievement and Eisenhower turned to winning over de Gaulle and Adenauer. After the Tories won the general election on October 8, Macmillan proposed an allied summit meeting to devise a common Western approach before meeting Khrushchev again.

The Eisenhower Administration wanted an East-West summit in early December, preceded by a Western summit as Macmillan suggested. [20] Although de Gaulle argued that not enough time remained to prepare for a December meeting, he really disagreed with Macmillan on the rationale for summit negotiations. De Gaulle considered a summit conference a solitary conclave where heads of government met to reach substantive decisions. He saw little chance for a Berlin settlement unless the Western powers modified their Geneva proposals still further and he certainly did not agree with Macmillan's suggestion for negotiating a new international statute for West Berlin. Moreover, he did not like the two-power nature of the *détente* he saw developing.

On October 21, the French Cabinet issued a communiqué requesting a delay in the summit conference with Khrushchev. It cited the

19. Hans Kroll, West German ambassador to Moscow in 1959, relates in his memoirs that Khrushchev—referring to himself—said, "resolving the German problem would be my crowning achievement." *The Washington Post*, August 20, 1967, p. A22.

20. *The New York Times*, October 18, 1959, p. I-1.

absence of "an effective reduction of tension" as reason enough for postponement.[21] It proposed broadening the agenda to stimulate the widest possible discussion, including issues relating to Southeast Asia, the Near East, and Africa. This statement ignored Eisenhower's and Khrushchev's claim that they had been able to reduce tension through their meeting at Camp David.

The real reason for de Gaulle's decision emerged a few days later. He wanted to try his own hand at reducing tensions and invited Khrushchev to a bilateral summit in Paris either in December or early in 1960. He followed the precedent set by Macmillan and Eisenhower. When Khrushchev accepted de Gaulle's invitation—he agreed to visit France at the end of March—Khrushchev placed de Gaulle on a plane equal to Eisenhower and Macmillan. De Gaulle intervened in the summit process to check Macmillan's drive for a settlement the French considered unacceptable and the two-power détente Eisenhower and Khrushchev envisaged.

Eisenhower regretted that no four-power summit would be possible before the end of the year. On October 28—clearly irritated by de Gaulle—he announced that the allied heads of government needed "to thrash out" matters and would meet in Paris in December.

Adenauer used the pause in the march toward the summit to scurry about Western Europe, coalescing opposition to a dramatic or substantive change in the status of Berlin. He went to London on November 17–19 to repair the damage of accumulated quarrels with the British. *The New York Times* reported "vigorous" and "forceful" discussions between Macmillan and him.[22] He went to Paris on December 1–2. On his return to Bonn, Adenauer announced that Bonn would not send an adviser to the summit with Khrushchev, hopefully preventing Pankow from assuming an advisory role. Observing Adenauer's diplomatic forays, Khrushchev protested in a Budapest speech that Bonn "is seeking to do everything to prevent an improvement in the relations between states and to discredit the foreign policy of the Soviet Union. Chancellor Adenauer is most active in this respect." [23]

On December 19–21, Eisenhower, Macmillan, de Gaulle, and

21. *Ibid.*, October 22, 1959, p. 6.
22. *Ibid.*, November 22, 1959, p. 39.
23. Embree, *op. cit.*, p. 202.

Adenauer met in Paris to consider the agenda, date, and place for the summit with Khrushchev. They decided to propose an agenda of three subjects: Germany and Berlin, disarmament, and East-West relations, and suggested April 27 in Paris as a time and place for the summit. They said they anticipated a series of summits extending beyond the Paris Conference, and left it to the foreign ministers and diplomatic working parties to draw up position papers before April.

Press reports of the meeting conflicted. First, the newspapers reported that de Gaulle and Adenauer had succeeded in persuading Eisenhower to withdraw the Geneva concessions made to Gromyko. The two continental leaders seemed to hope the summit in April would be largely exploratory. Second, the British told the press that nothing had changed. Eventually, the press learned that the four agreed to begin the Paris Conference with the Western peace plan of 1959. This procedure did not foreclose the Geneva concessions. The allies—in a compromise among themselves—decided to begin with their first proposal rather than their last one.[24]

Izvestiia called the Western summit a disaster and scored the Western powers for returning to their original Geneva peace plan. It blamed Bonn for this reversion. But Khrushchev replied favorably on December 26, endorsing the idea that the Paris summit should be the first of a series and asking that the date of April 27 be reconsidered to avoid a conflict with the May Day holiday in Moscow. The allies offered May 16, and Khrushchev accepted.[25]

24. *The New York Times*, December 21, 1959, p. 1; December 22, 1959, p. 1; December 29, 1959, p. 7.

25. As the administration pursued its negotiations strategy into a second year of talks, Acheson lectured it again on the risks involved:

"Now, what I am trying to do is to draw your attention to the nature of the conference to which Mr. Khrushchev has invited us. In other words, he's inviting us to confer with an idea of coming to terms about our own existence.

This is the kind of thing into which we are being led by the incredible view that any sort of a negotiation is good per se."

He thought Khrushchev already had succeeded in defining the talks as negotiations about the free city proposal for Berlin and a peace treaty for two Germanies.

Acheson again offered alternatives: (1) a defense force should be constructed "in accordance with the recommendations of SHAPE"; (2) the United States should make a public denial of the partition of Europe "to look forward to the time when government throughout Europe will have a decent basis in national acceptance, all measures of force and liberation aside"; (3) negotiations on arms limitations should be undertaken to bring nuclear power under interna-

4. *"Decline" of a Two-Power World*

In spite of de Gaulle's veto of an early summit and Adenauer's attempt to harden the Western position on Berlin, Khrushchev held to the course he had set with Eisenhower at Camp David. But in addition to de Gaulle and Adenauer, he now confronted—in the winter of 1960—internal opposition to his Berlin campaign. Senior army officers criticized his approach to the crisis because he relied too heavily, in their judgment, on extravagant public claims about Soviet strategic power to move the Western powers toward an accommodation over Berlin. Although the Soviet Union had developed boosters for throwing space satellites into orbit, it had not, as yet, produced ICBM's in terms of deployed hardware.[26] Khrushchev had gone so far as to formulate a new military policy substituting missiles for conventional military forces.[27] He also favored increased investment in the civilian economy to the detriment of the defense budget. The marshals remained unconvinced that Khrushchev could achieve a credible military posture in the Berlin crisis by relying on missiles alone.

On January 14, Khrushchev further alienated the marshals. In a speech to the Supreme Soviet, he announced a reduction in military manpower. He said the armed forces would have 1,200,000 fewer men by 1961. Military personnel, including junior and middle-grade officers, would be required to help "build socialism" in the civilian economy. He argued that the Soviet Union could afford a conventional force reduction because of its nuclear prowess and that the reduction would be a unilateral measure contributing to disarmament

---

tional control. Although the last two suggestions were vague, he probably intended to suggest that negotiations should be on issues other than those defined by the Soviet Union. *Ibid.*, November 19, 1959, p. 12.

Secretary Herter objected to Acheson's view of the crisis. Speaking to the press on November 24, Herter said he thought Acheson read the Soviet position as though it remained where it had been a year ago. Instead, Herter claimed, "Actually they have come a very long way from that." When questioned to explain, he said that since November 1958 the Soviets "have admitted our legal rights, admitted them several times, and completely. They have furthermore moved away from the threat of taking unilateral action." *Ibid.*, November 25, 1959, p. 6.

26. Horelick and Rush, *op. cit.*, pp. 64-65.

27. For a discussion of the marshals' opposition to Khrushchev's military policy, see Roman Kolkowicz, *The Soviet Military and the Communist Party* (Princeton: Princeton University Press, 1967), pp. 150-153.

—one up on the Western powers.[28] Unfortunately for Khrushchev, this speech generated heavy criticism of his ability to manage Soviet foreign policy.

Perhaps feeling the pressure of his domestic critics, Khrushchev—in the January 14 speech—revived the threat of a separate treaty with the DDR, and used it frequently thereafter to nudge the West toward a productive negotiating line. The State Department objected to this new pressure, but it still confirmed Eisenhower's visit to Moscow for June 10–19. At a reception for visiting Italian President Gronchi on February 8, Khrushchev objected to Gronchi's attitude toward the draft peace treaty: "If you are against a peace treaty, you are against peace." After this episode, Herter felt he had to say that Moscow's position on Berlin had hardened in recent months. A settlement seemed unlikely to him in the limited time of one meeting in Paris. At the most, he looked for "a meeting of minds" and the preparation of drafting instructions to the foreign ministers. Increasingly pessimistic about an early Berlin settlement, Herter tried to encourage consideration of other issues on the Paris agenda. He suggested that the disarmament discussions, due to begin in Geneva on March 15, might be considered at the summit.

In late February and early March, other incidents contributed to further deterioration of East-West relations. On February 21, *The New York Times* printed a story that Bonn and Madrid were considering the construction of supply bases in Spain for the Bundeswehr.[29] The West German Defense Minister, Franz Joseph Strauss, conducted his inquiry with Spain bilaterally rather than through NATO. Moscow charged that, contrary to Western protestations, the Bundeswehr was not effectively integrated into NATO. Strauss relented saying that Bonn would not negotiate a base agreement with Spain without NATO approval. Not until eight months later did Strauss' intentions in the controversy come to light. He engaged in the liaison with Spain to dramatize the lack of space in West German territory for an extensive enough supply system behind the NATO central front and to pressure the French into allowing German bases in France to which they finally consented.[30]

The U.S. revived the issue of the 10,000-foot ceiling for Berlin

28. *The New York Times*, January 15, 1960, p. 1.
29. *Ibid.*, February 22, 1960, p. 16.
30. *Ibid.*, October 25, 1960, p. 15.

air corridor flights. The Air Force requested these flights to demonstrate to the Soviets that for maximum efficiency in a Berlin Airlift the C-130 needed air space in the corridors beyond the ceiling. Herter approved the flights.[31] But the flights received publicity before they could be conducted. The Soviets declared that, if the United States wished to conduct flights above 10,000 feet, it would have to negotiate with the DDR. Established practice, they maintained, reserved the higher altitudes for Soviet and DDR aircraft. The publicity changed an operational proposal into a diplomatic affair. On March 2, Herter denied that any decision had actually been made to conduct the flights.

Khrushchev arrived in Paris on March 23. While traveling in France, he expounded the theme that Paris and Moscow should treat Bonn as a common enemy, obviously wanting to disrupt the Franco-German reunion and isolate Bonn. De Gaulle spoke quite bluntly to discourage him from assuming that he could make any gains excoriating Bonn or manipulating Berlin.[32] De Gaulle's visits to London, Ottawa, and Washington terminated a season of peripatetic diplomacy in preparation for the summit.

After an autumn of delay and a winter of increasing dispute, East-West relations deteriorated markedly during April. The bickering between Adenauer and Khrushchev degenerated into slander. Herter spoke bluntly about this quarrel, on April 5 in Chicago, and defended Adenauer. He reacted to Khrushchev's repetitive statements threatening a separate peace treaty as follows: "While he has been careful not to be too precise in his statements on this subject, the repetition of this threat cannot help but complicate the situation and affect adversely the international atmosphere."

The Soviets were highly agitated about Under Secretary of State Douglas Dillon's speech in New York on April 20.[33] Dillon spoke pessimistically about a settlement because, he said, "the Soviet view of Berlin is far removed from the facts." The DDR, he asserted, "is one of the outstanding myths in a vast Communist web of prodigious mythology," and he doubted that its leadership "could remain in power for a single day without the support of Soviet bayonets." He agreed that the Berliners lived in an abnormal situa-

31. *The Herald Tribune*, March 6, 1960, p. II-1.
32. *The New York Times*, April 3, 1960, p. 34.
33. *Ibid.*, April 21, 1960, p. 4.

tion. But he argued that all Germans lived with the partition of Germany—a "monstrous" abnormality demonstrated by the 2,300,000 East Germans and East Berliners in the last ten years who had "voted with their feet" against the regime and fled.

It is not clear why Dillon talked so outspokenly less than a month before the summit. The Administration may have concluded that the Soviets expected too much of the first summit, as their intermingling of threats and proposals once again indicated. Or Eisenhower may have felt he had to object to Khrushchev's renewed pressure tactics. To this effect, Dillon conveyed a warning:

> We have repeatedly informed Mr. Khrushchev that we will not negotiate under duress. Yet in his recent statements about his intentions to sign a separate peace treaty . . . unless an East-West agreement is reached on Berlin he is skating on very thin ice.
>
> But Mr. Khrushchev and his associates will be profoundly disillusioned if they assume that we will bow to threat or that we will accept their distorted picture of the German problem as a factual premise upon which to negotiate.

Mikoyan answered Dillon on April 23. He called it a cold war speech. He said he understood Dillon to be a wise man, "but even wise men say foolish things sometimes if they have something wrong with them." [34] Khrushchev answered in a speech at Baku on April 25. He turned Dillon's speech around to allege: "It comes out that the United States Government will not be willing to reach an agreement on disarmament and on the ways of improving East-West relations unless its view on the Berlin question is accepted." [35] Such views "put me on the lookout," he said. Dillon had not actually insisted on coupling other issues with a Berlin settlement, although Herter—to salvage some hope for the summit— had suggested coupling Berlin and disarmament in his Chicago speech.

5. "Collapse" of a Two-Power World

On May 5, Khrushchev announced to the Supreme Soviet that Soviet missileers had shot down an American plane in flight over the Soviet Union on May Day. Another American plane violating

34. *Ibid.*, April 24, 1960, p. I-35.
35. *Ibid.*, April 26, 1960, p. 20.

Soviet frontiers had been sighted but not destroyed on April 9. He asked a rhetorical question about the flights which revealed the sensitivity and seriousness with which the Kremlin leadership perceived the incident:

> Are they taken in order to exert pressure on us and to attempt to frighten us with their military superiority in order to undermine our determination to work for easing tension, to eliminate the cold war, and to put an end to the arms race?

With reassurance, he remarked to the Supreme Soviet:

> We can say to those gentlemen who sent the aircraft that if they think they can bend our knees and our backs by means of such pressure, this will have no effect on us. The Soviet Union has every means to give a rebuff to those who want to exert pressure in order to achieve a solution convenient to aggressors. In the name of the Soviet Government let me express thanks to the men of the military units who carried out with honor the task laid on them in defending the frontiers of our motherland.[36]

He did not, at this point, accuse Eisenhower personally of complicating summit negotiations. Rather he said: "Comrades, the impression is being formed that the aggressive actions . . . are a foretaste of the summit meeting." He went on, bitterly, at great length to abuse the United States for the incident.[37] The incident threatened to disrupt his whole policy course only a few days before the summit.

The United States National Aeronautics and Space Administration identified the aircraft Khrushchev spoke of as an unarmed U-2 weather observation aircraft. On May 7, Khrushchev announced that Soviet police had captured the pilot, Captain Powers, and that he had admitted that he overflew Russia on a photographic intelligence mission for the Central Intelligence Agency, not on a flight to observe the weather. Khrushchev accused Turkey, Pakistan, and Norway of hostility since Powers had flown from Turkey to Pakistan and had intended to overfly the Soviet Union from Pakistan to Norway. He

36. *The New York Times*, May 6, 1960, p. 7.
37. Recent actions of the administration other than the U-2 flights also distressed him. For example, he objected that Eisenhower had set a time for his departure from Paris, possibly leaving Nixon behind as a substitute, and he again criticized Dillon's speech. *Ibid.*, p. 6.

ridiculed NASA's explanation of Captain Powers' mission and said the wreckage of the U-2 would be publicly displayed in Moscow.[38]

The U-2 penetrated 1,000 miles into Soviet airspace before Soviet surface-to-air missiles (SAM's) destroyed it. This aspect of the affair caused Khrushchev acute embarrassment because the marshals who were his critics had argued earlier that the actual state of the country's defenses was much weaker than Khrushchev had boasted. Apparently, the Soviets did not have the means for bringing down the U-2 overflight of April 9. In Washington, officials managing the U-2 overflights could not explain how the Soviets had destroyed the flight of May 1. According to the manufacturer—Lockheed Aircraft Corporation—the plane could fly at an operational altitude of more than 90,000 feet. This flight capability exceeded the estimated reach of Soviet SAM's. If Khrushchev stated accurately that Soviet missileers struck the aircraft at 65,000 feet, the manufacturer speculated that an engine malfunction must have forced the U-2 down to within range of Soviet missiles. *The Washington Post* speculated that the relatively good condition of the aircraft's equipment on exhibit in Gorki Park indicated the U-2 had been shot down at a lower altitude than the 65,000 feet Khrushchev claimed. Later, on trial in Moscow, Captain Powers testified that he had been attacked at 68,000 feet.[39] When he returned to the United States in 1962 Powers said only that he had felt an explosion external to the aircraft.[40]

Within the administration, some officials argued that the United States should concede nothing more than regrets. Customarily, governments do not acknowledge intelligence activities. To protect the President, Allen Dulles, Director, Central Intelligence Agency, offered to accept full responsibility.[41] In a similar vein, the British suggested that too much of an explanation would damage Eisenhower's role at the summit. Others argued that the incident could not be ignored because of Soviet publicity and propaganda. They wanted the administration to announce that the President had not personally authorized the mission. The second group won Eisenhower over to their view.

Embarrassing NASA, which had been unaware of the actual mis-

38. *Ibid.*, May 13, 1960, p. 5.
39. *Ibid.*, February 17, 1962, p. 5.
40. *Ibid.*, March 7, 1962.
41. David Wise and Thomas B. Ross, *The U-2 Affair* (New York: Random House, 1962), p. 101.

sions performed by U-2's,[42] the administration admitted on May 7 that the pilot had performed an intelligence mission. A statement issued by the State Department read in part:

> As a result of the inquiry ordered by the President, it has been established that insofar as the authorities in Washington are concerned, there was no authorization for any such flights so described by Mr. Khrushchev.
>
> Nevertheless, it appears that in endeavoring to obtain information now concealed behind the Iron Curtain a flight over Soviet territory was probably undertaken by an unarmed civilian U-2 plane.[43]

The Department publicly justified the U-2 flight, speaking of the danger of surprise attack and the secrecy practiced by the Soviet government. For example, it noted that the Soviet Union had rejected Eisenhower's "open skies" proposal of 1955: "It is in relation to the danger of surprise attack that planes of the type of the unarmed civilian U-2 aircraft have made flights along the frontiers of the free world for the past four years."

However necessary the flights may have been, in blaming the Soviet Union for them, the statement appeared to be a mere countercharge in a war of words. Admittedly, Khrushchev placed Eisenhower in an awkward position, but Eisenhower's response publicly justifying espionage—sacrificed any prospect of a successful summit conference, as the British feared.

The Soviets lodged a formal protest on May 10, objecting to the administration's explanation that the United States had to conduct such flights because of the danger of surprise attack. The Soviets asked: "Does all this mean that, with the refusal of a number of states to accept this proposal for 'open skies,' the USA is attempting arbitrarily to take upon itself the right to 'open' a foreign sky?" A skillful riposte, this arguement placed the administration in an even more awkward position than at the outset. The Soviets insisted that the United States, in its statement of May 7, assumed responsibility for a premeditated policy of aircraft intrusions and refused to termin-

42. The highest officials in NASA were aware of the real missions. The briefing officer for the press was not. Eisenhower, *op. cit.*, p. 548n.

43. Senate Foreign Relations Committee, *Hearings, Events Incident to the Summit Conferences*, 86th Cong. 2nd Sess., p. 187 (hereafter referred to as *Hearings*).

ate "provocative invasions." They condemned the United States with
the help of the administration's own words:

> Thus the Government of the USSR concludes that the announce-
> ment that the flight was carried out without the knowledge and
> permission of the Government of the USA does not correspond
> to reality because in the very same announcement the necessity
> for carrying on intelligence activities against the Soviet Union
> is justified. This means that espionage activities of American
> aircraft are carried on with the sanction of the Government of
> the USA.[44]

In all of their accusations, the Soviets carefully accused "the Government of the USA" rather than the President himself.

The administration's public position justifying espionage flights
in general, although maintaining that the President did not authorize
particular flights quickly became untenable. The administration was
censured from two sides: from the Soviet Union for justifying flights
at all and from United States allies for not requiring presidential
authorization for all flights. On both counts, the administration
appeared irresponsible. Critics blamed Eisenhower for poor judgment in failing to ground the flights before the summit.[45] Lippmann
also blamed him for mismanagement for not being informed of
specific flights at the time.[46]

Secretary Herter issued another statement on May 9, reversing
the administration's position of May 7. The Department now argued
that the President did have general responsibility for all flights
even though he did not specifically authorize each specific flight:

> In accordance with the National Security Act of 1947, the
> President has put into effect since the beginning of his Admin-
> istration directives to gather by every possible means the infor-
> mation required to protect the United States and the Free World
> against surprise attack and to enable them to make effective
> preparations for their defense. Under these directives programs

44. *Ibid.*, pp. 196-198.
45. According to Wise and Ross, CIA ordered the flight of the U-2 for May 1
to photograph a suspected Soviet ICBM site under construction before a summer fog cover hid it from view. Ross, *op. cit.*, p. 10. Eisenhower said the data
to be acquired would not have been available at a later date. *The New York
Times*, May 26, 1960, p. 6.
46. Lippmann, *The Herald Tribune*, May 10, 1960, p. 16.

have included extensive aerial surveillance by unarmed civilian aircraft, normally of a peripheral character, but on occasion by penetration.[47]

The New York Times, the British, and the Soviets construed this statement to mean that the U-2 flights would continue.[48] An additional sentence supported this impression: "In fact, the United States has not and does not shirk this responsibility." The administration did not correct this impression because it did not want to appear to be retreating under pressure.[49]

Ordinarily when an intelligence operation is discovered, it is no longer useful and is discontinued. The U-2 flights seemed to be an exception when the administration decided to rationalize the operation. The Fulbright report, subsequent to an investigation of the entire episode, scored the unwisdom of the May 9 statement. Senator Fulbright contended that the statement made an honorable exit from the situation impossible for Khrushchev.

At his press conference on May 11, Eisenhower confirmed he had taken upon himself personal responsibility for the incident. He said Soviet secrecy—he might have said Khrushchev's claims of a missile gap favorable to the Soviet Union—justified the acquisition of information on military forces, "especially those capable of massive surprise attack . . ." He implied that Khrushchev's emphasis on the incident seemed contrived, and suggested that all the publicity about the U-2 should not be allowed to distract attention from the summit.[50]

On May 11, Khrushchev appeared at the public exhibit of the U-2 wreckage to express his horror at Herter's statement that Eisenhower himself had responsibility for the flight. He implied that the U-2 cast Eisenhower's visit to Moscow in doubt:

> You know my friendly attitude toward the President. My hopes have not been justified. I am a human being. I have feelings. The people of Russia are open-hearted. Can I urge the Russian people to greet him as a dear guest? The Russian people would

47. *Hearings*, p. 194.
48. *The New York Times*, May 10, 1960, p. 1.
49. Senate Foreign Relations Committee, *Report, Events Relating to the Summit Conference*, 80th Cong., 2nd Sess., p. 25 (hereafter referred to as *Report*).
50. *The New York Times*, May 12, 1960, p. 18.

say I was mad to welcome a man who sends spy planes over here like that.[51]

He said he would consult with Eisenhower in Paris about whether to place the incident on the summit agenda.

The State Department expected Khrushchev to raise the incident at the summit conference. It expected him to demand that the United States admit that espionage flights go against international law and jeopardize diplomatic relations. If Khrushchev made an issue of the incident in Paris, Eisenhower planned to counter with his "open skies" proposal. At this point, the conference would either be salvaged by an informal understanding that the incident should not be allowed to disrupt the conference or Khrushchev could use the incident to blame the United States for the failure of the summit.[52]

On May 14, Khrushchev arrived in Paris. Two days remained to settle the U-2 controversy before the summit began. In his arrival statement, he emphasized the importance of summit diplomacy. But he added:

> Though all the peoples desire the strengthening of peace and a détente in international relations, it is common knowledge that, particularly of late, influential quarters who are seeking to revive the cold war and hinder the invigoration of the international atmosphere have noticeably intensified their activities in certain countries. Let us hope that their efforts will yield no success.[53]

The Western foreign ministers discussed ways of avoiding further dispute over the U-2. Couve de Murville tactfully suggested to Herter that nothing more should be said about the necessity for flights. They all agreed Khrushchev should have to take the initiative and open the Berlin discussion. Adenauer arrived, conferred with de Gaulle, and departed before the Soviets raised a fuss about his presence in Paris.

Eisenhower and Macmillan arrived on May 15. Khrushchev made

51. *Ibid.*, p. 1.
52. *Ibid.*, May 15, 1960, p. 1. Already, Moscow had cancelled a scheduled visit to Washington of the Chief of Staff of the Soviet air force. *Ibid.*, May 14, 1960, p. 1.
53. *Ibid.*, May 15, 1960, p. 34.

no effort to see Eisenhower or Eisenhower to see him. Khrushchev appeared at the Elysée with Marshal Rodion Malinovsky, his Minister of Defense, and Gromyko. He spoke to de Gaulle in strong terms about the U-2 incident, but professed a desire for the success of the summit. In a day of frenetic diplomacy focused on the Elysée, Eisenhower and Macmillan called on de Gaulle to rehearse the parts prepared by their foreign ministers. Khrushchev saw Macmillan later and spoke as strongly to him as he had to de Gaulle. Through Macmillan and de Gaulle, therefore, Eisenhower had some inkling of Khrushchev's outburst the next day.

On May 16, the grand conference at the Elysée convened for its first and only session.[54] De Gaulle welcomed the conference and invited Eisenhower, as senior chief of state, to speak first. Khrushchev, nervous and pale, interrupted.[55] He said he did not consider the current session part of a summit conference. He considered it a preliminary meeting to determine whether appropriate conditions prevailed for a conference. He spoke at length, reviewing the "provocative act" committed by the "American Air Force." He protested that the administration had refused to retract the policy of the United States authorizing espionage flights over the Soviet Union. In effect, he said, the United States required him to negotiate under duress because "such actions will continue to be the national policy of the United States toward the Soviet Union." His voice rising, he asked:

> How can agreement be sought on the various issues which require a settlement with the object of reducing tension and eliminating suspicion and distrust between the states, when the government of one of the great powers bluntly declares that its policy is intrusion into the territory of another great power for purposes of espionage and sabotage and consequently, the aggravation of tension in relations between the powers? It is obvious that the proclamation of such a policy, which can be carried out only when countries are in a state of war, dooms the summit meeting to complete failure in advance.[56]

54. For a colorful description of this session, see Wise and Ross, *op. cit.*, pp. 150-158.
55. Western participants at the meeting said he seemed self-conscious about Malinovsky's presence. *Ibid.*, p. 151.
56. Embree, *op. cit.*, p. 254.

If Eisenhower wanted the conference to proceed, Khrushchev insisted that Eisenhower had to make amends and meet three conditions:

> In the first place, denounce the impermissible provocative actions of the American Air Force with regard to the Soviet Union and, in the second place, refrain from continuing such actions and such a policy against the USSR in the future. It goes without saying that in this event the government of the United States cannot fail to call strictly to account those directly responsible for the deliberate violation of the state frontiers of the USSR by American planes.

He added a fourth condition—that Eisenhower should "express regret." [57]

Khrushchev said that unless Eisenhower met these conditions, "the Soviet government sees no possibility of fruitful negotiations with the United States government at the summit." Not waiting for an answer, he went on to say that if the Eisenhower Administration failed to understand that no acceptable alternative to *détente* existed, then he would wait for another administration. He proposed postponing the summit for six or eight months, until after the presidential election in the United States.

He had good words for de Gaulle and Macmillan, regretting that the summit had been "torpedoed by the reactionary circles of the United States of America." He thought Eisenhower's visit to Moscow should be postponed.

Eisenhower responded with restraint—he exploded later at the embassy—to what he considered a brutal speech. He said Khrushchev misinterpreted the administration's statements on U-2 operations to infer a threat: "The United States had made no such threat. Neither I nor my government has intended any. The actual statements go no further than to say that the United States will not shirk its responsibility to safeguard against surprise attack." [58] For Khrushchev's information, Eisenhower declared he had issued a presidential directive suspending U-2 flights. They would not be resumed during his

---

57. *Ibid.*, pp. 255, 256.
58. *The New York Times*, May 17, 1960, p. 15.

administration.[59] Thus, he had already met Khrushchev's second condition before he heard it. He proposed an immediate discussion of the incident. If Khrushchev refused, Eisenhower said he would submit a new proposal for aerial surveillance to the United Nations Security Council. He accused Khrushchev of coming "all the way from Moscow to Paris with the sole intention of sabotaging this meeting on which so much of the hopes of the world have rested."

Macmillan told Khrushchev that Eisenhower's statement made it "absolutely clear" the flights were no longer United States policy, and that he should have no doubt in his mind that the summit would not be conducted under duress. De Gaulle proposed a private meeting of the four alone to see what could be done—a meeting without Malinovsky or Gromyko. In order to preserve some chance of an understanding, both Macmillan and de Gaulle were particularly concerned to prevent Khrushchev from publishing his statement. De Gaulle reminded Khrushchev that espionage by aerial means included Soviet satellites passing over France. At that remark, Khrushchev declared: "As God is my witness, my hands are clean and my soul is pure." In the ensuing discussion, Khrushchev queried: "What the devil pushed these people to fly over the Soviet Union?" De Gaulle replied: "There are many devils in the world and we are here precisely for the purpose of exorcising them." [60] Khrushchev refused all overtures, but indicated he would not leave Paris for two days.

After the meeting, Macmillan urged Khrushchev to reconsider and proposed a four-power agreement for abstaining from espionage. De Gaulle urged that no concessions be made to Khrushchev.[61] Gromyko assured the Western foreign ministers that unilateral action would not be taken against Berlin before another summit could be arranged. European critics of the administration, who believed Eisenhower had mishandled the U-2 incident, now felt Khrushchev had overplayed his hand by trying to humiliate Eisenhower.

On May 17, Lloyd prevailed upon Gromyko to revive the conference. Gromyko advised him to let things rest for the moment and

59. He did not announce this decision earlier because he wanted to reveal it when he revived his "open skies" plan. See his televised address of May 25. *Ibid.*, May 26, 1960, p. 6.

60. *Ibid.*, May 17, 1960, pp. 15, 16.

61. *Ibid.*, May 20, 1960, p. 2.

try to make headway in the next six to eight months toward another summit. Khrushchev informed de Gaulle by letter that he would not return to the Elysée unless Eisenhower met the Soviet conditions for negotiations. De Gaulle called another session of the summit anyway, and Soviet embassy officials inquired repeatedly by telephone whether de Gaulle considered the meeting a session preliminary to the summit or a summit session. The Western powers adhered to their position that the summit had already begun. Khrushchev did not appear. The three Western heads of government assembled, issued a statement noting Khrushchev's absence, and announced that de Gaulle had adjourned the summit conference.

Before leaving Paris, Khrushchev answered the charge that the Soviets should have been able to negotiate, since Eisenhower had suspended the flights. At a press conference, he claimed that Eisenhower's new directive applied to the remainder of his term of office only. Eisenhower had not renounced an aggressive policy, he argued. Nor had Eisenhower met the other three Soviet conditions.[62]

De Gaulle invited Eisenhower and Macmillan to a final meeting to discuss the immediate future, including "questions of common defense." In noting Gromyko's request for a Security Council meeting to consider the U-2 incident, they anticipated a difficult next few months. More immediately, they could not be certain what turn the Berlin crisis would take.

Khrushchev said he planned to return to Moscow via Berlin. To many American officials including Secretary of Defense Gates, Khrushchev's visit to Berlin—coming on the heels of his fit of temper in Paris—seemed ominous. The press speculated that he might sign a separate peace treaty on the spot in East Berlin. Secretary of Defense Thomas Gates ordered, from Paris, a world-wide alert of American military commands to test the military communications system from overseas. To Secretary Gates' relief, Khrushchev—sensitive to his critics in East Berlin, Moscow, and Peking—told his East Berlin audience on May 20 that:

We are realists and we will never pursue a gambling policy.
Under present conditions, it is worthwhile to wait a little longer and try to find a solution for the long-since ripe question

62. *Ibid.*, May 19, 1960, p. 8.

of signing a peace treaty with the two German states. This will not escape our hands. We had better wait, and the matter will get more mature.[63]

6. *Khrushchev's Behavior at Paris*

The public record suggested that had the U-2 incident not occurred or had it been managed differently by the administration, the Paris Conference might not have failed. The Fulbright report sympathized with Khrushchev's point, for example, that he had to act at a great disadvantage when the administration refused to disavow the flights.[64] Senator John Kennedy thought Eisenhower should have apologized to Khrushchev at the opening session. Postmortems in the Western press faulted the administration, claiming that Khrushchev left a way out on May 5 when he did not blame Eisenhower for the incident.[65] The May 7 State Department statement took advantage of that opening in saying Eisenhower had not authorized the flights. But the May 9 statement reversing this stance, the critics said, put Khrushchev in an impossible position because the administration challenged Moscow's authority over the Soviet Union's own air space.[66] Khrushchev built his case on this issue in his opening statement on May 16. And, in fact, Eisenhower realized—once he reached Paris—that the Soviets had misunderstood his position and told Macmillan and de Gaulle that the flights had been suspended even before he met Khrushchev at the first session.[67]

This critique of the administration's management of the incident is useful as far as it goes. It only scratches the surface, however, because it portrays Khrushchev as merely affronted and compelled to restore Soviet prestige. Actually, Khrushchev's problem went deeper than an affront to Soviet sovereignty. This critique of the administration is also misleading because it fails to mention how the Soviets themselves contributed to the failure of the conference. To say that Khrushchev reacted to administration blunders as best he could is too charitable a view of his behavior.

The critics acknowledged the other conditions required of Eisen-

63. Embree, *op. cit.*, p. 266.
64. *Report*, p. 25.
65. *Hearings*, p. 176.
66. *Ibid.*, p. 205.
67. Lippmann observed correctly that Eisenhower revealed the suspension order a week too late to have any effect. *The Herald Tribune*, May 17, 1960.

hower, but they de-emphasized them to imply that had Eisenhower announced the suspension of flights a week before the summit, Khrushchev might not have been driven to set additional conditions. To the contrary, the other conditions offered evidence that the Soviet position involved more than an attempt to recover prestige. The demands for condemnation of the Air Force and for punishment of those officials responsible for the incident were not conditions Eisenhower could meet. In particular, for him to punish the responsible officials would have been to punish himself because he had assumed responsibility for the flights.

Khrushchev made one statement about the U-2 incident in the opening session on May 16 which Ambassador Charles Bohlen, to his recollection, considered unique in the history of East-West conferences. Bohlen related: "He made one interesting reference . . . when he said that this was a matter that involved deeply the internal politics of the Soviet Union, a matter which he said was of great importance to them." [68] After the Paris Conference, the State Department compiled available evidence of recent events in Soviet internal politics to explain Khrushchev's intriguing remark. [69]

In the winter of 1960, internal opposition to Khrushchev grew. The army, supported by the air force, reacted severely to Khrushchev's program for reducing the level of armed forces personnel. The program severely affected the officer levels: Careers ended abruptly and the standard of living of many officers fell. [70] The marshals did not really accept Khrushchev's version of a massive retaliation policy rationalizing the release of military personnel. [71]

Harrison Salisbury reported that Khrushchev appointed party theoretician Mikhail Suslov to conduct an indoctrination campaign in order to persuade the armed forces to accept his program. [72] Suslov,

68. *The New York Times*, May 17, 1960, p. 16. Wise and Ross claim that the State Department interpreter present at the meeting translated Khrushchev's term as internal "policy," not "politics." The Russian term "politika" can mean either "policy" or "politics." *Op. cit.*, p. 156n.

69. *Report*, p. 16.

70. See Hanson Baldwin's report, *The New York Times*, May 19, 1960, p. 9.

71. According to Raymond Garthoff, Khrushchev compromised with the military on the defense program of January 1960. Even so, Malinovsky, for example, publicly qualified Khrushchev's statements about the program. See Garthoff's introduction to Marshal V. D. Sokolovsky, ed., *Military Strategy, Soviet Doctrine and Concepts* (New York: Frederick A. Praeger, 1963), pp. viii-ix.

72. *The New York Times*, May 17, 1960, p. 17.

apparently, did not win many adherents to the program because he used his assignment to form an alliance with the marshals against Khrushchev. Suslov's longstanding dislike for Khrushchev's domestic reforms converged with the marshals' outrage to produce an opposition affecting the strength of Kremlin factions.[73]

The opposition asserted itself in April with Suslov and Marshal Malinovsky at its head. Without announcement, changes were ordered in the Soviet military hierarchy seeming to favor Malinovsky.[74] An announcement in May indicated that Leonid Brezhnev, a Khrushchev protégé concerned with military affairs, had been promoted to a less critical position as Chief of State in April.[75] On May 4, the Central Committee reorganized the presidium to Khrushchev's disadvantage. The Central Committee reduced the number of Khrushchev's party secretaries in the presidium from ten to six. With a total presidium membership of fifteen, the six did not constitute the majority that ten did. Assuming the presidium ruled by majority vote, this change must have handicapped Khrushchev. Following these moves, the party-army conference in the Kremlin on May 11–14 reopened the issue of force reductions. But Khrushchev did not modify his defense program.[76]

Victor Zorza's account of Kremlin politics offered a reasonable explanation of why Khrushchev broke up the Paris Conference after he had consistently advocated summit diplomacy for achieving a Berlin settlement.[77] Zorza did not think Khrushchev's behavior could be accounted for by the existence of a simple majority against him in the presidium. The new majority in the presidium owed

---

73. Richard Löwenthal challenged Salisbury's opinion that Suslov opposed Khrushchev. He pointed to the fact, for example, that Suslov joined in Khrushchev's excoriation of Stalin at the Twentieth Party Congress in 1956 and that he supported Khrushchev against Malenkov, Molotov, nd Kaganovich—the "anti-party group"—in 1957. Löwenthal, "The Nature of Khrushchev's Power," *Russia under Khrushchev*, ed. Abraham Brumberg (New York: Frederick A. Praeger, 1963), p. 125. Boris Nicolaevsky disputed Löwenthal. He argued that Suslov misled his audience in his speech at the Twentieth Party Congress. Suslov did not criticize Stalin personally, only the policies associated with Malenkov in Stalin's time. For the same reason that he opposed Malenkov, he supported Khrushchev against the "anti-party group" in 1957. Nicolaevsky's case that Suslov was an unreconstructed Stalinist seems more persuasive. *Power and the Soviet Elite: "The Letter of an Old Bolshevik" and Other Essays*, ed. Janet D. Zagoria (New York: Frederick A. Praeger, 1965), pp. 274-275.
74. *The New York Times*, May 17, 1960, p. 17.
75. *Ibid.*, May 8, 1960, p. 1.
76. *Ibid.*, May 19, 1960, p. 1; also Garthoff in Sokolovsky, *op. cit.*, p. ix.
77. Victor Zorza, *Manchester Guardian*, June 2, 1960, p. 5.

its power to the Central Committee, where he believed Khrushchev still had considerable support even though he had lost a vote of confidence there. Two bits of evidence favored Zorza's thesis: (1) Khrushchev did not relent to veto the summit meeting and went to Paris anyway; (2) he did not modify the military policies which the marshals pressed him to revise.[78]

Khrushchev's opposition succeeded in disrupting the conference after he left Moscow. Zorza argued that the nature of Soviet politics is intensely bureaucratic, that the holder of power must be in Moscow manipulating the levers of authority to work his will. Mikoyan and Nikolai Podgorny, associates of Khrushchev who would be expected to defend him, were absent from Moscow at the time. Zorza suggested that the Central Committee, probably swayed by Suslov and the marshals, held a rump session in Moscow after Khrushchev departed and compelled him to change his position. Zorza reported that the statement which Khrushchev read out on his arrival in Paris was an altered version of the original he took with him from Moscow.

Very little of this account can be verified, of course, but it squares with what is known of Khrushchev's behavior before Paris. Even after Eisenhower, on May 9, admitted responsibility for the U-2 flights, Khrushchev did not attack him personally.[79]

Only at Paris and after did he attack him and present him with conditions he knew the President would not accept. Probably, Khrushchev did not come "all the way from Moscow to Paris with the sole intention of sabotaging this meeting on which so much of the hopes of the world have rested," as Eisenhower accused him. His opposition forced him to sabotage the meeting after he arrived in Paris. Judging by the special character of Khrushchev's rule—he did not succeed to Stalin's full powers—Zorza's account seems plausible.[80]

The hardening of Western policy in early spring added fuel to the fire of Khrushchev's opposition. When the administration decided to

78. The opposition probably sent Malinovsky to Paris as a reminder for Khrushchev to proceed gingerly. At the British Embassy on May 15, Khrushchev remarked to Macmillan: "Malinovsky insists on coming with me. . . . You're such a cunning old diplomat he thinks you'll twist me around your finger unless he's here." *The New York Times*, May 25, 1960, p. 11.

79. Nikita S. Khrushchev, *Statement and Replies to Questions, Gorky Park, Moscow, May 11, 1960* (New York: Crosscurrents Press, 1960), p. 10.

80. Robert Conquest's analysis coincided with Zorza's. See Conquest's *Power and Policy in the USSR* (London: MacMillan and Co., Ltd., 1962), pp. 390-391; see also P. B. Reddaway, "The Fall of Khrushchev," *Survey*, 56 (July 1965), 11 ff.

publicly defend Adenauer and strengthen its position on a Berlin settlement, Khrushchev could not ignore the implications for his project. Herter's April 5 speech did not offer him much hope and Dillon's April 20 speech must have upset him greatly. On April 23–24, Soviet Cultural Affairs Minister Zhukov, visiting in Washington, complained to administration officials and to Walter Lippmann that as early as March 15 United States policy visibly hardened and the "spirit of Camp David" seemed reversed. In mid-March, Zhukov said, Voice of America broadcasts began to sound hostile.[81]

Khrushchev received no support for a settlement from de Gaulle in his Paris visit or in what de Gaulle said in Ottawa and Washington. In his Baku speech replying to Herter and Dillon on April 25, he spoke warily about prospects for the summit. Sometime before the Baku speech, Khrushchev himself may have raised doubts about the summit. Summit diplomacy became increasingly awkward for him to defend.

To complete the circle of Khrushchev's enemies, the Chinese Communist party printed unusually critical commentary during April and May. On April 2, all Peking newspapers carried articles opposing Khrushchev's interest in *détente* and warned that the temporary interest of the Western powers in *détente* did not change the belligerent nature of imperialism.[82] As the summit approached, Mao Tse-tung himself, usually reticent, made five statements in ten days accusing the United States of war preparations. On May 15, he declared his support for summit diplomacy, but doubted it would produce significant results. As for the U-2 incident, he said:

> This incident reveals the true face of the United States, which under the phony flag of peace is actively preparing for aggressive war. . . .
>
> In the past, certain people have described Eisenhower as a person wholly devoted to world peace. I hope these people will be awakened by this incident.[83]

The "certain people" to whom he referred was, of course, Khrushchev. Chinese criticism undoubtedly provided additional fuel for Khrushchev's opposition in the Soviet Union.

81. *The New York Times*, May 16, 1960, p. 14.
82. *Ibid.*, April 3, 1960, p. 1.
83. *The Christian Science Monitor*, May 17, 1960, p. 1.

The formation of an internal opposition using a hardened Western policy and Chinese pressure to its advantage occurred well before the U-2 incident. The incident occurred in the context of a developing internal dispute about Khrushchev's whole approach to the Berlin crisis.

7. The U-2 and Berlin

The revelations of Soviet military weakness which the U-2 incident brought to the Central Committee's attention assisted Khrushchev's opposition. At one stroke, the incident supplied a battery of arguments for Suslov and the marshals to use in attacking Khrushchev's military policy and his foreign policy favoring *détente*. Clearly, the United States intended the U-2 flights to obtain photographic intelligence of Soviet military power.[84] Now the marshals knew that the American intelligence community knew something of the exaggeration with which Khrushchev spoke about Soviet missile power since the Soviet space satellites went into orbit in 1957. The Soviet Union probably did lose much of the prestige in intelligence circles Khrushchev had acquired for it when he deliberately tried to create the expectation that the growth of Soviet nuclear power had caused or was about to cause a shift in the military balance.

The U-2 aircraft demonstrated American technical superiority in the Soviets' own sky. Ordinarily, the U-2 could not be intercepted. The Soviets knew the U-2 as the "black lady of espionage." Evidence of its air intelligence capabilities displayed in Gorki Park demonstrated that the U-2 had obtained remarkably accurate photographic information. According to Secretary Herter, this aircraft had been in operation since 1956 and had conducted thirty or forty flights along or across Soviet borders.[85] Perhaps U-2 intelligence accounted for Secretary Gates' assurances in January and February 1960 that no "missile gap" would ensue unless the Soviets produced more missiles at a faster rate.[86] The U-2, through the quality of its per-

84. *The Washington Post*, June 12, 1960, p. E1; *The New York Times*, February 17, 1962, p. 5; March 7, 1962.

85. *The Washington Post*, June 12, 1960, p. E1.

86. In the winter of 1960, reports appeared in the press that the Soviet Union had as many as 100 missiles and the United States only three Atlas bases. These reports estimated that by 1961 the USSR would have 150 missiles deployed and the United States 50. *The New York Times*, January 16, 1960, p. 3; February 2, 1960, p. 1. In retrospect, Gates predicted the quantity and quality of future

formance, probably enabled the administration to restore some confidence in its own ranks by 1960, lacking since 1957, that the balance of military power had not yet shifted away from the United States because the Soviet missile program had not moved into the deployment stage.

The U-2 incident related directly to the Berlin crisis. Not only did it complicate the negotiation of a Berlin settlement, but as a reminder to Khrushchev of the Soviet Union's strategic vulnerability and as a rapporteur for the United States of the Soviet Union's relative strength, it took the wind out of Khrushchev's sails. The accuracy of the photographs must have startled him. The incident rendered his campaign against Berlin much less impressive. It should have cautioned him against trying to translate alleged missile production into political payoffs. For a policy dependent upon threats of deadlines and a separate treaty, the incident was a political disaster for Khrushchev. Inadvertently, the administration forced Khrushchev to a truce in the Berlin crisis.

8. The Dénouement of Dulles' Strategy

After the abortive summit, the Eisenhower Administration confronted a resurgence of Soviet diplomacy no longer restrained by summit expectations. In striving to put his own house in order, Khrushchev adopted the arguments of his opposition and became outspokenly bellicose toward the United States. He responded to a stand-off in the crisis maneuvering between East and West by switching to pressure tactics and verbal militance.

Izvestiia called Eisenhower incompetent. *Pravda* charged that he had been deceitful at Camp David. On May 23, in a bitter debate between Gromyko and Ambassador Henry Cabot Lodge in the United Nations Security Council, each blamed the other for what happened in Paris. In Moscow, Khrushchev ridiculed Eisenhower's tardy suspension of U-2 flights. Khrushchev went out of his way to deny rumors that Soviet internal pressures had forced him to sabotage the conference. The opposite was the case, he said: internal militaristic

---

Soviet missile strength rather accurately. He said that a "deterrent gap" would not develop even if a missile gap occurred and that missile estimates would have to be revised downward if the Soviets did not produce to capacity. He believed Soviet production intentions had to be weighed when estimating their missile inventory, as well as production capacity.

pressures in the United States had forced Eisenhower into a disastrous sequence of events.[87] The Soviet delegation in Geneva took steps to end the negotiations of a test ban treaty during Eisenhower's term of office. Khrushchev replied to a cable from the Democratic leadership of Congress which had urged him—when he was in Paris—not to postpone the summit: again, he blamed Eisenhower for all that happened and urged the Democrats to follow a course of *détente*. On June 3, he vilified Eisenhower saying he was capable only of being "director of a children's home." On July 1, Soviet fighter aircraft attacked an American RB-47 reconnaisance aircraft over international waters north of the Soviet Union, further straining relations.[88]

On June 12, *Pravda* wrote a defense of Khrushchev against "Leftist" critics including the Chinese Communists. It declared that "some persons" had called a policy of *détente* a deviation from Marxism-Leninism. On the contrary:

> Present day revisionists who ignore the general principles of the development of communism and who try to find their own path toward the establishment of socialism are concentrating their fire on the principles of Socialist construction in the U.S.S.R. and other Socialist countries, and are misinterpreting Lenin.[89]

This defense offered the most complete Soviet refutation to date of the Chinese argument that armed struggle rather than Soviet-style peaceful coexistence should rule the relationship with imperialism.[90]

Before the Eisenhower Administration left office, Khrushchev again reminded it of West Berlin's insecurity and allowed the DDR to sponsor new encroachments on the access routes. In the interim period, between May and December 1960, while the old administration waited for the new to be elected and organized, the DDR made gains in Berlin, demonstrating the handicap the United States had in operating without a fallback position for Dulles' original negotiations strategy.

In late summer 1960, Khrushchev authorized Ulbricht to impose a selective blockade of West German traffic on the access routes

87. *Ibid.*, May 29, 1960, p. 18.
88. *Ibid.*, July 2, 1960, p. 1.
89. *Ibid.*, June 13, 1960, p. 4.
90. *Ibid.*, p. 1.

beginning August 30. Ulbricht wanted to protest the rallies of two West German refugee organizations, scheduled for September 1–4 in West Berlin.[91] Pankow warned against misuse of the air corridors for transporting the membership of the refugee organizations. Military and West Berlin civilian traffic would not be affected, it said. The Western commandants in West Berlin immediately protested to the Soviet commandant in East Berlin that Pankow's action violated the quadripartite status of the city.

Pankow broke precedent and also closed the sector border between East and West Berlin by order of the DDR Interior Ministry, rather than by the customary order of the mayor of East Berlin. Previously, Pankow kept East Berlin separate in legal terms from the rest of the DDR, tacitly acknowledging the status of all-Berlin as a city under four-power rule. West Berlin and East Berlin were administered by their respective mayors and governments, a practice dating to the split in the city administration in 1948. In 1960, for the first time, Pankow treated East Berlin legally as part of the DDR.[92]

The West Berlin Senat subsidized transportation of members of the refugee organizations, all of whom had to arrive in West Berlin by air. Pankow lifted the blockade and the closure of the sector border as soon as the refugee organizations departed on September 4.

On September 8, the DDR once more unexpectedly imposed new restrictions on traffic to East Berlin. The restrictions were in the form of permits issued by the DDR Interior Ministry. In accepting West Berlin identity cards while refusing West German passports, Pankow unilaterally gave West Berlin a separate legal status—the status reflected in the free city proposal. Since Bonn opposed a separate status for West Berlin, it would not allow West Berliners to use their identity cards to obtain permits for crossing into East Berlin. Thus, the effect of the new DDR restrictions was a ban on travel by West Berliners to East Berlin. In addition, Ulbricht demanded removal of the Western garrisons by 1962. American Ambassador Walter Dowling, in Bonn, denounced the measures and drove into East Berlin to show the flag.

Ulbricht's move proved awkward for the Western powers to counter. They retained an interest in East Berlin, given their continuing interest in preserving the occupation status of the entire city. But they

91. *The New York Times*, August 31, 1960, p. 8.
92. *The Christian Science Monitor*, September 2, 1960, p. 2.

could do little in practice to enforce the occupation regime in East Berlin. The employment opportunities and political and economic contrast West Berlin offered to East Berliners and East Germans gave the Western powers some limited influence. Since the ban affected only West Berliners' travel to East Berlin, East Berlin employees continued to work in West Berlin.

The imposition of border controls by the DDR in September 1960 foreshadowed the more comprehensive control of all traffic to East Berlin in August 1961. The future could not, of course, be foreseen. As a trend of events issuing from the unresolved Berlin crisis in consonance with Macmillans' estimate after Paris that there would be "new threats and new dangers," the DDR ban painfully reminded the allied missions in Berlin of their inability to stop the DDR when Pankow chose its ground carefully.

Bonn resorted to economic countermeasures on September 30. It announced it would void the new interzonal trade agreement just negotiated in August, scheduled to take effect on January 1. This action threatened to halt a mutual $500,000,000 annual trade flow. Bonn must have hoped that Pankow would desire the trade more badly than the travel restrictions and would fix its priorities accordingly. On November 7, Ulbricht retaliated, imposing inspection requirements on West Berlin manufactures in transit to West Germany allegedly to prevent "war materials" shipments.

By December 1, Bonn had second thoughts and proposed restoring the new trade agreement, provided Pankow lifted West Berliner travel restrictions to East Berlin. Bonn apparently had reason to believe that the DDR would be interested enough in the continuation of interzonal trade to agree to a *quid pro quo*.[93] Pankow hinted at an interest in negotiations. When the two sides met, however, the East German representatives showed no interest in relating the question of interzonal trade to the East Berlin travel ban.

On December 18, Ulbricht threatened to blockade a portion of West German traffic to West Berlin after January 1, precisely what Bonn most feared. He said he planned to close the rail lines operating between West Berlin and points West.[94] Ulbricht's threat related the trade question to the East Berlin travel ban, although in exactly the opposite way Bonn preferred. He also raised the specter of full

93. *Ibid.*, December 2, 1960, p. 4.
94. *The New York Times*, December 19, 1960, p. 10.

blockade when he asserted that the New York Agreement of 1949 which restored ground traffic to Berlin after the first blockade depended upon the vitality of the interzonal trade agreement. This assertion carried great risks for Ulbricht because, if he violated the 1949 agreement, the Western powers—as signatories—could become directly involved.

Barely ten days before the expiration of the old trade agreement, on December 21, Bonn and Pankow formulated a compromise. Bonn conceded the DDR need not lift the East Berlin travel ban if Pankow gave assurances to lift it at an undefined future time. Pankow conceded it would remove its controls on West Berlin's "war materials" shipments to West Germany. On December 29, the two parties restored the new trade agreement scheduled for January 1.

The compromise for restoring the interzonal trade agreement revealed that Bonn agreed not to insist on its original demand for abolition of the East Berlin travel regulations in return for Pankow's assurance that the ban would not be permanent. Bonn did not effectively counter the new travel restrictions of September 8. Ulbricht successfully compelled Bonn to choose between access to East Berlin or access to West Berlin. As expected, Bonn chose the latter. The settlement illustrated the difficulty Bonn faced in attempting to apply a commercial threat to a situation in East Berlin beyond its reach.

The decisive juncture in the series of moves between Bonn and Pankow occurred when Ulbricht threatened another blockade of West German traffic to West Berlin to begin January 1. If Bonn could have resisted that threat, it might have been able to make its own commercial threat stick. To resist, it needed American support.

If the United States initially supported Bonn's attempt to bring pressure to bear on Pankow, the United States obviously did not offer to help in calling Ulbricht's bluff. Or if Bonn made its initial move strictly on its own initiative, the United States did not offer to help at the last minute. In any event, the United States could not have offered to help even if it preferred because it did not have in hand sufficient conventional armed forces to mount a challenge to another Berlin blockade. The lack of an American strategy for falling back on conventional forces to defend West Berlin affected Bonn's negotiating posture because American support for Bonn in a blockade—the extremity to which Bonn had to drive the matter to prevail—would be severely limited.

The entire period between May and December 1960 amounted to a fallback situation in which the United States had exhausted both conventional and summit diplomacy to resolve the Berlin crisis. The local problem of defending West Berlin that the administration had de-emphasized when Dulles inaugurated his policy for a negotiated solution came back to haunt the administration in its last days. The United States found itself in a fallback situation without any fallback strategy.

PART III

Berlin Strategy, the Wall, and the Blockade of Cuba

CHAPTER 5

Kennedy Inherits the Crisis

In 1961, the crisis began all over again. Khrushchev raised the same issues, this time with greater urgency. The new administration set about planning more flexible military means for defending West Berlin and reconstructing the Geneva negotiating proposals. But it worked under a significant handicap because Khrushchev had become impatient precisely when Kennedy needed time to develop his own policies. When Khrushchev renewed his threats in June, he set off another "deadline" crisis. Unlike 1958, this "deadline" produced a cycle of military demonstrations. Each side quickly countered the military moves of the other with moves of its own.

In midsummer, the DDR began literally to be drained away by a loss of population caused by Pankow's internal policies and stimulated by renewal of the crisis between Moscow and Washington. The DDR's predicament undoubtedly embarrassed Khrushchev. The administration in Washington worried that the population of East Germany might revolt—as in 1953—entangling the great powers in a war each would rather avoid. Both Khrushchev and the administration were relieved when Pankow in August succeeded in stopping the drain of manpower escaping through West Berlin, although the particularly brutal way in which Pankow halted the population flow shocked the administration. Pankow did not rely on administrative measures, but chose to build a concrete wall directly opposite the sector border facing West Berlin in the city center. Eventually, it erected a barbed wire fence around West Berlin to the north, west, and south. The

Berlin crisis continued, but with a difference. The Soviets seemed to take heart from Pankow's success in Berlin. The administration sensed that it had been tested by Moscow and failed even though it had avoided a direct confrontation. Inadvertently, the powers turned a corner, and the accumulation of their miscalculations obscured the way ahead.

1. The New Pressures on Khrushchev

The longer the Berlin crisis continued, the more it occurred in tandem to the Sino-Soviet dispute. The Berlin crisis became protracted, in part, because of Khrushchev's preference for a negotiations strategy and a penchant for summit diplomacy. The Chinese Communists opposed these methods, and tried to stiffen Khrushchev's approach. Moreover, they opposed a negotiated *détente*—even though Khrushchev's objective in seeking *détente* was to prevent West German nuclear armament—because it presupposed a two-power world.[1]

As early as December 1959, Peking publicized an attack on American foreign policy as a foil for an attack on Khrushchev. For example, Peking argued that Dulles' flexibility and movement toward Berlin negotiations meant nothing more than a mere change of cold war tactics and could not be seriously exploited by the Communist world. According to the Chinese, the Eisenhower Administration rejected Khrushchev's Berlin policy, notwithstanding Khrushchev's view to the contrary.[2] In the weeks preceding the Paris Conference, Peking initiated a public ideological debate with Moscow. A rush of official statements emanated from Peking in April. The ninetieth anniversary of Lenin's birth furnished an occasion for the debate. The timing of the statements indicated Peking's foreboding that Khrushchev would strike a bargain with Eisenhower in Paris somehow at China's expense.[3]

In the politics of the dispute, for example at the Moscow conference

1. The history of the Sino-Soviet dispute can be traced back to the earliest period of the Chinese Communist Party (CCP). Suffice it to say here that Peking had been critical of Khrushchev before 1959, but had not decided until then to vigorously publicize the issue. See G. F. Hudson, Richard Löwenthal, and Roderick MacFarquhar, *The Sino-Soviet Dispute* (New York: Frederick A. Praeger, 1969), p. 58.

2. A. M. Halpern, "Communist China and Peaceful Coexistence," *China Quarterly*, July–September 1960, p. 21.

3. Hudson, Löwenthal, and MacFarquhar, *op. cit.*, pp. 81-82.

of world communist parties in November 1960, Khrushchev prevailed. The content of the debate, however, revealed weaknesses in Khrushchev's approach to the Berlin crisis which became increasingly apparent as the Berlin crisis continued. The Chinese raised doubts about the effectiveness of using missile power to achieve political payoffs in foreign policy. On the other hand, they did not seem to be sufficiently skeptical about their own alternative. Armed struggle bore great risks and might not be any more successful than Khrushchev's approach. Before the summit conference of 1960, Peking had warned Khrushchev that his approach would fail: "U.S. imperialism holds nothing but venom for the peace efforts of the socialist camp headed by the Soviet Union." Peking accurately stated: "The fact is, even after the Camp David talks and even on the eve of the East-West summit conference, we see no change at all in substance in U.S. imperialist war policy, in the policy carried out by the U.S. Government and by Eisenhower personally." [4]

By implication, the Chinese expected greater benefits from the use of force than from the threat of force mingled with a strategy of negotiation. They, of course, could contemplate the use of force in the Far East with greater equanimity than the Soviets could in Europe and undoubtedly appreciated Moscow's problem to some extent. It would not do for Moscow to launch a war of "national liberation" in the NATO region. But the questions the Chinese raised illuminated an incipient problem in Khrushchev's Berlin policy. If Khrushchev could not move the Western powers with methods short of the outright use of force, he would not make any gains. Yet, if he did employ force, he would risk defeat of his whole enterprise because a war in Europe, no matter how it began, could readily develop into a nuclear holocaust.

2. Khrushchev's Impatience

After his inaugural, President Kennedy instructed Ambassador Llewellyn Thompson in Moscow to inform Khrushchev that the new administration would need time to prepare for Berlin negotiations.[5] The Soviets preferred not to wait and reopened the Berlin crisis with an *aide-mémoire* to Bonn on February 17. They complained of hav-

---

4. Hudson, Löwenthal, and MacFarquhar, *op. cit.*, pp. 112-113.
5. Theodore L. Sorensen, *Kennedy* (New York: Harper & Row, 1965), p. 542.

ing to wait for the administration to put its house in order, insisting that the issue not be postponed until after the West German elections in September 1961. "It is now obvious," they said, "that all the time-limits have expired for understanding the need to sign a peace treaty and thereby solve the problem of the occupation status of West Berlin, making it a free city." [6] They still desired an interim Berlin settlement, "pending the conclusion of a peace treaty," if all powers understood that the interim period would be strictly limited and that at the conclusion a peace treaty had to be signed.

In March, when Thompson saw Khrushchev, the Chairman referred the ambassador to the *aide-mémoire* to Bonn, saying he placed a high priority on a Berlin settlement.[7] The Warsaw Pact meeting at the end of March underlined this priority.[8] On April 10, Khrushchev told Walter Lippmann he urgently wanted a peace treaty.[9] He insisted that the status of the DDR be consolidated and the frontiers of Germany defined before Bonn acquired nuclear weapons. Lippman had the impression Khrushchev wanted a "showdown."

The war in Laos and the Cuban exiles' disaster at the Bay of Pigs occupied the administration until late April. Sensitive to Khrushchev's pressures, the White House announced on May 19 that Kennedy would meet Khrushchev in Vienna, June 3–4. When Kennedy and Khrushchev conferred, they discussed other subjects as well as Berlin, but they had their most disagreeable discussion on that subject. In the end, Khrushchev left the President with a memorandum creating another "deadline" crisis. The memorandum identified the Federal Republic as a threat to mankind.[10]

The Berlin issue was central in the memorandum. Soviet terms for an interim settlement appeared more demanding than Gromyko's last proposal at Geneva. Gromyko had allowed eighteen months for the work of a mixed German Committee in the interim period. In the June 1961 memorandum, the Soviets proposed six months as "quite sufficient" for Bonn and Pankow to negotiate their differences. They expressed impatience because the issue had "matured." The "interchangeable threat mechanism,"—Secretary Herter's term for Gro-

6. Embree, *op. cit.*, p. 291.
7. *The New York Times*, March 18, 1961, p. 5.
8. *Ibid.*, March 31, 1961, p. 1.
9. Walter Lippmann, *The Coming Tests with Russia* (Boston: Little, Brown and Company, 1961), p. 23.
10. The text of the memorandum is in *Documents*, pp. 642-645.

myko's shrewd device linking a threat to Berlin with the Soviet peace treaty proposal—remained intact.

Urgency characterized the Soviet memorandum of June 4. The entire document read as a complaint of delay. Khrushchev, reporting in Moscow on the Vienna Conference, confirmed this impression: "We ask everyone to understand us correctly: The conclusion of a peace treaty with Germany cannot be postponed any longer. A peaceful settlement in Europe must be attained this year." [11]

Khrushchev had committed his prestige to resolving the Berlin issue with the Eisenhower Administration more than two years earlier and his efforts had not produced a settlement. He revived the effect of a deadline to restore to himself the lever he needed for bringing pressure to bear on the United States. Khrushchev's reference to "this year" meant that by December 31, 1961, he would try to settle the issue.

3. *Kennedy's Thoughts on Berlin*

The revival of the Berlin crisis was untimely for the new administration. Kennedy had charged in his presidential campaign that the Eisenhower Administration would leave office without having resolved outstanding foreign policy problems and, worse yet, without having provided the military forces needed for grappling with them. [12] Kennedy became the spokesman of the old administration's critics— Acheson for example—and pointed out the imminence of a "missile gap" and the inadequacies of existing conventional forces. [13] After taking office, he did not confirm the existence of a "missile gap" because he discovered that the Soviets had actually fielded only a few ICBM units in spite of Khrushchev's earlier boasting about "serial production." [14] But he did express dissatisfaction with the condition of the armed forces, both nuclear and conventional. Dulles' massive retaliation policy had produced a great dependence on unprotected nuclear weapons and had cut back conventional forces in numbers

11. *Documents*, p. 663.

12. Kennedy remarked in 1959: "The next administration will have to deal with the Russians over Berlin, and with the Chinese over Quemoy, with relatively deteriorating military strength—this is what alarms me most." John F. Kennedy, *The Strategy of Peace*, ed. Allan Nevins (New York: Harper and Brothers, 1960), p. 216.

13. *Ibid.*, pp. 33-45.

14. *The New York Times*, February 17, 1961, p. 1.

and in readiness. After a quick defense review in February, Kennedy requested Congress to correct these deficiencies.

The military policies of the new administration also deflated Khrushchev's military policy. Khrushchev's policy stressed the self-defeating nature of nuclear war to disarm the Western powers psychologically. Secretary of Defense Robert McNamara borrowed terms and concepts from conventional war to argue the case that nuclear war need not be self-defeating, strictly speaking. He also argued that old-fashioned conventional war had a place in the nuclear age. In rejecting Dulles' military policy, the new administration also rejected Khrushchev's, an event which impressed the Soviet marshals more than it impressed Khrushchev.

The administration's messages to Congress of March 28 and May 25 proposed amendments to the fiscal 1962 budget for funding the survival capabilities of strategic offensive forces: to expand and accelerate the Polaris and Minuteman missile programs, to provide an airborne alert program for one-eighth of the bomber forces and ground alert for one-half of the bomber forces, to construct a bomb-alarm system and "invulnerable and continuous command posts and communication centers." [15]

McNamara proposed increasing forces for conventional war. He wished to possess the means for extensive warfare below the nuclear threshold when and where the Soviets or Communist Chinese entered a vital area without employing nuclear weapons. The administration requested funds for broad improvements in conventional weapons and equipment, air and sealift capability, fighter aircraft, and increases in armed forces personnel and training. In the May message, just before the Vienna Conference, Kennedy proposed a reorganization, modernization, and re-equipment of Regular Army divisions, the Army Reserve, and the Marine Corps.

Kennedy's emphasis on military readiness in the winter and spring of 1961 ironically produced more pressure on Khrushchev to accelerate the Berlin crisis. An unfavorable environment developed in the first months of 1961 from which the administration labored all year long to extricate itself. The new administration had to take remedial defense measures. But as soon as it did, the Soviets felt compelled to respond, requiring another round of remedial measures by the United States. Kennedy moved toward a military ordeal in

15. *Ibid.*, March 28, 1961, p. 16.

the Berlin crisis, all the while struggling to avoid it. By 1961, Khrushchev had little interest in slow-motion negotiations, in contrast to his stance in March 1959, when he had consented to the Geneva foreign ministers' conference.

The general outline of Kennedy's Berlin policy emerged in his election campaign. He clearly favored negotiations:

> We must plan a long range solution to the problems of Berlin. We must show no uncertainty over our determination to defend Berlin—but we must realize that a solution to the problems of that beleaguered city is only possible in the context of a solution of the problems of Germany and, indeed, the problems of all Europe. We must look forward to a free Berlin, in a united Germany in a Europe where tensions and armaments have been reduced . . .[16]

The sentiments expressed in the last sentence seemed indistinguishable from the British position favoring a Berlin settlement in the context of zonal arms limitations.[17]

Speaking in December, 1959 of "a long range solution" for Berlin, Kennedy first meant to say he had hopes for a Berlin *modus vivendi:* "I think there is perhaps an area where we could both make some agreement which would respect the relative position of both of us in that section of Europe, and still permit Berlin to live easier." [18] Specifically:

> I think, hopefully, we would like to get a commitment, perhaps guaranteed by the United Nations, to reaffirm the concept of a corridor into Berlin and therefore free access to it, which would be controlled either by the United Nations or by the West Germans and the Berliners or by England, France, and the United States. In return for that, we might agree to some thinning out of troops in Berlin, but that would be rather meaningless because there are not many there now anyway. We might agree to cease propaganda activities.[19]

16. Kennedy, *op. cit.*, his speech of June 14, 1960 reprinted at the front of the book.
17. The British developed a close relationship with the new administration. Kennedy got on well with Macmillan. And the Prime Minister appointed David Ormsby-Gore, a long-standing friend of Kennedy's, as British ambassador to Washington. Sorensen, *op. cit.*, pp. 558-559.
18. Kennedy, *op. cit.*, p. 214.
19. *Ibid.*, p. 212.

Like Macmillan, the insecurity of the access routes bothered Kennedy. He recognized that a proposal for internationalizing them depended upon convincing the Soviets that the United States would assume high risks to preserve the Berlin occupation regime: "But you cannot possibly get an agreement there unless they think that we mean what we say; that if they attempt to drive us out, directly or indirectly, it would mean war, which could spread to the world. If that is clear, then possibly we could." [20]

Kennedy's discussions of Berlin led him back to the development of further military resources as a way of persuading the Soviets that "we mean what we say." At Geneva in 1959, the United States proposed to negotiate a Berlin settlement focusing on the internationalization of the access routes. It failed at that time because the Soviets had not yet been convinced the Western powers would settle for some version of the free city proposal. Kennedy had more reason to be hopeful for a settlement—more reason than Dulles or Macmillan had— if he prepared an obvious fallback position.

Second, "a long range solution" for Kennedy involved a *modus vivendi* with the DDR. In 1959, he spoke of thinning out troops in Berlin and of curtailing propaganda emanating from Berlin, two of Pankow's demands. He referred to "the necessity for the East German government to have increased status—the importance of East Germany to the Soviet economy and its political system . . ." [21] He believed that the Soviet Union regarded diplomatic recognition and consolidation of Ulbricht's regime as a vital interest of its own. In 1959, Kennedy said he thought Secretary Dulles' Berlin policy "was a little too rigid and unyielding to changing currents in European policies," too closely aligned with Adenauer as though Dulles believed that Willy Brandt's opposition socialist party might never come to power. Kennedy sympathized with Averell Harriman, who urged the United States to acknowledge DDR authority without extending diplomatic recognition to it. [22] Accepting the DDR, Kennedy thought, would encourage "nationalism" in Eastern Europe. Kennedy's position on the DDR inferred a policy of two Germanies within the framework of the older policy supporting Bonn as a NATO ally.

Third, in 1959 Kennedy intended "a long range solution" to include

20. *Ibid.*, p. 214.
21. *Ibid.*, p. 212.
22. *The New York Times*, July 13, 1959, p. 1.

an interim Berlin settlement, formally awaiting the day when the Soviet Union would end the cold war, and actually de-emphasizing Berlin as a traditional source of conflict. In 1957 Kennedy had rejected Dulles' "emphatic reaffirmations of the imminent collapse of Soviet totalitarianism," [23] and anticipated a time when the Soviet Union would be compelled to mellow. In 1960, Kennedy said:

> If our military power remains paramount . . . then it might be possible to encourage the Russians and Chinese to say farewell to arms. We can then expect the competition would shift to non-military spheres. It will then be a struggle between the two systems: . . . which system of political, economic, and social organization can more effectively transform the lives of the people in the newly emerging countries.[24]

Kennedy made these statements on Berlin before he won the Presidency. They indicate the point from which he began thinking about the Berlin crisis after Khrushchev renewed the conflict. From available evidence, his thinking did not seem to undergo a radical change on Berlin while in office. He had mixed feelings about Berlin. He recognized the value of military readiness. But he also qualified Acheson's argument for readiness because he really desired and preferred a negotiated settlement as he sketched it in 1960.

4. *The Vienna Conference*

The Vienna Conference illustrated Kennedy's greatest worry in 1961, namely, that his administration's revision of the United States defense posture would give Khrushchev the wrong impression and lead to a military "showdown" over Berlin. Kennedy decided to go to Vienna and try his hand at extricating his administration from an environment dominated by military matters. He wanted to stimulate political movement in the crisis. More accurately than he probably surmised at the time, Kennedy put his finger on miscalculation as the central theme of the Berlin crisis. By 1961, Soviet miscalculation was old and deep. Kennedy did not succeed in changing it at

23. John F. Kennedy, "A Democrat Looks at Foreign Policy," *Foreign Affairs,* 36 (October 1957), 46.
24. James MacGregor Burns, *John F. Kennedy, A Political Profile* (New York: Harcourt, Brace, World, 1961), p. 271.

Vienna. But he recognized the nature of the crisis early in his administration.

Kennedy did not revive summitry as a means of reaching diplomatic settlements. His predecessor's experience at the Paris Conference dimmed any expectation of that kind of result. He simply took advantage for his own purposes of the pattern of personal contact set by Macmillan, Eisenhower, and de Gaulle. After Vienna, Kennedy had no interest in continuing the practice of summit meetings.[25] He preferred substantive talks conducted by skilled negotiators.

At Vienna, Kennedy had little occasion to engage in constructive diplomacy with Khrushchev. He had to expend his energies vainly trying to warn Khrushchev off a collision course over Berlin.[26] Khrushchev astounded Kennedy with the Soviet memorandum of June 4. Kennedy tried to convince Khrushchev that the Soviets would never succeed in converting West Berlin into a free city. To persuade him, Kennedy drew the issue as narrowly as possible, focusing on the security of the access routes and saying that the United States would, if absolutely necessary, go to war to keep access to Berlin open.[27] Khrushchev said he had heard this kind of intimidation before from Eisenhower. Kennedy concluded that verbal warnings did not impress Khrushchev, and decided to push military contingency planning in earnest once he returned from Vienna.[28]

Initially the administration was uncertain in predicting the intensity with which the Soviets would revive the Berlin crisis. Secretary of State Rusk suggested to the NATO Council that the publicity the Soviets gave to the June 4 memorandum would be one index of their intentions.[29] If they published it for maximum public exposure, he believed a serious crisis probably loomed ahead. If they did not, private bargaining to achieve a settlement might be possible. Moscow published the memorandum on June 10.[30]

Kennedy went back over the contingency plans he had asked Acheson to formulate in the spring. The administration entered a phase of intense planning, anticipating a severe deterioration in relations with Moscow. Kennedy clearly sounded distressed about

25. Sorensen, *op. cit.*, pp. 551-552.
26. *The New York Times*, June 5, 1961, p. 1.
27. *Ibid.*; Sorensen, *op. cit.*, pp. 585-586.
28. *The New York Times*, June 6, 1961, p. 1.
29. *Ibid.*, June 12, 1961, p. 1.
30. *Ibid.*, June 11, 1961, p. 1.

the outcome of the Vienna Conference when he spoke to the country on June 6.[31]

On June 15, Khrushchev again gave the United States six months to come to terms. He went out of his way to ridicule Kennedy's sense of obligation to West Berlin and therefore, indirectly, Kennedy's warning in Vienna that the United States would go to war over the access routes:

> In the conversations with me, President Kennedy, and as a matter of fact other Western representatives, referred to the fact that the Western powers bear some sort of obligations to the residents of West Berlin and that these obligations cannot be affected even by the conclusion of a German peace treaty. It is natural to ask, however: What obligations they feel must be maintained if all of them follow from the surrender of Hitler Germany and from the provisional Allied agreements and, consequently, can be valid only until the peace treaty is signed. What is more, there are in general no special Allied commitments with regard to West Berlin. The Allied obligations applied to the entire territory of Germany, and it was precisely these agreements that were grossly violated by the Western powers.[32]

Ulbricht dramatized the insecurity of the access routes when he threatened to interrupt air access as well. Asked at a press conference on June 15 about the effect of a peace treaty on Tempelhof airport, the West Berlin terminus of the air corridors, Ulbricht replied: "Actually this does not depend on me. Perhaps, the airport will close itself down."[33] He demanded contractual arrangements with the DDR to manage air traffic: "Can you imagine that it would be possible to maintain air traffic without an orderly air safety service? Such an air safety service must now be agreed upon with the representatives of the state exercising air sovereignty."[34]

5. *Formulation of a Berlin Strategy*

Before Vienna, Kennedy gave Acheson the task of preparing a line of action for the Berlin crisis. Acheson recommended arming, and argued a commanding case for mobilization. He clashed with others

31. *Ibid*, pp. 646-651.
32. *Documents*, p. 661, 663.
33. *Documents*, p. 659.
34. *Ibid.*, p. 658.

around the Cabinet table who believed that the possibilities for negotiation had not been entirely exhausted.[35] Kennedy did not accept all of Acheson's recommendations because he did not want to exclude negotiations. Kennedy preferred to proceed along two tracks simultaneously: partial mobilization coupled with overtures for negotiations. Kennedy hoped the military measures would give Khrushchev an incentive to negotiate.[36]

Kennedy mixed the options. He led with negotiations while noticeably preparing military forces as a reserve card. Eisenhower and Kennedy both preferred negotiations, but Kennedy introduced factors of higher risk in the crisis for Khrushchev to ponder. He mixed options to raise risks without allowing them to get out of control and hopefully to give the Soviets pause to consider the risks to themselves. He used the identical mixed method over a year later in the Cuban missile crisis. In that crisis, he mixed options, leading with the least provocative action first—a naval blockade—and preparing an invasion force—the troops in Florida—in an obvious reserve move.

Avoiding complete reliance on a negotiations strategy, Kennedy could slowly increase pressure, play for time, and hope Khrushchev would back down. But mixing options cost Kennedy, too. Since his preferences lay with negotiations rather than with a cycle of military demonstrations, the mixed strategy might prove ineffectual if Khrushchev played on Kennedy's known preferences. In not making an either/or choice—in not waiting to talk about negotiations until Khrushchev changed his attitude, as Acheson urged—Kennedy ran the risk of blunting the effect of the higher-risk strategy he actually armed the country to employ. His preferences were too obvious for effective bargaining. He risked garbling the message he wanted Moscow to hear.

Acheson argued that an undiluted high-risk approach had the merit of making an unmistakable commitment to Berlin for the benefit of Soviet calculation. It sounded a "loud and clear" message. No strategy would be very effective unless it demonstrated that West Berlin mattered more to the United States than to the Soviet Union, that the United States would assume greater risks in protecting the city than the Soviet Union would in attacking it. Kennedy believed

35. Debate within the administration focused on the question of how much emphasis the arming option recommended by Acheson should receive. Arthur M. Schlesinger, Jr., *A Thousand Days: John F. Kennedy in the White House* (Boston: Houghton Mifflin Co., 1965), pp. 380-390.

36. Schlesinger, *op. cit.*, pp. 380-383.

Acheson's approach carried unacceptable risks because positions would harden and repercussio..s from incidents would be more difficult to control. Worse yet, the Soviets might overreact, believing the United States wanted a war. Acheson admitted that the approach he recommended might lead to war. But the alternative, Acheson insisted, was a possible misunderstanding which could lead, inadvertently, to war. The administration emphasized the risks of acting in Berlin. Acheson stressed the danger in not acting.

All arguments aside, on July 25, in a public address, Kennedy detailed the decisions his administration had reached.[37] They embraced a mix of options. The military side caught the public eye, and, indeed, his address seemed more precise on that side. Actually, the President placed equal emphasis on negotiations. His Berlin strategy included four elements: (1) a definition of the threat to Berlin, (2) a description of United States interests in Berlin, (3) a request for congressional authorization to mobilize selected military units, and (4) a proposal for negotiations.

Speaking about the first element, he said that Khrushchev's Berlin policy posed a wider threat than to Berlin alone: "The immediate threat to free men is in West Berlin. But that isolated outpost is not an isolated problem. The threat is world wide. Our effort must be equally wide and strong and not be obsessed by any single manufactured crisis." In effect, his speech provided the broadest possible rationale for partial mobilization, and set the crisis in a global strategic context. Assistant Secretary of Defense Nitze explained the importance of the global context for the administration's Berlin strategy in September:

> The point is that we can offset a local preponderance of Communist strength by a determination to apply Western strength on terms other than those selected by the Soviets. Soviet tanks across the autobahn to Berlin would interpose at only one of the many points throughout the world where the important or vital interests of the Soviet empire are vulnerable.[38]

In other words, the administration proposed to defend West Berlin with a strategy which would expand the area of confrontation and

---

37. *Documents*, pp. 694-701.
38. Paul H. Nitze, Address before the Association of the United States Army, Washington, D.C., September 7, 1961, *Department of Defense News Release*, No. 919-61, p. 2.

escape the restricted area of the Berlin enclave. The United States would retaliate in kind elsewhere—against Soviet shipping to Cuba, for example. Matching a blockade of Cuba for a blockade of the Berlin access routes, all Soviet or East European traffic enroute to the Caribbean could be halted at sea. Or, Soviet traffic on the high seas could be halted at random. The administration studied a long list of nonmilitary countermeasures as well, for example, the pending agreement for reciprocal commercial air flights could be postponed; cultural, athletic, and scientific exchanges discontinued; the embargo on strategic exports to bloc countries tightened; or Soviet accounts in the United States frozen.[39] Any or all of these actions would not immediately relieve West Berlin, but the administration regarded them as a useful sign of resolve.

The second element of the Berlin strategy appeared in Kennedy's description of United States' interests in Berlin itself. Kennedy explicitly mentioned (1) the military presence of the United States in West Berlin; (2) access and egress for the American garrison; (3) the security and viability of West Berlin. The United States, he said, considered each of these a vital interest. Kennedy omitted any reference to East Berlin.[40] To seal his pledge, the President identified the safety of the United States with the safety of the West Berliners: "Soviet strategy has long been aimed not merely at Berlin, but at dividing and neutralizing all of Europe, forcing us back to our own shores." [41]

Kennedy's description of United States interests—drawing a line from which the Soviets would keep their distance—obliquely contained a threat of war if they approached the line. The administration could not reach any other conclusion in the circumstances. The United States remained dependent, as always, on nuclear retaliation to ensure its commitment to West Berlin. The American garrison constituted a guarantee of the commitment. In an August press conference, Kennedy expressed himself more candidly on this point:

39. *The New York Times*, July 27, 1961, p. 9.

40. Kennedy had already declared on July 19: "The real intent of the June 4 *aide mémoire* is *that East Berlin, a part of a city under Four Power status, would be fully absorbed into the so-called 'German Democratic Republic'* while West Berlin, even though called a 'free city,' would lose the protection presently provided by the Western powers and become subject to the will of a totalitarian regime." (My emphasis.) *Documents*, p. 689.

41. *Ibid.*, p. 696.

I am quite aware that Berlin is, from a military point of view, untenable, if it were subjected to a direct attack by the Soviet Union. What we hope would prevent that direct attack is the awareness of the Soviet Union that we mean to defend our position in West Berlin, and that American troops, who are not numerous there, are our own hostages to that intent.[42]

The second element preserved a remnant of Dulles' massive retaliation policy the administration would rather have repudiated.

The third strategic element in Kennedy's speech reflected the administration's attempt since March to relieve the heavy dependence on nuclear weapons that the country's defense posture had acquired during the Eisenhower years. Kennedy requested a mobilization and deployment of additional armed forces to provide conventional military options for defending West Berlin. Short of the national mobilization recommended by Acheson, the President requested the Congress to authorize an increase in the draft; an order to call to duty certain ready reserve units, air transport squadrons, and Air National Guard tactical air squadrons; an increase in the Army's total authorized strength and in the Air Force and Navy active duty strength; and a reactivation of certain aircraft and ships. He also requested a supplementary appropriation, half of which "is needed for the procurement of non-nuclear weapons, ammunition, and equipment."

This increase in conventional military forces originated in Acheson's report which recommended that another Berlin blockade be challenged, at some point, on the ground.[43] Specifically, Acheson proposed that a military task force should implement a probe along the *autobahn* from Helmstedt, at the western end, in the direction of West Berlin to clear obstructions from the roadway and to test Soviet reactions. Earlier in July, Kennedy had directed McNamara and Nitze to draw up military contingency plans expanding on the idea of applying gradual, nonnuclear military action on the road to Berlin. Plans for an *autobahn* probe operated as a corollary to the general

42. *The New York Times*, August 31, 1961, p. 10.
43. Acheson recommended a ground probe rather than complete reliance on an airlift. *Ibid.*, June 1, 1961, p. 10. Hanson Baldwin, however, thought that the administration also planned an air probe. These operations would begin after the Soviets turned back a test convoy or airlift ostensibly for the supply and reinforcement of the American garrison in West Berlin. *Ibid.*, August 13, 1961, p. 5; Schlesinger, *op. cit.*, p. 382.

NATO startegy advocated by the administration—the strategy of "flexible response"—as Generals Taylor and Norstad called it. Kennedy projected a new NATO strategy to replace the 1954 strategy which merely applied the massive retaliation policy of Secretary Dulles to the central front in Europe.

Similar to the "pause" concept in the "flexible response" strategy, the *autobahn* probe would grant Moscow time to reverse itself and restore the status quo. The proposed NATO strategy envisaged a pause for conventional warfare, perhaps thirty days, at the central front. The administration intended the NATO "pause" to serve as an initial Western response to a Soviet strike through the central front at isolated points or in limited strength. The "pause" concept differed in one major respect from its probe corollary. The NATO strategy had a nonnuclear, defensive orientation. By contrast, an *autobahn* probe required the Western powers to mount an offensive with nonnuclear forces, penetrate East Germany, and move toward West Berlin.

In April 1962, Nitze argued that the probe would raise the threshold of nuclear war, therefore contributing to the credibility of the administration's declared intention to defend West Berlin:

> There are enough NATO forces to mount a really serious nonnuclear probe in the air corridors or along the autobahn in the event of Soviet actions against Western interests in Berlin. That probe can be thrown back only by the massive application of Soviet power in a major fight against NATO forces, which in turn would surely bring on a Western nuclear response . . . it simply is not credible that we or anyone else will respond to a given small step with the immediate use of nuclear weapons.[44]

The probe would serve a double function: (1) as an extraordinary military action it could be implemented, theoretically, without the United States resorting to nuclear weapons, and (2) as a demonstration of intent, it would warn the Soviets that, if they repulsed the probe, nuclear weapons would be employed.

Relative to the fourth and last element of the Berlin strategy, Kennedy expressed his concern that inadvertent war could not be ruled out in spite of a strategy for the controlled application of force. For example, the Soviets would have to perceive the *autobahn* probe

44. Paul T. Nitze, Address before the Amerika-Gesellschaft, Hamburg, Germany, April 11, 1962 (mimeograph), pp. 9-10.

as a probe and not as the first step in an attack on the Soviet Union. Kennedy said he believed that "misjudgment" had been the principal factor in modern wars.[45] So he argued that the function of diplomacy in the Berlin crisis should be to keep talking. Diplomacy should, at a minimum, operate as a kind of strategic communications system. And, hopefully, a continuous dialogue between Washington and Moscow would lead to a settlement of the crisis. The President indicated that the State Department had started preparations for negotiations.

These four elements formed a strategy both more flexible and credible as a defense of West Berlin than simply threatening nuclear war. The strategy organized a wide range of countermeasures to use when verbal warnings proved insufficient, and it loosened United States dependence on nuclear war for defending West Berlin. The administration also hoped the Berlin strategy would serve as a pilot project for convincing the NATO Council of the value and feasibility of conventional military options in the nuclear age. The Pentagon intended to use the Berlin crisis as a handy rationale for achieving a *de facto* revision of official NATO strategy.[46]

The Berlin strategy, essentially a strategy of carefully phased escalation, held a nuclear threat in reserve.[47] Depending on circumstances, escalation might be a lengthy, slow-motion process. If units of the Group of Soviet Forces in Germany (GSFG), for example, blocked the Berlin access routes, the process might begin with one or

45. In his July 25 speech, he said:
"Three times in my lifetime our country and Europe have been involved in major wars. In each case serious misjudgments were made on both sides of the intentions of others, which brought about great devastation. Now, in the thermonuclear age, any misjudgment on either side about the intentions of the other could rain more devastation in several hours than has been wrought in all the wars of human history."
Documents, p. 701.
46. For a discussion of McNamara's search for conventional military options, see William W. Kaufman, *The McNamara Strategy* (New York: Harper and Row, 1964), chapter 2. See also Bernard Brodie's critique of the "conventional option," in "The McNamara Phenomenon," *World Politics*, 17 (July 1965), 680-684.
47. Herman Kahn has a mock Berlin crisis escalating through twenty or more levels in *On Escalation: Metaphors and Scenarios* (New York: Frederick A. Praeger, 1965), pp. 34-35. Kahn defines escalation as "an increase in the level of conflict in international crisis situations." He also defines it as "competition in risk-taking, or at least resolve, and a matching of local resources, in some form of limited conflict between two sides." *Ibid.*, p. 3.

more of the Western powers submitting the crisis to the United Nations Security Council.[48] Failing United Nations action, selective economic countermeasures could be imposed. Failing civil actions, at some point later an *autobahn* probe would be executed. Failing that, the Western powers would still have the option of using nuclear weapons locally in East Germany before resorting to general war. The length and slowness of the process would allow Moscow as much time as possible to correct originally optimistic calculations and halt its undertaking. The strategy required a cautious, sophisticated handling of events to stimulate appropriate fears of a wider war without events rushing toward that point. The administration designed the strategy to activate Moscow's desire to avoid war over Berlin and simultaneously to preserve its own options as long as possible.

The very fact that the administration decided to develop a strategy and raise forces for relieving West Berlin without having to turn immediately to nuclear weapons provided a useful warning to Khrushchev. The President's address and the activity to which it led were a sign of energy the Soviets could not fail to take into account. The actions necessary for communicating an intent to assume higher risks were "loud" enough for communication purposes. Unfortunately, they were not as "clear" as they might have been because of the administration's inclination to mix options.

6. *European Reactions to the Strategy*

Kennedy's address of July 25 proved as noteworthy for what he did not say as for what he said. His most significant omission related to the absence of an allied consensus on the strategy. When he announced "a series of decisions by the administration," he could only say there had been "a series of consultations" within the alliance. For the most part, the strategy was a unilateral one. No consensus existed because each ally had a different view of the function military forces should serve in the crisis.

The British, for example, argued against an *autobahn* probe. The administration preferred to raise the nuclear threshold and delay the introduction of nuclear weapons in a confrontation. The British wanted to hold the threshold where it had been since 1954 when

48. At one point, Rusk said that this first move would be taken to engage "the conscience of the world." *The New York Times*, July 24, 1961, p. 1.

NATO lowered it on the central front. Correspondingly, they much preferred activating Soviet fears of war at the outset rather than through a long process of heightening tension. Rather than a probe with conventional forces, the British argued for the first use of tactical nuclear weapons.[49] Tactical nuclear weapons, they argued, would serve the same purpose as a probe: to persuade the Soviets to escalate or withdraw. The British tried to make a distinction between tactical and strategic nuclear weapons which the administration thought might be lost in practice once NATO crossed the nuclear threshold. They would not consent to significant troop increases to support an *autobahn* probe.[50] The British were, however, eager for negotiations to begin.

Bonn and Paris viewed the administration's strategy in the context of the larger German problem.[51] They did not criticize Kennedy's effort to broaden the scope of the Berlin question and expand the area of crisis operations. Indeed, to these two allies, the narrow application of the strategy only to West Berlin—Kennedy said nothing about East Berlin—seemed to contradict the wider definition Kennedy gave for the threat to Berlin. They agreed with the British that the nuclear threshold should remain where it had been since 1954.[52] Bonn held doubts about the feasibility of controlling escalation and considered the geographical and population environment of the po-

49. *Ibid.*, June 1, 1961, p. 10; *Report on Defense*, 1961, 1288 (London: Her Majesty's Stationery Office, 1961), p. 6.
50. *The New York Times*, July 23, 1961, p. 25. The administration requested the British to return one division to West Germany. Other than adding certain technical support troops and increasing training for their troops already in West Germany, the British never did meet this request. Indeed they could not meet it under the "New Look" security policy of 1957 which depleted their conventional forces to pay for their nuclear deterrent. Even the technical supplement sent to the British Army of the Rhine required some stretching of forces. H. A. De-Weerd, *Britain's Defense New Look Five Years Later*, Rand Paper 2562, The Rand Corporation, Santa Monica, California, March 1962, p. 3; William P. Snyder, *The Politics of British Defense Policy* (Columbus: Ohio State University Press, 1964), pp. 39-40.
51. *Statement by French Foreign Minister Maurice Couve de Murville* before the Senate on December 5, 1961, Ambassade de France, Service de Press et d'Iformation, N. 170A, December 6, 1961.
52. At the Oslo meeting of NATO foreign ministers in May, Von Brentano said that if the Soviet Union attacked, the alliance should "not hesitate to use atomic weapons in order to stop aggression against Berlin." *Ibid.*, May 11, 1961, p. 6. A similar statement by Strauss was reported: "It would give me holy terrors, if I were to hear that a conventional attack was to be met only with conventional weapons."

tential theater for conventional warfare—central Germany—unfavorable for ground operations. Bonn and Paris much preferred to rely on plans for the immediate use of tactical nuclear weapons to deter the Soviets from provocations in the first instance. They perceived little need to reopen negotiations with Moscow to avoid miscalculation.[53] In the Continental view, the Soviets would understand a ready nuclear posture as the clearest expression of Western intentions.

The administration's Berlin strategy remained unilateral. The United States succeeded in raising the nuclear threshold on the central front only to the extent it strengthened and increased its own conventional forces. It requested Bonn to accelerate the planned increase of seven German divisions to reach the NATO goal of twelve divisions for the Federal Republic, and it also expected West Germany to bear a greater portion of the costs accruing from the maintenance of American forces in West Germany.[54] Agreeing to a larger financial contribution, Adenauer and Defense Minister Strauss acted slowly in raising additional troops because they did not want to tamper with their defense policies before the federal elections of September 1961.[55]

The French returned two divisions from Algeria to metropolitan France, retaining them on French soil rather than at the central front.[56] The British refused to add another division to their Army of the Rhine. The administration lobbied for a force level on the central front of thirty active and thirty reserve divisions, an increase of nine active and undoubtedly more than nine reserve divisions over the 1961 level.[57] By the end of 1961, General Norstad had about twenty-five active divisions under his command through the addition of one previously scheduled West German division and augmented United States forces.[58]

53. *Ibid.*, August 5, 1961, p. 3.
54. *Ibid.*, July 23, 1961, p. 1.
55. Adenauer did not agree to increase the length of the West German military service from twelve to eighteen months until he conferred with Kennedy in November, 1961. *Ibid.*, November 27, 1961, p. 1. By the end of 1961, Bonn had raised 80,000 additional personnel not all of whom were designated to the ground forces. *Ibid.*, December 31, 1961, p. 32.
56. *The Washington Post*, June 30, 1961, p. A1.
57. In 1961, the force level at the central front stood at about twenty-one incomplete active divisions. Alastair Buchan, *NATO in the 1960's* (New York: Frederick A. Praeger, 1960), p. 90.
58. The administration improved the quality of the Seventh Army, added 50,000 troops, transferred sixteen tactical air squadrons—equivalent to 300 aircraft—to the Seventeenth Air Force in West Germany, and pre-positioned 100,000 tons of equipment for additional deployments as necessary. *The New York*

The administration had no greater success in securing advance agreement from its allies on contingency planning in support of the strategy. As early as May 1961, it talked up the advantages for the NATO governments, particularly for Washington, London, Paris, and Bonn—those immediately involved in the crisis—to commit themselves to contingency plans before military action became necessary.[59] For a strategy requiring a sophisticated handling of events in a crisis, preplanning seemed very desirable. A quick but well-considered response in conditions of rising tension might make a significant difference in controlling events. The administration did not feel it could delegate the ultimate decisions for peace or war to an inter-allied committee. But it wanted to recognize the legitimate demands of its allies for participation in the decision-making process and used the Ambassadorial Group in Washington—responsible for quad-ripartite contingency planning—as a participatory forum.[60]

If multilateral planning decisions could be reached, the administration intended to adapt itself to those decisions and to request the same of the other three governments. If an agreed level for the nuclear threshold, for example, could roughly be determined in planning, operational decisions might follow more readily and would have the diplomatic merit of multilateral approval. As it happened, the strategic differences between allies which would have become painfully apparent in a crisis surfaced in the discussion of contingency planning. The Ambassadorial Group became the forum of a futile attempt by the United States to multilateralize the administration's Berlin strategy.[61] The strategy remained unilateral because the other governments refused any binding commitments, preferring to leave them-

Times, September 9, 1961, p. 1; October 12, 1961, p. 1; Kaufmann, *The Mc-Namara Strategy*, p. 113.

59. *The New York Times*, June 1, p. 1. At the beginning of the Berlin crisis, in 1959, contingency planning was conducted on a tripartite basis. Eventually, Bonn was added to the group because—aside from the U.S. Seventh Army—the Federal Republic possessed the largest and most readily available military resources for the implementation of agreed plans.

60. Max Freedman described the "special committee" conducting the planning in a later column: "Allies Debate Priorities in Combating Berlin Menace," *The Chicago Sun Times*, October 21, 1962, p. 9; see also Alastair Buchan, *Crisis Management, The New Diplomacy*, The Atlantic Papers, NATO Series II, The Atlantic Institute, Boulogne-sur-Seine, April, 1966, pp. 36-39.

61. The crucial issue of raising the nuclear threshold went unresolved. *The New York Times*, November 16, 1962, p. 5. Deputy Under Secretary Murphy described an equally frustrating experience in tripartite Berlin planning in 1959 and 1960. *Op. cit.*, pp. 437-438.

selves free to manage in unpredictable circumstances. While the United States did not get all that it wanted from the Ambassadorial Group, allied diplomats and military officials valued the Group as a place to air substantive differences.

The administration, of course, preferred a united front. It pressed hard to raise allied force levels and to obtain agreed-upon plans for an *autobahn* probe. When the Western foreign ministers met in Paris on August 5–6, they could only agree "in principle" to add manpower and equipment to their conventional forces.[62]

7. The Summer Crunch

In the summer of 1961, both the administration and the Kremlin made preparations for an East-West clash after December 31, although both preferred the negotiations track for its lesser risks. Khrushchev turned once again to public threats and bluster to induce the Western powers to negotiate. On June 21, the twentieth anniversary of Hitler's invasion of the Soviet Union, Khrushchev dressed himself in the uniform of a lieutenant general—his wartime rank— to deliver a blistering speech. He implied that the Soviet Union soon would begin a nuclear testing demonstration. On June 28, he informed the Western powers that economic contingency plans would fail: "Threats of discontinuing trade cannot, of course, prevent us from signing a German peace treaty."[63] On July 8, Khrushchev acknowledged the administration's March and May requests for supplemental defense appropriations, reversing his program for reducing Soviet force levels announced in January 1960. He also authorized an increase in Soviet defense expenditures.[64] In effect, the Soviet marshals got their way as tensions rose. The Soviets did not respond in kind after Kennedy's third request for supplemental appropriations on July 25, although Khrushchev complained on August 7 that "military hysteria is now being drummed up in the United States."[65]

Khrushchev preferred negotiations, but events of his own making

62. *The New York Times*, August 6, 1961, p. 1.
63. Nikita Khrushchev, *The Soviet Stand on Germany* (New York: The Crosscurrents Press, 1961), p. 57.
64. *Ibid.*, p. 65.
65. *Ibid.*, p. 87. On July 6, Malinovsky boasted—in the style of Khrushchev— that the Red Army had reorganized to equip all units with "rocket weapons" and that missiles of all types had become the Soviets' primary striking force. *The New York Times*, July 15, 1961, p. 2.

overtook him. In his speech of August 7, he referred to West Berlin as a "convenient loophole to obstruct the development of the GDR as a socialist state." He charged that the Western powers wanted to subvert the DDR: "Stop gentlemen. We know exactly what you want, what you are after; we shall sign a peace treaty and close your loophole in the GDR!" [66] The refugee traffic from the DDR into West Berlin increased phenomenally in the summer of 1961. The more Khrushchev talked of closing the "loophole," the greater the traffic became. Those East Germans who contemplated flight read his statements as their last chance. In July, 30,000 East Germans fled and in the first twelve days of August 20,000 more arrived in West Berlin. [67]

Although Khrushchev stimulated the traffic, the traffic flow actually resulted from Ulbricht's decision to reorient the economy toward a system of cooperative labor and collective farming. This decision represented Ulbricht's second major attempt to remake the economy of the DDR along Soviet lines. His first attempt, in the early 1950's, failed when workers resorted to strikes or deliberately cut production and farmers underproduced. One such strike on the issue of work-norms led to the popular uprising of June 17, 1953. The state delayed the "construction of socialism" until 1959 when, after a six-year respite, it put workers and farmers into a forced march once again. This second program of socialist economic development focused initially on collectivizing the farms. The farms were reorganized, officially, within three months in 1960. Farmers again slowed production, migrated to the cities, or fled to West Berlin. Thus, the agricultural economy ran short of manpower, resulting in a supply crisis when fields went unharvested. In 1961, the state enacted a new labor code to lower costs and increase production, but also worsening labor conditions. Workers were greatly agitated by the code, and joined the farm population, protesting or fleeing to West Berlin. [68]

The crisis in agriculture generated the rise in refugee traffic which, in turn, compelled Pankow to find some means of halting the traffic. The state had an alternative: it could have abandoned the economic changes generating the traffic. But this time the state opted to press on with the new economic policy rather than return, as in 1953, to

66. Khrushchev, *The Soviet Stand on Germany*, p. 123.
67. Phillip Windsor, *op. cit.*, p. 237.
68. For the history of Pankow's domestic economic policies, see Stephan Thomas, "Beyond the Wall," *Survey*, 44/45 (October 1962), pp. 54-65 and Evelyn Anderson, "East Germany," *Survey*, 42 (June 1962), pp. 96-106.

the old economic order which the industrial and agricultural labor force preferred.

Ulbricht implored the Kremlin to help him close the "loophole." Khrushchev counseled caution because he could not be certain whether the United States would intervene or encourage an East German revolt in retaliation, even though it had not aided the uprising of 1953 or the Hungarian revolution of 1956. Moscow knew the Western powers worried about the traffic and the instability of East Germany.[69] The Soviets probably did not know what to make of Kennedy's July 25 speech in which he said nothing about East Berlin. They noticed at Vienna that Kennedy seemed more concerned about the practical aspects of Western access to West Berlin than about any other issue in the Berlin crisis.[70]

Pankow established checkpoints on the highways leading to East Berlin and West Germany in late July.[71] By August 1, it had erected a series of three checkpoints to process refugees traveling by train to East Berlin: one at the local station, one enroute, and one at the terminal in East Berlin.[72] Sometime between August 1 and August 5, Ulbricht flew to Moscow, pleading for authorization to block all the refugee routes to West Berlin.[73] The Kremlin leaders must have

69. Rusk, for example, discussed the subject intermittently with the British and French ambassadors in Washington. *The New York Times,* July 14, 1961, p. 1.

70. Describing what Kennedy said to Khrushchev at Vienna, Reston reported on June 4:

"The President placed his emphasis in this question not on the legal question whether the Soviet Union had any right to recognize Communist East Germany as a sovereign government, but on the practical question of getting necessary supplies through the Communist territory to West Berlin. He insisted this was not only a right of the Western powers, as a result of their conquest of Germany, but a duty to the 2,200,000 people of West Berlin, assumed not only by the United States, Britain and France but also by the Soviet Union. This was interpreted by some Communists here as an indication that the President was concerned not about the recognition of East Germany by Moscow, but only about freedom of access to Berlin, regardless of who controlled the checkpoints on routes between West Germany and the former German capital."

Ibid., June 5, 1961, p. 1.

71. *Ibid.,* July 28, 1961, p. 2.

72. *Ibid.,* August 2, 1961, p. 2. Earlier in July, Pankow made a determined effort to prevent more than 60,000 East Berliners from working daily in West Berlin. *Ibid.,* July 8, 1961, p. 5. This effort drew another ineffectual protest from the Western commandants as a violation of the quadripartite status of East Berlin. *Ibid.,* August 4, 1961, p. 1.

73. *Ibid.,* August 5, 1961, p. 6.

relented while Ulbricht was in Moscow, because on August 6 Warsaw Pact representatives met in Moscow to approve Ulbricht's proposals.[74]

On August 7, Khrushchev said that the Red Army would mass opposite the Federal Republic's frontiers in any serious contingency.[75] Also, on August 7, he assured the Western powers that he would not blockade West Berlin. By August 9, Pankow had failed to curtail the traffic using controls applied internally in the DDR. Ulbricht indicated that further measures would be necessary. On August 11, the DDR legislature—the Volkskammer—ratified Ulbricht's proposed measures to halt "the head hunting and man-trade organized by West Germany and West Berlin." [76] Khrushchev reappointed the prestigious Marshal Ivan Konev to Konev's former command of the Warsaw Pact forces.[77]

The Western powers did not significantly respond to the movement and busy atmosphere in the Eastern camp.[78] The Western foreign ministers, meeting in Paris, did not produce an official reaction to the refugee traffic, although they discussed the problem.[79]

On August 11, Khrushchev roared that, if war came, "the culture and arts of Italy" would be destroyed, "the Acropolis might be in the line of fire." Directing his verbal blitz toward official Washington, he said:

> Come to your senses, gentlemen! I appeal to those who have not lost the faculty of thinking calmly and soberly and on whom the development of the international situation depends. There was a time when the American Secretary of State Dulles brandished thermonuclear bombs and followed a policy of "from positions of strength" with regard to the socialist countries. He followed this policy with regard to all states which disagreed with the imperialist claims of the United States. That was barefaced atomic blackmail, but it had to be reckoned with at the time because we did not possess sufficient means of retaliation,

74. *Ibid.*, August 6, 1961, p. 1.
75. *Ibid.*, August 8, 1961, p. 1.
76. *Ibid.*, August 12, 1961, p. 4.
77. *Ibid.*, August 11, 1961, p. 1. Konev had opposed Khrushchev's reduction of the armed forces, but, the curtailment of that program apparently closed the rift between them.
78. The State Department, for example, expressed the opinion that economic countermeasures in response to Khrushchev's threats would be premature at this point. *Ibid.*, August 5, 1961, p. 1.
79. *Ibid.*, August 6, 1961, p. 1.

and if we did, they were not as many and not of the same power as those of our opponents. But today the situation has changed radically. And specific conclusions must be drawn from recognition of the fact that the capitalist countries are unable to force their ideology, their way of life on us, cannot compel the socialist countries to turn back. It is necessary to follow a reasonable policy on our essentially small planet which man can now circle 17 times in 24 hours.[80]

Look! We have Lunar II. So, two can play "barefaced atomic blackmail," he seemed to say.

Ulbricht forced Khrushchev's hand. Now Khrushchev actually had to act on the favorable shift in the military balance he had talked incessantly of since 1957 and apply it to the circumstances of the Berlin crisis. To date, he had avoided specific applications, arguing that the matter "will get more mature." Clearly, the "loophole" had to be closed or the DDR would collapse. So he gambled, talking loudly, moved troops around in East Germany, and agreed to a line of action, probably very closely coordinated between Moscow and Pankow.

On August 13, a little after midnight, Pankow published the declaration which the Warsaw Pact had approved on August 6:

> The present traffic situation on the borders of West Berlin is being used by ruling quarters of the German Federal Republic and intelligence agencies of NATO countries to undermine the economy of the GDR. The government bodies and military concerns of the German Federal Republic, through deceit, bribery, and blackmail, induce certain unstable elements in the GDR to leave for West Germany. These deceived people are compelled to serve with the Bundeswehr, and recruited for the intelligence agencies of different countries to be sent back to the GDR as spies and saboteurs.

Fixing blame for the DDR's internal problem on Bonn, the declaration authorized Pankow to act:

> In the face of the aggressive aspirations of the reactionary forces of the German Federal Republic and its NATO allies, the

80. Khrushchev, *The Soviet Stand on Germany*, p. 145. The Soviets had just succeeded in orbiting a manned capsule, Lunar II, for a new record in space feats.

Warsaw Pact member states cannot but take necessary measures to guarantee their security and, primarily, the security of the GDR in the interests of the German peoples themselves.

The governments of the Warsaw Pact member states address the Peoples Chamber and Government of the GDR, and all working people of the GDR, with the proposal to establish an order on the borders of West Berlin which will securely block the way to the subversive activity against the socialist camp countries, so that reliable safeguards and effective control can be established around the whole territory of West Berlin, including its border with democratic Berlin.

The declaration assured the Western powers that they would not be affected by the DDR action:

It goes without saying that these measures must not affect existing provisions for traffic and control on communication routes between West Berlin and West Germany.[81]

Simultaneously with the declaration, Pankow issued a decree [82] establishing border controls: (1) East Germans could cross the West Berlin borders only with "special permission," that is, not at all; (2) East Berliners would be required to obtain a "special permit" for crossing into West Berlin, that is, they could no longer cross over; (3) West Berliners would have to show their identity cards to enter East Berlin, making the 1960 travel ban permanent; [83] (4) "Revanchist politicians and agents of West German militarism" would be barred from East Berlin; (5) "former decisions on control"—the 1960 travel ban—remained valid for West Germans entering East Berlin; (6) non-Germans would be unaffected. Simultaneously with both the declaration and the decrees, DDR troops began to construct barricades at the sector border between East Berlin and West Berlin and to control all traffic moving between the two parts of the city. By this and subsequent actions, the troops effectively halted the refugee traffic.

The "wall" went up gradually, not all of a sudden, suggesting that Pankow and Moscow were uncertain what the administration's re-

---

81. *Documents*, p. 722.

82. *Ibid.*, pp. 724-725; for detailed description of the wall episode in Berlin, see the West Berlin daily, *Der Tagesspiegel*, August 15, 1961, pp. 3-7.

83. Pankow rescinded this provision later in August, preventing West Berliners from crossing at all.

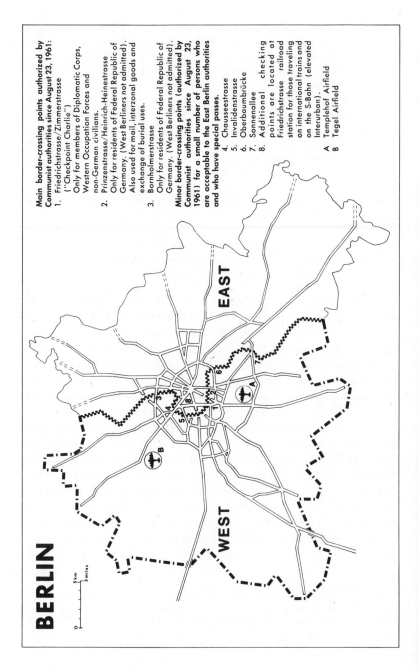

BERLIN

0 — 5 km
0 — 3 miles

WEST

EAST

A

B

Main border-crossing points authorized by Communist authorities since August 23, 1961:

1. Friedrichstrasse/Zimmerstrasse ("Checkpoint Charlie")
   Only for members of Diplomatic Corps, Western Occupation Forces and non-German civilians.

2. Prinzenstrasse/Heinrich-Heinestrasse
   Only for residents of Federal Republic of Germany. (West Berliners not admitted). Also used for mail, interzonal goods and exchange of burial uses.

3. Bornholmerstrasse
   Only for residents of Federal Republic of Germany. (West Berliners not admitted).

Minor border-crossing points (authorized by Communist authorities since August 23, 1961) for a small number of persons who are acceptable to the East Berlin authorities and who have special passes.

4. Chausseestrasse
5. Invalidenstrasse
6. Oberbaumbrücke
7. Sonnenallee
8. Additional checking points are located at Friedrichstrasse railroad station for those traveling on international trains and on the S-Bahn (elevated Interurban).

A Templehof Airfield
B Tegel Airfield

action would be.[84] The "order on the borders of West Berlin" began as barbed wire supported by troops and antipersonnel carriers. Then the pavement and streetcar tracks were torn up. Finally, on August 18, cement blocs were built into a wall on the Potsdamer Platz. The operation proceeded slowly. Many streets and crossing points remained open after August 13. The Western powers did not know how substantial or permanent the armed border would be until it arose over time. This approach to constructing the border compounded Washington's problem of defining the situation. It also would have made it easier for Moscow to halt the operation, if the United States had desired some way to block it.

When Pankow and Moscow perceived in the days following August 13 that the Western powers would not make any rash or unexpected moves, the construction proceeded with more confidence and speed. Eventually, only a few streets remained passable and these served more as gates than as open thoroughfares. Barricades were extended north and south of the city center to a length of twenty-five miles, dividing the city into halves. Eventually, land behind the wall was cleared, more obstructions built, and watchtowers raised. The sector border became a frontier similar to the demarcation line between East Germany and West Germany. In addition, barricades were placed between West Berlin and East Germany, thus encircling West Berlin.

Pankow's action effectively terminated the quadripartite status of East Berlin, partially fulfilling Khrushchev's threat of November 10, 1958, that the Soviet Union would abandon the remaining occupation agencies. Western military patrols continued the practice of entering East Berlin, although Pankow eventually reduced the number of entrances for them to one—Checkpoint Charlie. The patrols, permitted only because the Soviets desired reciprocal entrance to West Berlin to change the guard at the Red Army war memorial, remained as a token of East Berlin's former status. Later, the American commandant in Berlin refused to allow East Germans to process the documents of American diplomatic personnel entering East Berlin, and denied himself entrance.[85] His action severed relations on the official level

84. James L. Richardson, *Germany and the Atlantic Alliance: The Interaction of Strategy and Politics* (Cambridge: Harvard University Press, 1966), pp. 286-287.

85. *The New York Times*, December 24, 1961, p. 1.

between the four-power commandants within the city and forced communications between them into roundabout channels.

8. *The First Strategic Test*

The administration did not regard the events of August 13 and the following days as a test of its Berlin strategy.[86] It greeted the walling-up of the sector boundary with relief because this action prevented a highly sensitive issue, the refugee traffic, from backing the United States and the Soviet Union into a war. The administration observed that the exodus of East German refugees through West Berlin, agitated by Khrushchev's threats against the city, eroded the manpower resources of the DDR. Officials worried that if Pankow took drastic action throughout East Germany, another popular uprising might very possibly occur. Bonn, in turn, might feel it had to respond,[87] and, inexorably, West German intervention would force the hand of Washington and Moscow. This reasoning explained the administration's silence before August 13. The White House refrained from encouraging any uprising.[88]

A more careful examination of the event followed the initial sense of relief. The administration had not prepared for the contingency of an East German uprising, and it had no contingency plans available for responding to the events which actually occurred.[89] Secretary

86. The immediate response of the White House portrayed the event as "a dramatic confession of Communist failure," as a Soviet propaganda defeat. *Ibid.*, August 16, 1961, p. 1.

87. Adenauer never favored unilateral intervention in 1961 any more than he had in 1953. He reacted moderately on August 13, expressing support for Western efforts to cope with the situation. *Ibid.*, August 14, 1961, p. 1.

88. *Ibid.*, August 10, 1961, p. 1; cf. Smith, *op. cit.*, pp. 262, 265.

89. That a lack of planning existed is evident from Geoffrey McDermott's description of official reaction in West Berlin on August 13. McDermott was the British minister in Berlin in 1961:

"On August 13, we were all concerned together to devise the best measures we could against the Communist outrage which it was clear to us might have incalculable consequences. Far away in their capitals officials and politicians began to think. In Berlin the first reaction was to call a committee meeting, which was hardly calculated to terrify the enemy. Our troops there, all 10,000 of them, were put on the alert. We decided on a protest to our Soviet 'colleague' in East Berlin and recommended a further protest by the Western governments to the Soviet Government. Good paper stuff. After Willy Brandt had arrived to join our deliberations, we went on discussing for hours what effective practical conteraction we could

Rusk issued a public statement on August 13. He protested, but he made a distinction between events in East Berlin and United States interests in West Berlin. He passed over the quadripartite status of all-Berlin as a hollow convention.

Available information indicates that measures taken thus far are aimed at residents of East Berlin and East Germany and not at the allied position in West Berlin or access thereto. However, limitation on travel within Berlin is a violation of the four power status of Berlin and a flagrant violation of the right of free circulation throughout the city.[90]

The Western Commandants did not make a protest until August 15.[91] By that time, the Senat and population of West Berlin expressed serious dissatisfaction with the absence of an effective response to the final division of the city. In a letter to Kennedy, Mayor Brandt warned that "more defensive tactics" would give the Soviets the impression that it was only "a matter of time" until they could sever West Berlin's connections to the Federal Republic. Another blockade would leave West Berlin "like a ghetto." He also said:

The legal sovereignty of the East Berlin government has been recognized by acceptance as far as the restrictions of the crossing points and access to the East sector are concerned. This I deem a serious turning point in the city's post-war history as there has not been since the blockade. The decisive issue is that the West has always insisted on the four power status.[92]

To mollify the West Berliners, Kennedy asked Vice President Johnson to fly to West Berlin on August 18 and ordered a Seventh Army battle group in West Germany to proceed to West Berlin on August 19.[93]

---

launch. The fact is, we were all of us stupefied and almost as much taken by surprise as everyone else."
Berlin: Success of a Mission (New York: Harper and Row, 1963), p. 33. Sorensen frankly admits that Kennedy had to improvise a response. *Op. cit.*, p. 594. See also Schlesinger, *op. cit.*, pp. 394-395.
90. *Documents*, p. 725.
91. *The New York Times*, August 16, 1961, p. 1.
92. *Ibid.*, August 20, 1961, p. 6. For a study of the Berliners' reaction in the 1961 crisis, see Kurt L. Shell, *Bedrohung und Bewährung: Führung und Bevölkerung in der Berlin Krise* (Threat and Trial: Leadership and People in the Berlin Crisis) (Köln, 1966).
93. *Ibid.*, August 19, 1961, p. 1.

In a note to the United States on August 23, Moscow abruptly threatened to interrupt air access, inflaming the crisis still further.[94] The White House issued an immediate and vigorous warning to the Soviets not to interfere with military or civilian access.[95] With the announcement from Moscow on August 30 that the Soviet Union would resume nuclear testing, the administration concluded that the Kremlin leadership had misjudged the United States response to the wall.[96] Kennedy announced on August 30 that General Clay would return to West Berlin to restore public confidence and prevent the local situation from deteriorating any further, and that the Western foreign ministers would meet again in Washington to accelerate contingency planning.[97] Moscow's resurgent burst of pressure—as it drew confidence from successfully closing the West Berlin "loophole"—did not terminate until October 17.

In effect, on August 13, Moscow tested the administration's Berlin strategy and found it less than expected. The strategy never connected with the events which happened because it excluded planning relevant to closure of the border. But substantial implications followed from this exclusion. The Soviets learned that the strategy pertained to the worst potential contingency affecting the Western position in West Berlin rather than to the most likely contingency at the time—Soviet and East German action against the refugees.[98] Since early July, the East German exodus had risen to alarming proportions. The administration, increasingly aware of the exodus, did not invoke the strategy because it did not want to make a bad situation worse. The very fact that the strategy did not apply when the administration confronted a Berlin contingency served as a test of the strategy. Moscow inadvertently tested the strategy for what it omitted. After August, the Soviets knew what the strategy ruled out, and therefore, the narrowness of the administration's interests in Berlin. They

---

94. The note gave the administration the impression that, having sealed off East Berlin, the Soviet Union would go further to separate West Berlin from West Germany. *Documents*, pp. 753-755. See *The New York Times*, August 25, 1961, p. 1, describing the administration's hopes that the border closure would satisfy Moscow's desire to stabilize East Germany.

95. *Documents*, pp. 755-757.

96. *The New York Times*, August 31, 1961, p. 1.

97. *Ibid.*, p. 10.

98. Reporting from West Berlin, Sydney Gruson quickly concluded that the

had yet to find the real strength of the strategy, but they discovered what the United States would grant without a contest.

The Soviets probably had not been completely clear what the Kennedy administration retained of the old NATO policy on Germany, particularly since negotiations had not begun. They probably wondered about the American commitment to German unity, the centerpiece of Bonn's foreign policy. If a commitment still existed, the administration could not be relied upon to discourage an East German uprising. If not, a step toward sealing the division of Germany could be taken without unacceptable risk. When the DDR succeeded in walling up the sector border, the Soviets confirmed for themselves that the administration's commitment to Bonn had serious limits attached to it.

In fact, the United States had not qualified its general commitment to Bonn.[99] But the summer crunch revealed the administration's preference for a *de facto* policy acknowledging two-Germanies. This preference appeared, not in the administration's reluctance to use military force to stop the wall from being built—no one advocated that. Rather, it appeared in the distance separating the administration's position on the Berlin crisis from Bonn's interest in East Berlin and nonrecognition of Pankow. By contrast, as late as November 1960, Bonn tried to intervene in Pankow's traffic regulations for West Berliners entering East Berlin. The Eisenhower Administration probably also preferred a mild two-Germanies policy, as revealed in Dulles' agent theory.

The response to the summer crisis probably encouraged Khrushchev to push for a peace treaty. He probably perceived just a short step for the administration to go from an implicit policy of two Germanies to an explicit one. But the administration did not plan to take that step. After the incidents in August, it became increasingly

United States planned for the wrong contingency: "What now seems clear, and what the West seems to have underestimated is that access to West Berlin from the East, rather than access from the West, had become paramount in Khrushchev's mind." *Ibid.*, August 18, 1961, p. 2.

99. The commitment in the Paris Protocols of 1954 took the form of a declaration to recognize the Federal Republic as the only representative of all-Germany. Outright repudiation of the protocols would have abrogated the alliance with Bonn. Adenauer wrote to Kennedy expressing his misgivings that any further Western reverses in Berlin would produce a neutralist trend in West German politics. *The New York Times*, August 30, 1961, p. 1.

difficult for the administration to convince Moscow that Soviet proposals were unacceptable. Further, the role of West Berlin in East-West politics now appeared irreparably altered. The city felt more isolated than at any other time in the postwar era, when it was an outpost of the cold war and an "escape hatch" for East Germans.[100]

9. The Gamble that Paid Off

The closing of the sector border on August 13 eliminated the last significant vestige of the quadripartite status of East Berlin—the opportunity for civilian travel between East Berlin and the western sectors. At the Geneva Conference in 1959, Couve de Murville referred to the intersector traffic as an indicator of the city's residual unity.[101] The Soviets had separated East Berlin administratively from West Berlin in 1948,[102] but many East Berliners continued to work and find their amusement in West Berlin. This practice dated from the original *de jure* regime based on the four-power occupation protocols of 1944, implemented by the victors of the Second World War. Since 1945, the Western powers adhered to the quadripartite status of the city as the legal basis of the occupation regime, but retained an interest—admittedly a limited one—in the freedom of movement for all Berliners.

Pankow's move on August 13 extended its own *de facto* regime in East Berlin to cover exceptions to its rule deriving from the *de jure* regime. It effectively removed this ambiguity in the Eastern status quo. Perhaps it is too sinister to suggest that Pankow took advantage of the economic disorder in the DDR to settle outstanding legal and political issues pertaining to the status of East Berlin. Theoretically, Pankow could have continued to maintain the refugee control system at the entrances to East Berlin from East Germany, established early in August.[103] This system did not affect the status of East Berlin, but it did not, of course, prevent East Berliners from crossing into West Berlin. And apparently it did not work effectively enough to halt the

100. Sebastian Haffner wrote that West Berlin still represented the "head" of the German "animal" whose existence prevented the final consolidation of the DDR as a coherent state. "The Berlin Crisis," *Survey*, 44/45 (October 1962), p. 43. Fritz René Allemann was more skeptical. He argued that on August 13 West Berlin lost its function as a symbol of German unity. "Berlin in Search of a Purpose," *Survey*, 61 (October 1966), pp. 129-138.
101. *Foreign Ministers Meeting*, p. 181.
102. Windsor, *op. cit.*, pp. 109-116.
103. *The New York Times*, August 2, 1961, p. 2.

traffic from East Germany. When Moscow authorized Pankow to close the sector border in the city center, they both settled three issues in one move. They halted the loss of manpower important to the DDR economy, they put an end to the political embarrassment which the preference of many East Berliners for work in West Berlin revealed, and they effectively denied the quadripartite status of the Eastern sector.

Desire and necessity seemed to have conjoined for Pankow. The administration in Washington did not sympathize with the desire of Pankow to wall up the population of the DDR. It did respect the necessity of the Soviet Union to prevent a complete collapse of the DDR. The Kremlin could not anticipate whether the United States would be guided more by dislike for Pankow's desire than respect for Pankow's necessity. It could not exclude an emotional response to the measures taken against the refugees. For this reason alone, something of a gambling element can be detected in the building of the wall. The Eastern side proceeded cautiously, building the wall slowly, yet acting uncertainly and, it believed, with risk. It gambled and won because the United States controlled its emotions and bowed to necessity.

For the United States to have reversed the equation and compelled Pankow to separate desire from necessity—compelled Pankow to devise a means of halting the traffic without damaging the quadripartite status of East Berlin or of abandoning its economic program altogether—the United States would have had to intervene in the last resort at the sector border before the process of wall-building reached an irreversible stage. But the question of intervention never really arose in Western circles because no planning had been done to anticipate Pankow's move. A gap remained between a vague feeling of wanting to stop Pankow's gross measures and actually intervening because no one could, on the spur of the moment, now connect the two. In the absence of planning, the administration could argue more easily from necessity and assert that intervention had to be out of the question.

McDermott, British minister in Berlin, argued the case against intervention rather eloquently:

> If General Clay had been in Berlin I have little doubt the tanks would have rolled that day. And this course of action was dis-

cussed at length at our meeting. But we decided against it and I do not believe it would have done any lasting good even though it might have boosted the Berliners' morale for a time. For though there was no actual wall to knock down that first day, we should have had to mow down ranks of scruffy-looking but quite well-armed East Germans, and their barbed wire. Whether the East Berlin population had then risen or not the Russians could not possibly have allowed us to occupy their sector of Berlin. Their powerful forces, very much at the ready, would have gone into action. There would have then ensued at best a battle, in which the Western garrisons were bound to be defeated and forced to retreat to their sectors; at worst, a war.[104]

He revealed the sentiment on which his case rested when he said of Berlin in general: "It is not worth a war." [105]

His argument amounted to a war scare, placing too much weight on the possibility of war. A powerful argument can be made from the war factor alone to the exclusion of all other factors. The decisive point in McDermott's argument was his assumption that the Soviets "would have gone into action," if the Western powers had intervened. Two Russian GSFG divisions moved into the vicinity of Berlin in mid-July. They were reported near at hand on August 13, equipped with armor and artillery.[106] McDermott identified the fact of their presence with an assumption of their use. Undoubtedly, Konev placed them there to convey the message McDermott perceived. Without access to Soviet state archives, however, the question remains whether the Soviet officers in charge actually had orders to move into Berlin and to shoot to kill if the allies opposed "scruffy-looking but quite well-armed East Germans." Rumors persisted for years after August 13, 1961, that the East German troops at the sector border that day had not been issued ammunition.

If the debate in allied circles focused on only one form of intervention, "at best a battle, . . . at worst a war," undoubtedly intervention seemed rash. In considering the question of intervention, a planner presumably would place massive, battle-fighting intervention at one end of a scale and other forms of intervention in between that and acquiescence. Perhaps selected countermeasures borrowed from

104. McDermott, *op. cit.*, pp. 33-34.
105. *Ibid.*, p. 130.
106. *The New York Times*, July 19, 1961, p. 1; August 14, 1961, p. 1.

the administration's Berlin strategy had a place—out-of-area response, shows of force, civil actions. Planning is a very rational process. A crisis is not. All that can be profitably suggested, long after emotions have cooled, is that planning for an East Berlin contingency might have been useful at the time because the uncertainties were not all on the Western side. Moscow and Pankow faced real uncertainties as well.

The circumstances were uniquely awkward for the United States. And the factor of surprise operated decisively. Kennedy's first reaction late on August 12, Eastern Daylight Time, was: "Is this our first knowledge of their action? With all that cement and stone going up, why didn't we know about it before?" [107] Even if the administration had not anticipated the contingency, with more time, an *ad hoc* response might have been devised. In the circumstances, not even that could be considered. Intervention would have had to come quickly to be effective.

Two reasons accounted for the lack of planning. First, the administration planned for the worst contingency against West Berlin, anticipated sometime after Khrushchev's deadline elapsed at the end of the year. The planners worked within a six-month schedule. For example, the Pentagon did not schedule additional forces to arrive in Europe until autumn. More important, the administration's position of nonintervention illustrated a preferred policy of two Germanies which remained unarticulated, but present nonetheless in its perception of the crisis. When the chips were down, the United States acknowledged the actions of the DDR to maintain itself as a viable political entity. In the context of an implicit policy to support Bonn and tolerate Pankow, the quadripartite status of East Berlin was a blind spot.

107. Edward Weintal and Charles Bartlett, *Facing the Brink: An Intimate Study of Crisis Diplomacy* (New York: Charles Scribner's Sons, 1967), p. 211.

CHAPTER 6

Geneva II:
An Elusive Settlement

KENNEDY tried to get negotiations moving in the summer of 1961. In spite of his preference for negotiations, circumstances compelled him to give his initial attention to the military side of the crisis. First, the United States possessed inadequate military resources for the Berlin crisis, so he requested congressional authorization for limited mobilization and other measures to strengthen conventional military forces. Second, Pankow's construction of a wall through Berlin required a morale-boosting military show of force by American troops in West Berlin. The mobilization and the show of force were inevitably dramatic. Thus, the administration appeared much more belligerent than Kennedy wanted it to be. Not to be outdone, the Soviets responded with nuclear testing, as a counter to the administration's conventional military armament, and with severe harassment in and around Berlin as a counter to the American show of force in West Berlin.

This state of affairs displeased and worried Kennedy. The crisis seemed to be deteriorating before negotiations could even begin. The Department of State prepared proposals enabling Kennedy to explore openings for a settlement along the lines of his earlier thoughts on Berlin.[1] Kennedy directed Rusk to disentangle the proposals from

1. Schlesinger, *op. cit.*, pp. 386-390.

inter-allied discussions where they were stuck [2] and suggested to Khrushchev that Rusk and Gromyko together explore a solution. Khrushchev agreed because he himself much preferred a negotiated settlement to a sharply deteriorating exchange of demonstrations full of risk.

The negotiations in 1961–1962 bore little resemblance to the Geneva Conference of 1959. They were less formal and relatively narrow, focusing more directly on a few essential elements of a Berlin *modus vivendi*. Gromyko did not tie an interim Berlin settlement to the work of a mixed-German committee. Moreover, the settlement both sides discussed did not have a time limitation in spite of the provision in the Soviet memorandum of June 4 for a six-month limit to an interim settlement. The administration abandoned the idea of an interim settlement as a means of compromise in favor of another means focusing negotiations on the access issue which Kennedy regarded as the crucial one. It revived the proposal presented by Herter and Lloyd at Geneva for internationalizing the access routes. The United States started the diplomatic game in 1961 on its own wicket.

The negotiations progressed through four stages, in each of which the administration pushed the access proposal as far as it would go. In the first stage, Rusk explored Gromyko's attitude toward the access routes, tentatively discussing ways of correcting the ambiguity and variance in current access practices. In the second, Ambassador Thompson made a serious attempt in Moscow to get a settlement with the access proposal. In the third stage, a relatively productive exchange with Gromyko led Rusk to believe that the proposal might be acceptable to Gromyko. For the fourth stage, then, the administration prepared the outline of a settlement founded on the access proposal and garnished with points of interest to Moscow. By this time, however, the administration had pressed both Bonn and Moscow over a period of seven months to the limits of what they were willing to compromise. The whole enterprise collapsed from the weight of increasing Soviet skepticism and Adenauer's outspoken opposition.

1. *Kennedy Strives to Avert War by Miscalculation*

Kennedy's speech of July 25, his mobilization speech, included a nonmilitary section:

2. *Ibid.*, p. 398.

But I must emphasize that the choice is not merely between resistance and retreat, between atomic holocaust and surrender. Our peacetime military posture is traditionally defensive; but our diplomatic posture need not be. Our response to the Berlin crisis will not be merely military or negative. It will be more than merely standing firm. For we do not intend to leave it to others to choose and monopolize the forum and the framework of discussion. We do not intend to abandon our duty to mankind to seek a peaceful solution.[3]

Kennedy endorsed Herter's 1959 proposal "to remove any actual irritants in West Berlin," providing Moscow understood that the United States would not negotiate away the city's "freedom." He went out of his way to remark:

We recognize the Soviet Union's historical concerns about their security in central and eastern Europe after a series of ravaging invasions, and we believe arrangements can be worked out which will help meet those concerns and make it possible for both security and freedom to exist in this troubled area."[4]

This statement seemed to hint that Kennedy wanted to revive Macmillan's proposals for force reductions in Central Europe accompanying a Berlin settlement. Indeed, not much new ground remained for another diplomatic effort to cover.[5]

Negotiations were delayed because the Western powers no longer could agree that they were desirable. When the Western foreign ministers met in Paris on August 5–6, Rusk and British Foreign Secretary Home argued strenuously for a united diplomatic front. Von Brentano and Couve de Murville opposed negotiations. They predicted that a diplomatic initiative, in the context of Khrushchev's gross standing threats, might very well be misunderstood in Moscow as a sign of faltering confidence in the long-term stability of West Berlin.[6] Rusk rejoined that he wanted to explore the possibility of

3. *Documents*, p. 699.
4. *Ibid.*
5. *The New York Times*, August 1, 1961, p. 1.
6. *Ibid.*, August 7, 1961, p. 1. A veteran of the 1959 Geneva Conference, Von Brentano felt most reluctant to endorse proposals for a settlement separating the Berlin question from the problem of German unity. *Ibid.*, August 1, 1961, p. 2. But the administration would not allow Bonn to block the resumption of negotiations. *Ibid.*, August 5, 1961, p. 3.

negotiating before Khrushchev worked himself into a corner where he would feel compelled to act on his threats.[7]

When Vice President Johnson—enroute to West Berlin—conferred with Adenauer in Bonn, the Chancellor said he had changed his mind and agreed now that negotiations should begin.[8] Adenauer probably perceived that, if Moscow could be entangled in negotiations, the West might achieve a moratorium or at least a delay in unilateral DDR or Soviet moves causing undesirable changes—the Berlin wall, for example—in the Berlin status quo. Events in mid-August had the opposite effect on de Gaulle. He flatly refused to negotiate when the Soviets were acting unilaterally.[9] In September, he talked openly of countermeasures if the Soviets tried to change the status of Berlin any further.[10] The other three allies decided to proceed without him.

Khrushchev, increasingly impatient with the delay, had alternately been demanding a four-power peace treaty or threatening a separate one ever since the Vienna Conference. On August 4, Khrushchev instructed the Western powers that they really had only two alternatives: either negotiate or confront unilateral changes in Berlin.[11] After Ulbricht and he brought off unilateral changes on August 13, Khrushchev had the satisfaction of knowing that for the purposes of future negotiation the Western powers could not speak meaningfully of the quadripartite status of all-Berlin. And he could certainly anticipate greater stability within the DDR. Mikoyan taunted the Western powers: "You may not like the GDR . . . but you will have to ask them for a pass if you want to enter Berlin. Without it you will not get through. No one can fight over this. Only a lunatic would fight over this."[12] To underline the lunacy of war, Moscow an-

7. *Ibid.*, August 5, 1961, p. 1.
8. *Ibid.*, August 20, 1961, p. 3.
9. *Ibid.*, August 24, 1961, p. 1.
10. At a September press conference, de Gaulle said: "It is true, I repeat, that on the spot, in Berlin, the act of force which would be undertaken could bring some advantage to the Soviets, as it would obviously be difficult for the Western powers to act from such a distance on the soil and in the sky of the former German capital. But the Western powers could well fight back on the seas and in the skies traveled by Soviet ships and planes, which would also be far from their bases. There would then be an exchange of wrong doings which undoubtedly would not end to the benefit of the Soviets." *Major Addresses, Statements, and Press Conferences of General Charles de Gaulle*, p. 141.
11. *The New York Times*, August 5, 1961, p. 1.
12. *Ibid.*, August 2, 1961, p. 5.

nounced a resumption of nuclear testing and naval maneuvers involving nuclear detonations.[13]

In late August or early September, Kennedy instructed Ambassador Thompson to invite the Soviets to open negotiations.[14] He extended the invitation at a time when relations between Moscow and Washington had reached an abysmal low. Hostilities around Berlin were more intense than they had been at any time since 1949. Soviet and East German military personnel interfered with air access, using "buzzing" tactics in the air and blinding search lights from the ground trained on incoming planes.[15] Assistant Secretary Nitze declared: "The Communists should understand that though democracies have great patience and forebearance, there eventually comes a point where one more straw will break the camel's back of that forebearance. Any interference with our essential rights in Berlin must be viewed by us as the straw that breaks the camel's back." [16] The State Department released documentation dating from 1945 and 1946 which displayed the original agreements in the Air Directorate of the four-power Control Council creating air corridors for access from the West.[17]

On September 13, the administration called public attention to the presence of both Rusk and Gromyko in New York for the session of the United Nations General Assembly, and said: "This will provide an opportunity for serious talks about Germany and other problems if the Soviet side proves willing." [18] Moscow responded enthusiastically, stating that Gromyko would be prepared to enter into "a relevant exchange of opinions." Thompson prearranged this exchange of announcements. He invited Gromyko a week previously to meet with Rusk in New York, and Khrushchev endorsed the meeting.[19] Von Brentano and Couve de Murville were not enthusiastic about a Rusk-Gromyko meeting. Thus, the communiqué issued at the September 16 foreign ministers' meeting in Washington read that Rusk would make an effort "to ascertain if there exists a reasonable basis

13. *Ibid.*, August 31, 1961, p. 1; September 2, 1961, p. 1.
14. *The New York Times*, September 6, 1961, p. 8.
15. *Ibid.*, September 15, 1961, p. 1; September 10, 1961, p. 3.
16. Nitze, Address before the Association of the United States Army, p. 2.
17. *Documents*, pp. 787-791.
18. *Ibid.*, p. 793.
19. *The New York Times*, September 15, 1961, p. 1.

for negotiations with the Soviet Union." [20] To work around French opposition, Rusk agreed to call the negotiations "exploratory," having in mind, nevertheless, to do more than explore. Home planned to meet Gromyko also.[21]

According to James Reston, Kennedy was preoccupied in late summer with the danger of Soviet miscalculation in the Berlin crisis.[22] He commissioned his brother, Attorney General Robert Kennedy, to state publicly that Moscow should be under no illusions that the United States would not employ nuclear weapons if necessary to defend West Berlin.[23] Kennedy hoped that Rusk would convey to Gromyko the administration's firm convictions and serious intent about Berlin. Kennedy reasoned, not very optimistically, that if the Soviets proved willing to discuss Western proposals on Berlin and if they seemed to appreciate the gravity of interfering with access then he might legitimately have hopes for a *modus vivendi*.[24] Kennedy initiated a private correspondence with Khrushchev in September to help negotiations along and to keep them alive.

Rusk and Gromyko met on three separate occasions in New York in late September. Their meetings were, in effect, the first stage of negotiations. Gromyko appeared to be quite aware of the risks involved and said the Soviet Union would delay its year-end deadline if negotiations began in earnest.[25] Rusk and Home, equally forthcoming, quickly got down to the essentials of a solution. Rusk proposed arrangements for removing the ambiguity and insecurity of civilian access to West Berlin.[26] By focusing on the access routes, Rusk had in mind the following: (1) that the four powers would guarantee Western access to Berlin; (2) that Pankow would adhere to the four-power guarantees in a separate agreement with the Soviet Union; and (3) that transportation officials from Bonn and Pankow

20. *Documents*, p. 801.
21. *The New York Times*, September 16, 1961, p. 1.
22. See Reston's report *ibid.*, September 25, 1961, p. 1. See also Kennedy's address to the General Assembly. *Documents*, pp. 803, 804, 810-811; Richard H. Rovere, "Letter From Washington," *The New Yorker*, September 23, 1961, pp. 82-88.
23. *The New York Times*, September 25, 1961, p. 1.
24. *Ibid.*, September 18, 1961, p. 1.
25. *Ibid.*, October 1, 1961, p. 1; *Ibid.*, September 24, 1961, p. 1.
26. *Ibid.*, September 28, 1961, p. 1. In a press interview on August 20, Rusk asserted that the four powers had a responsibility even for civilian traffic, not simply military convoys. *Documents*, p. 751. He remained unenthusiastic about broad proposals pertaining to German unity. Schlesinger, *op. cit.*, p. 399.

would settle on a new arrangement for civilian access, underwritten by additional four-power guarantees.[27]

When Gromyko spoke vaguely of guarantees for West Berlin, Rusk and Home tried to determine whether he meant access guarantees. And to offer him some incentive to guarantee new access arrangements, Rusk suggested limitations on arms in Central Europe as a *quid pro quo*.[28] Gromyko did not give on the essentials. Again he demanded a reduction in the allied garrisons and a recognition of the line between East and West Germany and the Oder-Neisse line as frontiers of the DDR.[29]

On October 6, Kennedy invited Gromyko to the White House and pressed him for access guarantees. Gromyko reiterated the Soviet position that access would be guaranteed if the United States signed a peace treaty, formally recognizing the DDR.[30] To this standard response Kennedy said: "You have offered to trade us an apple for an orchard. We don't do that in this country." [31] Kennedy said afterward that Gromyko seemed willing to continue the exchange—the only encouraging sign he could detect.[32]

2. *"But Mr. President, the Soviets Will Misunderstand"*

Basically, the administration had decided, if necessary, to go to war—a limited, carefully orchestrated, non-nuclear war—to prevent Soviet encroachment on the Berlin access routes. It proposed negotiations to communicate that decision and, on the basis of mutually recognized dangers in the Berlin crisis, to negotiate a settlement or, at least, a stand-down in Berlin. At a White House luncheon for the Western foreign ministers when they were in Washington in mid-September to review contingency planning, Couve de Murville challenged the administration's methods for dealing with Moscow. Implicitly, he predicted Kennedy would fail. He argued that the President's decision to go to war, if necessary, would not be well understood if the President also strenuously took the initiative to open

27. *The New York Times*, September 29, 1961, p. 1; October 1, 1961, p. 1; December 5, 1961, p 1.

28. The French later objected that Rusk went this far. *Ibid.*, October 15, 1961, p. 4.

29. *Ibid.*, October 6, 1961, p. 4.

30. *Ibid.*, October 9, 1961, p. 1.

31. *Ibid.*, October 7, 1961, p. 1.

32. *Ibid.*, October 12, 1961, p. 1.

negotiations. Negotiations in the current atmosphere could be mis-construed in Moscow to mean that the West would trade the unassail-able legal status of West Berlin, as France considered it, for a new convention implicitly or explicitly extending diplomatic recognition to the DDR. Kennedy said that because he had decided to accept the risks of war he had an obligation to do what he could to avoid it. But Couve thought negotiations would obscure Kennedy's basic decision.[33]

Paris perceived the Berlin crisis as Khrushchev's crisis. Kennedy, by contrast, believed the crisis would not be Khrushchev's for long if Khrushchev proceeded to sign a separate treaty placing the West in the dilemma of either choosing war or complying. But the French thought, if Khrushchev did sign a treaty, the Soviets would be in the same dilemma. Moscow would have to choose between upholding Pankow's authority on the access routes—an act of war— or returning to the status quo. The French were convinced Khrushchev would not go to war over Berlin. Or, they said, if they were wrong, Khrushchev could not be stopped by negotiations. Kennedy did not deny the logic of this argument. He just did not believe he could trust Khrushchev to perceive the situation so rationally. After the New York meetings had concluded, the French argued that Gromyko's adamant attitude in his talks with Rusk proved that the Soviets were not impressed.[34] In any event, de Gaulle would not participate in allied planning for negotiations, although he remained fully represented in military planning. The administration probably had little incentive to sym-pathize with the French position after October when Khrushchev lifted his deadline and agreed to negotiate.

Kennedy also had no end of trouble with Bonn. He tried to live with France's absence, but he needed Bonn's support to give the administration's proposals credibility in Moscow. The press reports about the Rusk-Gromyko meetings in late September alarmed Bonn. Sidney Gruson in *The New York Times* reported that the administra-tion soon would demand changes in Bonn's Eastern policies. Bonn, he said, would lose its customary veto over American foreign policy. Certain advisers around Kennedy, according to Gruson, wanted to revise the status of West Berlin and the access routes in exchange for some form of recognition for Pankow coupled with Central European arms limitations. Gruson said that this group prevailed over other

33. Reston in *ibid.*, September 18, 1961, p. 1.
34. *Ibid.*, October 16, 1961, p. 3.

advisers who believed that concessions merely postponed a resolution of the crisis.[35] General Clay also stirred up the press, remarking that Bonn should think seriously of revising its relationships with Pankow, if it really desired a united Germany.[36] Clay, a friend of West Germany, tried in this way to warn the West Germans of the trend of administration thinking. These rumors oversimplified Rusk's views and upset Kennedy because they aggravated his relations with Bonn. Since a government had not yet been formed in Bonn following the elections of September 17, they complicated internal politics in West Germany, as well. Adenauer, now without a parliamentary majority, struggled for almost two months to create a coalition cabinet.[37]

During the Rusk-Gromyko meetings, Von Brentano exclaimed loudly offstage that Bonn would not underwrite the division of Germany by recognizing the DDR.[38] What provoked Von Brentano were the inquiries he had received from Washington soliciting Bonn's views of the arrangement for civilian access Rusk had in mind. For example, would Bonn be willing to negotiate with Pankow to reach a detailed agreement on civilian access? Rusk wanted a new arrangement supplementing, not overturning, the West's legal access rights.[39]

The Secretary argued within the councils of the administration, as Dulles had before him, that Bonn should negotiate with Pankow because West Germany—through the interzonal trade agreements— regularly conducted negotiations anyway.[40] If Bonn objected to direct negotiations between the Western powers and Pankow, he thought Bonn itself could negotiate without affecting the question of recognition. Von Brentano and Adenauer opposed Rusk's plan, thinking the United States terribly insensitive to its interests. To their way of thinking, negotiations with Pankow were always a necessary evil to be conducted as inobtrusively as possible. They perceived that Rusk's proposal would change the character of existing contacts with Pankow, raising the status of the contacts without receiving or even demanding anything from Pankow in return to rationalize granting

---

35. *Ibid.*, September 12, 1961, p. 7.
36. *Ibid.*, September 23, 1961, p. 1.
37. Peter H. Merkl, "Equilibrium, Structure of Interests and Leadership: Adenauer's Survival as Chancellor," *The American Political Science Review*, 56 (September 1962), 634-650.
38. *The New York Times*, September 27, 1961, p. 20.
39. *Ibid.*, October 6, 1961, p. 1.
40. *Ibid.*, October 1, 1961, p. 4.

the concession. Why concede anything before Pankow actually agreed to improve access, they asked.

Bonn eventually agreed to talk with Pankow provided the four powers enclosed the committees for the talks as creatures of the four powers. Bonn vetoed the arms limitations measures Rusk wanted to attach to a Berlin settlement. In general, the West Germans proved unwilling to move very far from the Western peace plan of 1959.[41]

3. Why Did Khrushchev Relent?

Khrushchev withdrew his December deadline for a peace treaty on October 17, the first day of the Twenty-second Party Congress. This date marks the end of the sequence of military actions and reactions, beginning in March with the administration's first defense message and accelerating after Vienna with Kennedy's partial mobilization speech. The American measures to mobilize and improve conventional military forces enraged Khrushchev. Kennedy believed he had to warn Khrushchev, but Khrushchev did not perceive Kennedy's moves as a warning. He thought Kennedy wanted to blackmail him. To remind Kennedy of the extremely vulnerable position the United States held in West Berlin, the Soviets resumed nuclear testing in September, even though Khrushchev had told Kennedy at Vienna that the Soviet Union would not be the first to test. Moscow's campaign of harassment in the Berlin air corridors ran parallel to the testing program. The demonstration and counterdemonstration tapered off when Khrushchev seemed satisfied that he had made his point and, more importantly, when the administration initiated a serious diplomatic effort through Rusk, indicating a willingness to talk.

The administration felt enormously relieved by Khrushchev's announcement lifting the December 31 deadline. But some officials went too far. They suggested that the mobilization, albeit a limited one, turned the tide, that Khrushchev became reasonable because he realized the risks involved in a collision course and corrected his miscalculation.[42]

Mixing options is not likely to produce unmixed effects. The effect on Khrushchev of the administration's persistent efforts to negotiate

41. *Ibid.*, October 14, 1961, p. 1.
42. Sorensen, *op. cit.*, pp. 592-593.

also played a role in his October 17 announcement. If Khrushchev wanted negotiations and pursued a collision course as a calculated risk for getting them, the success of the mobilization—hailed within the administration—is not apparent. He was not a defeated man if he got the negotiations he wanted.

Evidence suggests that Khrushchev believed that the Soviet Union had matched the United States in crisis posturing and maneuvering, and had persuaded it to enter serious negotiations. His basic long-term calculations in the crisis, therefore, remained uncorrected. First, Khrushchev strenuously rejected any implication that he could be intimidated by Kennedy. John J. McCloy, Kennedy's special assistant for arms control and disarmament matters, happened to be Khrushchev's guest at Sochi in the Crimea, the Chairman's holiday retreat, when Khrushchev received word of the President's July 25 speech announcing partial mobilization. Khrushchev told McCloy he considered the speech a virtual declaration of war. He turned on McCloy heatedly, insisting that if war occurred, Kennedy would be the last president of the United States! Kennedy, he warned, should not try to move him with threats. He said he still believed in the President's good sense to resolve their differences with peaceful means.[43] McCloy carried Khrushchev's rage and warning back to Kennedy. Second, in early August, Khrushchev proceeded in collaboration with Ulbricht to terminate the flow of refugees into West Berlin. Their success probably diluted the effect of Kennedy's speech even if Khrushchev had originally been impressed with it. Third, Khrushchev replied, in kind, to Kennedy's actions. He broke the moratorium on nuclear testing and let Konev harass air traffic into West Berlin.

In his speech to the Party Congress on October 17, Khrushchev publicly concluded that his warning and counterdemonstration had paid off. Referring to the Rusk-Gromyko discussions, he said: "These talks left us with the impression that the Western powers were showing a certain understanding of the situation, and that they were disposed to seek a settlement of the German problem and the issue of West Berlin on a mutually acceptable basis." [44] In this context, he said that he had already informed the Western powers of his willingness to negotiate in good faith and that negotiations should focus on

43. Schlesinger, *op. cit.*, p. 392.
44. *Pravda*, October 18, 1961, p. 2.

disengagement of armed forces in Central Europe, a ban on nuclear weapons in both Germanies, and access guarantees for West Berlin.[45]

Judging by his outburst to McCloy, his success with the Berlin wall, and his own counterdemonstration, Kennedy's bid to negotiate rather than his plans for mobilization persuaded Khrushchev to withdraw the deadline. Khrushchev looked for Kennedy to make a decision to negotiate. The American mobilization and the Soviet counter-demonstration concluded because each power mistakenly believed it had effectively conveyed the message it wanted the other to hear—Kennedy, although still with some qualms, that he had armed to parley; Khrushchev, that he could not be bullied. Negotiations offered the only way to resolve the crisis, according to the two leaders. Because each misjudged the reason for the other's desire for negotiations, he misjudged the results to be expected from parleying.[46]

4. *"Exploratory Talks" and the Second Strategic Test*

At the annual December meeting, December 13–15, Rusk and Home discussed with the NATO Ministerial Council the next step in East-West negotiations. Fourteen NATO foreign ministers—all but Couve de Murville—agreed to an active approach to negotiations, indicating that the "exploratory" discussions should be rather substantive notwithstanding French objections. The pattern of the "fourteen-and-the-one," or "the empty chair"—NATO without France—so prominent in the late 1960's, appeared as early as December 1961 over the issue of Berlin negotiations. Discussions would begin in January 1962, without France and with a reluctant Federal Republic.[47] On Decem-

---

45. *The New York Times*, October 13, 1961, p. 1.

46. During the period of relative quiet after October 17, Khrushchev suddenly turned on the Scandinavians. On October 30, he demanded consultations with Helsinki on measures of mutual defense against a possible NATO attack, basing the demand on a 1955 treaty of "mutual assistance" with Finland. He denounced Norway's and Denmark's cooperation in the newly organized NATO Baltic command shared with the Federal Republic. Sweden was also accused of collaboration with Bonn. The administration wondered if Moscow wanted to recruit Helsinki for recognizing the DDR. Whatever the motive, President Urho Kekkonen of Finland and Khrushchev agreed on November 26 to postpone "mutual assistance." The side-show ended as abruptly as it began. Khrushchev hinted that his intention had been to thwart the participation of Bonn in the new Baltic command. This purpose also appeared in the communiqué of his meeting with Kekkonen. There was little evidence of specific claims against Finland itself. *Ibid.*, November 25, 1961, p. 1; November 26, 1961, p. 4.

47. *Ibid.*, December 13, 1961, p. 1; December 16, 1961, p. 1.

ber 22, in Bermuda, Kennedy and Macmillan agreed that Ambassador Thompson in Moscow should act as agent of the alliance for conducting talks with the Soviets.

While Thompson studied his instructions, Secretary Rusk explained what he considered the reason for negotiating. The administration, he said, had made the decision to defend West Berlin at "whatever cost." "That decision remains the basis on which we intend to explore the possibilities of a peaceful resolution of the Berlin crisis." And

> Since George Washington first enjoined the American people to recognize a connection between the maintenance of adequate military strength and the maintenance of the peace, our history has underlined that the danger of war is greatest when potential enemies are in doubt about the capacity of nations to defend their vital interests, about their will to defend them, or about how they define their vital interests. All three of these conditions for a peaceful resolution of differences are heightened in a world where the use of nuclear weapons may quickly come into play once conflict begins at any level.[48]

Thompson would address himself to removing Soviet questions or doubts about the United States capacity, will, and interests in the Berlin crisis.

The next stages through which the negotiations passed may be labeled according to the negotiators involved: the Thompson-Gromyko series of meetings from January 2 to March 6, the almost daily Rusk-Gromyko discussions on the periphery of the Eighteen Nation Disarmament Conference in Geneva from March 11 to March 27, and the Rusk-Dobrynin meetings of April 16 to May 30.

On January 2, 1962, Ambassador Thompson called on Gromyko and initiated the second stage of negotiations since September. Thompson had instructions to try for a settlement to be ratified by a foreign ministers' conference. On January 3, *The New York Times* reported from Washington: "The talks are expected to continue for some time and officials here are no longer interested in quibbling over whether this amounts to 'exploratory probes' or 'preliminary negotiations.' It is not tea party gossip, they say." [49]

---

48. Dean Rusk, "Some Issues of Contemporary History," *The Department of State Bulletin*, 46 (January 15, 1962), 83-88.

49. *The New York Times*, January 4, 1962, p. 3.

Thompson and Gromyko met five times altogether.[50] An analysis of the meetings reveals that Thompson presented a two-point position. In the first point, he tried to emphasize that the United States and the Soviet Union shared an interest in avoiding war over Berlin. He did not have to belabor the point because Gromyko knew already that the United States, to remain in Berlin, depended ultimately on a decision to go to nuclear war. For all intents and purposes, the ambassador identified the issues in the Berlin crisis with the danger of nuclear war.

The second point the ambassador presented followed from the first. Given a common desire to avoid war, he proposed a settlement focusing on the access issue—the *casus belli* for the administration. Thompson inquired if the Soviets would offer guarantees for the security of the routes. Depending on Gromyko's answer, he was ready to suggest traffic arrangements with the DDR. A *modus vivendi*, as the administration conceived it, would have to take account of the DDR's interests as well as the Soviet Union's. Although the Thompson-Gromyko meetings never progressed to the stage where a compromise formula respecting the interests of both sides could be introduced, both negotiators knew that the administration had a specific proposal in mind.[51]

Thompson had instructions to propose the establishment of a Berlin International Access Authority. The authority, by four-power agreement, would become traffic manager on the access routes and administrator of facilities in Berlin necessary for traffic control. The authority would not supplant the legal title of the Western powers over the access routes. Secretary Rusk said it should facilitate the flow of traffic, to determine who could or could not travel to West Berlin. On April 26, Rusk described the authority as follows:

50. The meetings were held at the Soviet Foreign Ministry on January 2, January 12, February 1, February 9, and March 6.

51. Kennedy had made the following statement to Aleksie Adzhubei, editor of *Izvestiia* and Khrushchev's son-in-law, in an interview on November 28: "in attempting to work out a solution of the problems which came about as a result of World War II, we don't want to increase the changes of World War III. All we wish to do is maintain a very limited—and they are very limited—number of troops of the three powers in West Berlin and to have, for example, an *international administration of the autobahn* so that goods and people can move freely in and out" (my emphasis). *Ibid.*, November 29, 1961, p. 18. Khrushchev publicly rejected the proposal on December 9. *Ibid.*, December 10, 1961, p. 20.

. . . on our side we see no incompatibility between free access and the local responsibilities and authorities of those in the area through which access would move. In other words, we see a situation where no interference by one with the other is entirely possible, but that does not get into the question of recognizing the GDR.[52]

Soviet guarantees for access security would be embedded in the charter of the organization. Thompson also proposed including Pankow and Bonn as charter members.[53]

Thus, the administration outlined this compromise in the Thompson-Gromyko meetings: Soviet guarantees for security of the access routes in exchange for East German membership in the access authority. The United States would gain uninterrupted access for civilian and military traffic and the Soviet Union indirect recognition for the DDR. Since the administration could not recognize the DDR formally—because of the alliance with Bonn—and the Soviets could not formally deny DDR claims, an international organization provided a simple and convenient medium for resolving the crisis. This solution assumed, however, that the parties would be motivated to make the access authority function because of a common interest to avoid war over the access issue.

The Soviets were not particularly impressed with Thompson's proposal. Gromyko responded stiffly, presenting all the well-worn Soviet proposals on West Berlin. His behavior indicated that he regarded the meetings with Thompson as a forum to threaten and demand acquiescence in the Soviet position. He made it quite clear that the Soviet Union had no desire for a *modus vivendi,* except one resulting from the most severe kinds of concessions by the United States.

Gromyko dismissed Ambassador Thompson's first point, stating that the removal of the last war's vestiges—namely, the military presence of the United States in West Berlin—was of more concern to him than avoiding a hypothetical war in the future. Gromyko refused to let any recognition of the danger of nuclear war lead him into serious consideration of Thompson's proposals. By taking this position, he reversed Thompson's point to imply that the United

52. *The Department of State Bulletin,* 46 (May 14, 1962), 798.
53. *The New York Times,* April 14, 1962, p. 2.

States would bring war upon itself, if it adhered to its own position. He argued that it could easily avoid war by removing its identification of the Berlin crisis with the danger of nuclear war.

Reversing Thompson's first point, Gromyko conceded Thompson's second point. Given a common desire to demilitarize West Berlin, he thought one could deal accordingly with the access issue. Gromyko said the Soviet Union would be willing to give the United States guarantees for the security of the access routes. If Thompson viewed this remark in isolation from others Gromyko made, Gromyko's statement appeared to be a positive response to Thompson's efforts. Indeed, in the context of the administration's access proposals, Gromyko's statement could be construed as an encouraging sign of movement in Kremlin policy. But Gromyko showed little interest in Thompson's position as a whole.

To Moscow, the United States seemed to be delaying a settlement by alternately expressing a desire to avoid war and presenting access proposals unacceptable to the Soviet side. Khrushchev's impatience was not abated by the proposals Thompson conveyed to him through Gromyko. On February 7—before the fourth Thompson-Gromyko meeting—Konev renewed air harassment in the corridors. He conducted a protracted military probe in depth to test the administration's resolution to defend the access routes to West Berlin.

Soviet harassment in the air corridors included reserving air space and filing flight plans for Soviet military aircraft; flying Soviet MIG's into the path of allied aircraft; buzzing Pan American, British European Airways, and Air France flights to West Berlin; dropping metal chaff to interfere with allied radar facilities; and causing sonic booms in the Berlin flight zone. This activity continued intermittently from February 9 until March 29. In retaliation, General Clay and Mayor Brandt boarded a military transport to fly in the north corridor at the time and altitudes the Soviets had reserved for February 9. American, British, and French military transports flew daily in the air spaces reserved by the Soviets.[54] Civil airlines maintained scheduled flights.

The Soviet program of air harassment, in conjunction with Gromyko's sternness at the meetings with Thompson, worked to make a shambles of the administration's proposal for an International

54. *Ibid.*, February 10, 1962, p. 1; George Bailey, "The Gentle Erosion of Berlin," *The Reporter*, 26 (April 26, 1962), 18-19; Ausland, *op. cit.*, pp. 67-73

Access Authority. Gromyko conceded guarantees for access in the proposed charter of this Authority in the same period when Soviet pilots in the corridors tried to remove the legal conditions upon which Western access stood. Moscow declared that air harassment demonstrated the legal right of Soviet aircraft to fly in the corridors at will.[55] For this purpose, the pilots did not actually need to disrupt traffic. They only had to fly in the corridors without Western permission. This illegal Soviet behavior eroded Western legal title to the access routes, enabling the Soviets to assert their legal title. In this sense, Gromyko's willingness to guarantee access appeared as an assertion of power and authority to grant access privileges—reminiscent of Marshal Zhukov's assertion on the same subject in 1945.

In the Thompson-Gromyko meetings, Gromyko invariably returned to the free city proposal as the central issue. He did not argue that the Soviet Union should have exclusive title to West Berlin. He insisted, instead, that the Western powers should not have exclusive title to it. Ostensibly, Gromyko argued that the occupation regime should be abolished in favor of a new title for the legal existence of the city. Thompson discerned without any difficulty, however, that the free city proposal served as a facade for the most disturbing aspect of Gromyko's position. The Soviet Union appeared to be disinterested in a settlement the United States could willingly accept, but to be intent upon coercing the United States into a settlement largely on Soviet terms. The free city proposal was a measure of Soviet confidence that the United States would eventually relent. Gromyko demanded nothing less than the military presence of the Soviet Union in West Berlin or an end to the United States military presence. He seemed to be trying to call the administration's bluff.

The administration was not bluffing. The President intended the initial and continuing response to air harassment—flying military transport planes through the corridors—to warn the Soviet Union of the risks of harassment. Although General Clay recommended fighter escorts for allied aircraft as a stronger form of warning, the administration agreed with the British that as long as the harassment did not

55. On February 16, the Soviet Embassy in East Berlin stated: "We control the air corridors and inform the Western powers that we will be using them whether they will fly in them as well. We will take no action to stop them but they will be responsible for accidents." *The New York Times*, February 17, 1962, p. 5.

disrupt normal air traffic, military transports were effective enough.[56] Aside from written and oral protests to Moscow,[57] the administration successfully made its point—through General Norstad's skillful management—in a moderate military fashion, leaving the forbidding decision to escalate to the Soviets.[58] The Thompson-Gromyko stage of negotiations concluded with a military demonstration by the Soviet Union and a counterdemonstration by the United States on the access issue, tightening the diplomatic deadlock.

Before consideration of the next stage, the Federal Republic's attitude should be noted in order to anticipate why Bonn finally vetoed the negotiations later in May. The Soviets provoked an incident in January 1962 which demonstrated how uncomfortable Bonn felt in consenting to the negotiations that it did not really favor. On January 3, *The New York Times* reported that the Soviet Union had presented a memorandum to the West German ambassador in Moscow, Dr. Hans Kroll.[59] In the memorandum, the Soviets offered the prospect of bilateral negotiations between Moscow and Bonn on outstanding areas of dispute between the two governments. They intimated that a trade agreement of "ocean-sized" proportions could be arranged.

Evidently, the Soviets wished to create the impression that Bonn negotiated directly with Moscow without Thompson's knowledge. To complicate matters, Ambassador Kroll had a reputation for favoring limited bilateral relations and he had in fact approached the Soviet government in November on his own initiative. The Soviet memorandum thus came as a sequel to Kroll's November contact, although Kroll himself believed the memorandum took advantage of his contact to sow distrust among the Western allies.[60] *The New York Times*

---

56. *Ibid.*, February 17, 1962, p. 5. *The New York Times* reported that American fighter escorts were on five-minute alert at Ramstein Air Force base. *Ibid.*, March 13, 1962, p. 12.

57. *Ibid.*, February 16, 1961, p. 3.

58. Kennedy restrained his comments at his press conference on February 21: "I'm hopeful that the Soviet Union and ourselves will be able—as I've said from the beginning—to reach an accommodation, because obviously, any interference with these kinds of rights, or rights which may be on the autobahn, all these things carry with them hazards which none of us should welcome, if we look at the possible end of the road. So I would not make any judgment . . . I merely hope that it would be possible for them to desist." *Ibid.*, February 22, p. 10.

59. Actually, Kroll received the memorandum on December 27, 1961. *Ibid.*, January 4, 1962, p. 3.

60. *Ibid.*, March 3, 1962, p. 1. Kroll had discussed a five-point plan for a Berlin settlement with Khrushchev on November 9, 1961. *Ibid.*, November 10, 1961, pp. 1, 10; January 8, 1961, p. 1.

jumped to the conclusion that the "Kroll incident" indicated that Bonn said one thing through Ambassador Thompson acting for NATO and another through Ambassador Kroll.[61] Actually, the four allied ambassadors in Moscow maintained continuous communication among themselves, and Kroll apprised Thompson at the time of his conversations with Khrushchev.

To avoid confirming the impression that Bonn wished to subvert the Thompson-Gromyko meetings, Adenauer declared that Bonn had nothing to hide. He published the memorandum—which he did not accept as a serious proposal anyway—and the Foreign Office announced that Kroll would be dismissed in the near future. Nevertheless, Adenauer did not rebuke the ambassador and described him later as "a valuable man." [62] And, after conferring with de Gaulle in February, Adenauer himself suggested a pause in the talks between Thompson and Gromyko. He remarked that Thompson should not negotiate endlessly, particularly when the proposed International Access Authority involved unnecessary concessions.[63]

Bonn held to an ambiguous position and did not completely oppose the administration's efforts for a settlement for at least three reasons. Most obvious, Bonn could not change Kennedy's desire to reduce the risks inherent in the crisis. Second, Soviet propaganda urgently stressed that the Berlin crisis had to be resolved before the alleged resurgence of German militarism developed to provoke war, so Bonn did not wish to appear to substantiate Soviet propaganda by obstructing a peaceful settlement. Third, Adenauer relied on de Gaulle to play obstructionist. The communiqué of the February meeting between Adenauer and de Gaulle reflected a meeting of minds. In retrospect, since Adenauer asserted himself unambiguously in opposition to the negotiations in May, perhaps he should have done so earlier. He misled the Kennedy Administration, which did not sense the full extent of West German opposition to the negotiations.

5. The Second Geneva Conference

On February 22, Rusk announced he would head the United States delegation to the Eighteen Nation Disarmament Conference at Geneva

61. *Ibid.*, February 20, 1962, p. 9.

62. *Ibid.*, May 8, 1962, p. 1. Bonn lost another ambassador before the American-Soviet negotiations drew to a close. The administration objected to the attitude of Adenauer's ambassador in Washington, Dr. Grewe, toward the talks and asked for his recall. Schlesinger, *op. cit.*, p. 403.

63. *The New York Times*, February 21, 1962, p. 1.

in March. He indicated he would arrive four days before the con-
ference began and would be ready to discuss the Berlin crisis with
Gromyko.[64] His announcement opened the third stage of negotiations.
On March 5, the Soviets announced that Gromyko would meet with
Rusk in Geneva.[65] Although the State Department issued a public
statement describing the International Access Authority proposal,[66]
Gromyko requested a discussion of a broad range of issues. While
Pravda denounced the proposal for an access authority,[67] Poland
proposed a revised version of the Rapacki plan for establishing a de-
nuclearized zone in Central Europe.[68] In a letter to U Thant, United
Nations Acting Secretary General, Gromyko endorsed the Polish
proposal. Thus, the third stage of the Berlin negotiations, taking
place at a conference for general disarmament, appeared as a side
discussion of regional disarmament.[69] Diplomacy revived in a wider
context with freer play. The military confrontation in the air corridors continued through the entire course of the conference.

At Geneva in March, Gromyko proposed to Rusk the creation of an
international authority over the access routes to West Berlin. He
adopted the language of the administration's proposal without moving any closer to it than his previous offer of access guarantees. Not
surprisingly, the Soviet version of an access authority described
access to the free city of West Berlin. The authority itself would
arbitrate access disputes arising from DDR control of the routes.[70]

64. *Ibid.*, February 22, 1961, p. 1.
65. *Ibid.*, March 6, 1962, p. 1.
66. *The Department of State Bulletin*, 46 (March 5, 1962), 463-464.
67. *Pravda*, March 9, 1962, p. 7.
68. *The New York Times*, March 13, 1962, p. 1.
69. In presenting the United States plan for general and complete disarmament, Rusk employed terms which were equally applicable to his view of the
Berlin crisis:
  "Let us, then apply ourselves to the task of this conference soberly, sys-
  tematically, and realistically. Let the need for disarmament provide the
  momentum for our work. Let us follow every promising path which might
  lead to progress. . . .
  And let us not permit this conference, like its predecessors, to become
  frozen in deadlock at the start of its deliberations. Surely, it need not do
  so. The obstacles to disarmament agreements—tending to divide us into
  rival aggregations of power—might at long last begin to yield to the over-
  riding and shared interest in survival which also can unite us for peace."
United States Arms Control and Disarmament Agency, *Disarmament: The New
U.S. Initiative*, Publication 8, September, 1962, p. 38.
70. Ulbricht publicized the Soviet proposal on March 24. *The New York*

In keeping with the Geneva Conference and Khrushchev's objectives in the Berlin crisis, Gromyko also proposed a disarmament plan for East and West Germany, including renunciation by the Germans of any production or acquisition of nuclear weapons, an agreement to deny bases for "foreign" nuclear weapons, and a nonaggression treaty.[71]

Rusk reacted to Gromyko's proposals in a mixed fashion. First, he promptly rejected them. Second, he noticed that no hardline statements accompanied the proposals, as they had in Gromyko's sessions with Ambassador Thompson. Third, Gromyko gave him a very full exposition of the Soviet position and, in discussing a specific proposal, clarified the Soviet view of the access issue. Fourth, Gromyko agreed to continue the Berlin negotiations, designating Soviet Ambassador Dobrynin in Washington to carry on. For the Secretary, then, his meetings with Gromyko were useful, although certainly not conclusive. In light of the great disappointment expressed by the State Department when the negotiations collapsed later in April, Rusk must have come away from his talks with Gromyko in March relatively optimistic about the chances of a minimal agreement.[72] *The New York Times* reported that the Soviet delegation went to great lengths to encourage the impression Moscow would not crowd the administration at this point.[73] The communiqué to which Rusk and Gromyko agreed at the conclusion of the Geneva Conference contained the following

---

Times, March 25, 1962, p. 32. As he described it, an arbitration authority composed of governments formally extending diplomatic recognition to the DDR in a peace treaty would hear appeals when access disputes occurred. The DDR would not be a member of the authority, although the treaty would establish the free city of West Berlin. The Soviet Union would mediate between the authority and the DDR. This scheme paralleled suggestions Rusk made to Gromyko in September for a four-power access arrangement and a separate Soviet-DDR peace treaty with the Soviet Union as a party to both. *Ibid.,* November 14, 1961, p. 1.

71. *Ibid.,* March 23, 1961, p. 1.

72. At his press conference on March 30, Kennedy expressed some encouragement at the outcome of the Geneva Conference: "I think both sides have proceeded with a good deal of care because they realize it is important and therefore could bring about, we hope, a very happy solution, though none has been forthcoming, but could have if miscalculations or mistakes [sic] made by anyone, it could bring about a very happy one. So that we proceed with care and we welcome the care with which others may proceed." *The New York Times,* March 31, 1962, p. 12. Cf. *ibid.,* April 14, 1962, p. 1.

73. *Ibid.,* March 27, 1962, p. 1.

sentence: "Their conversations have been both useful and frank, and some progress has been made in clarifying points of difference.[74]

If Rusk left Geneva on a note of cautious optimism, so did Gromyko, although for different reasons. Throughout the Geneva Conference, the Soviets continued their program of harassment in the air corridors to Berlin. They probed on two fronts: the diplomatic effort in Geneva probed for flexibility in the administration's access proposal; the military effort in the access routes probed the boundaries of the administration's advertised war decision which, presumably, lay at the bottom of its access proposal. Moscow suspended the two efforts simultaneously at the end of the Rusk-Gromyko meetings in Geneva.[75]

The Soviets probably thought they found evidence at Geneva that the administration was inhibited by its reliance on a nuclear defense of Berlin. Judging by Gromyko's behavior in the meetings with Thompson, they considered the administration to be bluffing. Then, Konev launched an air harassment operation, perhaps to determine whether they had a correct impression. The military probe probably seemed satisfactory enough to them, but not conclusive because Norstad continued to fly military transports. Now, at Geneva, Rusk negotiated under conditions of military duress in the air corridors. Indeed, after lodging a protest at the first meeting, Rusk—at Kennedy's direction—proved willing to discuss access issues while the Soviets actually threatened Western access rights.[76] The Soviets traditionally relate their diplomacy to military power more closely than the United States generally does and are prone to believe other powers do the same. They also consider the context of events as important as events themselves. Thus, Khrushchev may have regarded Rusk's behavior at this juncture in the negotiations as indicating a lack of confidence during the crisis, a worry about the vulnerability of West Berlin. In any event, the Soviet delegation at Geneva went out of its way to be conciliatory to the American delegation. And later, after the negotiations had failed in May, the Soviets expressed disappoint-

74. *The Department of State Bulletin*, 46 (April 16, 1962), 625.
75. The conference ended for Rusk and Gromyko on March 27. The harassment stopped on March 29.
76. *The New York Times*, March 12, 1962, p. 1; March 15, 1962, p. 1. Rusk personally preferred not to discuss access issues when Konev employed military duress in the corridors, but went to Geneva at Kennedy's request. Ausland, *op. cit.*, p. 73.

ment and anger, implying that they had been proceeding on an assumption which then proved incorrect.

Gromyko probably agreed to the communiqué with as much cautious optimism as Rusk. When Gromyko presented his proposals for an international authority and regional disarmament plan, Rusk rejected them. Nevertheless, Gromyko noted that Rusk preferred to avoid a complete breakdown in the discussions, and the American delegation actively solicited peripheral agreements when no agreement proved possible on Berlin.[77] Above all, Rusk wished to continue the Berlin negotiations in Washington. The more Rusk persisted for a settlement, the more he probably misled Gromyko into thinking that the administration wanted to escape the risks of war and settle for what it could get. Instead of convincing Gromyko of its will and capacity to make the decision to go to war, Rusk may have convinced him that the administration would do everything in its power to avoid it. Gromyko probably concluded that if he could make his own position even more attractive without essentially changing it, if he could think of a respectable way to cover a United States retreat, then Rusk might be receptive. When Rusk, while yet rejecting the Soviet position, accepted the language of the communiqué that the conversations had been useful and that some progress had been made, Gromyko may have interpreted the communiqué to mean that the administration would move—at last—toward the Soviet position.

The New York Times recorded the misunderstanding at Geneva. Describing the behavior of Rusk and Gromyko, the correspondent in Geneva wrote: "Their manner suggested that they felt themselves on the way toward one of the most unusual compacts of the Cold War, for they had found themselves in apparent agreement that there was not likely to be a Berlin agreement soon and they had reached a tacit agreement not to acknowledge this." This report reflects the views of the American and British delegations, not the Soviet delegation, because those delegations wanted the "tacit agreement" mentioned. The Soviets wanted an explicit agreement. The problem with tacit agreements is that they may be so tacit they really do not exist, particularly one that denies an "apparent agreement" not to have an agreement! The report is an example of how the United States mis-

77. *Ibid.*, March 14, 1962, p. 1.

judged Soviet intent, identifying the Soviet position with the United States' own desire for a tacit *modus vivendi*.[78]

McDermott, former British minister in Berlin, claims that as early as January 1962 Rusk expressed some optimism about the outcome of negotiations.[79] If McDermott is correct, a misjudgment arose early, and explains the root of the problem with the negotiations track. In itself, the administration's attempt to communicate its will and capacity to defend West Berlin presumed that verbal clarity about the administration's war decision would contribute to the formulation of a settlement.

The Soviet Union and the United States misunderstood each other at Geneva because each did not accept the other's position at face value. They ignored the surface and perceived motives beneath the surface to which they thought they could subscribe when, in reality, the obvious features of their positions indicated their real positions. The Soviet Union, despite all its bombast, meant what it said. The United States also demonstrated its position in the military duel with Konev in the air corridors and in pressing for a settlement through Rusk in Geneva. Both governments meant what they said, but were so intent upon their own positions that they tended to project an interest in them to the other side.

6. Washington between Two Vetoes

After an extended period of diplomatic probing in Geneva, the two delegations retired to their capitals to think through the fourth stage. The administration prepared for stage four with the expectation of Soviet concessions, particularly with the suspension of Soviet harassment in the air corridors. It discounted the possibility that the suspension of harassment might be the result of Soviet expectations of concessions.

Proceeding from the expanded discussion of the third stage, the State Department prepared a series of proposals, centering on the access issue, but linking arms limitations devices to it. Rusk probably explored some of these proposals with Gromyko on a tentative basis at Geneva. The State Department had five proposals:

---

78. *The New York Times*, April 1, 1962, cited in Laszlo Hadik, "The Berlin Question 1942–1962, A Historical Summary," unpublished MS, Institute for Defense Analyses, Washington, D.C. 1963.

79. McDermott, *op. cit.*, p. 54.

1. The establishment of an International Access Authority.

2. An agreement by the United States and Soviet Union to forego transferring nuclear weapons to governments currently not possessing them.

3. An exchange of nonaggression declarations between NATO and the Warsaw Pact.

4. The establishment of committees composed of West Germans and East Germans in equal numbers to maintain "technical" contacts between two Germanies.

5. An arrangement for a permanent conference of deputy foreign ministers of the four powers to meet regularly to review the remaining issues in Berlin.[80]

The other proposals derived from the International Access Authority proposal. If Soviet assent to the *modus vivendi* incorporated in the charter of the authority could be achieved, the two governments might very well embroider the basic agreement to include two military and two diplomatic measures. A mutual desire to avoid nuclear war over the access issue could readily lead to a nonproliferation agreement and pledges of nonaggression. The technical committees and the deputy foreign ministers' conference would continue the process of settlement on two levels, resolving any further details and, perhaps, future Berlin crises.

The State Department anchored these proposals in the occupation status of West Berlin. The administration planned to reiterate that the DDR should be granted membership in the access organization. Membership would not constitute diplomatic recognition because the administration did not consider an international organization a government. To emphasize the international character of the authority, the United States planned to suggest a membership of thirteen representatives: five Western ones from the allied powers in West Berlin, the Federal Republic, and West Berlin itself; five Eastern ones from the Soviet Union, Poland, Czechoslovakia, the DDR, and East Berlin; and three neutral ones from Austria, Switzerland, and Sweden.[81] The Department expected the membership provision to be

80. *Ibid.*, April 14, 1962, p. 1.
81. *Ibid.*, April 21, 1962, p. 1.

controversial because the Soviets had long contended that the DDR included East Berlin. Furthermore, decisions of the authority would be by simple majority and Austria, Switzerland, and Sweden, officially neutral, considered themselves part of the West and might not be willing to hold decisive roles in majority voting.

The Department anticipated Bonn's objections by stressing non-recognition of the DDR in the first proposal and in the third as well, where declarations would be exchanged rather than a treaty formulated which Pankow would sign. The second recalled Bonn's pledge in 1954 not to acquire nuclear weapons for independent use. The fourth proposal—to establish committees for technical contacts between Bonn and Pankow—originated in Western discussions at the Geneva Conference of 1959, a proposal Bonn had approved at the time. The fifth—for a permanent Berlin conference at a lower level—also was considered at the 1959 conference.

Rusk planned to meet Dobrynin on April 16. Before the administration could begin a fourth stage of discussions with the Soviets, it needed to be certain that Bonn would not interpose strenuous objections, particularly to arms limitations. The State Department informed Bonn of the five proposals on April 10, requesting approval by April 12.[82] Unfortunately, the Department asked Bonn to respond favorably and gave little time for objections. In the Department's view, the United States had not changed its basic position, and Bonn had been kept informed of the discussions in Geneva.

In Bonn, however, Adenauer perceived enough change in emphasis to require new study of the proposals, and he also recognized that the Foreign Office needed more time than two days for a new study. Unfortunately, he had a written acceptance prepared and returned to the State Department within the alotted time. It appeared that Bonn acquiesced, and the Department seemed satisfied that Adenauer gave his approval.

On April 13, a press leak in Bonn publicized all five proposals, giving the Soviets therefore the substance of the proposals for the fourth stage before Rusk even had a chance to present them for confidential bargaining.[83] Originating in Bonn, the press report also

82. Originally, the Department set a twenty-four-hour deadline. It extended the deadline another twenty-four hours at Adenauer's request. Joseph Alsop, *The Washington Post*, May 11, 1962, p. A21.

83. *The New York Times*, April 14, 1962, p. 1.

conveyed an impression that the West Germans strongly opposed the proposals. Adenauer had not given this impression to the State Department the previous day. The Department assumed that the leak originated in Adenauer's parliamentary group, whom he had informed of the proposals.

The State Department, conceding the general accuracy of the report, did not regard the incident lightly. *The New York Times* stated that Rusk was "greatly upset." [84] In a letter to Foreign Minister Schroeder in Bonn, he accused Bonn of a breach of confidence.[85] On April 15, State protested to Ambassador Grewe in Washington that the incident appeared to be a deliberate attempt to disrupt the fourth stage of the Berlin negotiations,[86] particularly because Adenauer's reply to the proposals had not indicated serious opposition. Grewe apologized, denying, however, that the government in Bonn officially sanctioned the leak. Schroeder, responding to Rusk's letter, reiterated Grewe's statement that his government should not be held responsible. Adenauer said he considered the Secretary's accusation of a breach of confidence a personal affront.[87]

The incident of April 13 left the administration weakened and embarrassed because it could not construct a meaningful settlement without West German support. Rusk simply marked time when he met Dobrynin on April 16. To obtain Bonn's support after an incident unpleasant to both Washington and Bonn required a more discerning and less hasty approach by the State Department and a more candid statement of views by Bonn. The Department publicly indicated that Rusk would not make any proposals to Dobrynin which did not have West German approval. Kennedy, obviously angry with Bonn, insisted in no uncertain terms that negotiations continue, hopefully with a better understanding in Bonn.

Part of the difficulty in Bonn resulted from the composition of the new coalition government. Schroeder, replacing Von Brentano as foreign minister, looked more favorably on Berlin negotiations than his predecessor did. Adenauer, and Von Brentano now in the Bundestag, were at odds with Schroeder. The Foreign Office would say one thing only to have the Chancellery contradict it.

84. *Ibid.*, p. 2.
85. *Ibid.*, May 15, 1962, p. 1.
86. *The New York Times* used the term "sabotage" in describing the effect of the incident on the negotiations. *Ibid.*, April 14, 1962, p. 1.
87. *Ibid.*, May 15, 1962, p. 1.

Rusk met Dobrynin again on April 23 for a "procedural" meeting.[88] The Secretary stalled until he could coordinate his negotiating position with Schroeder during the NATO Foreign Ministers' conference at Athens in early May. His conversations with Schroeder produced the results Rusk wanted. Adenauer publicly agreed that Rusk should continue his meetings with Dobrynin, and Rusk assured Schroeder that no proposals would be made which were unacceptable to him.[89]

While Rusk talked with Schroeder—who represented one faction in the Bonn government—Von Brentano—representing the other faction—called on Kennedy to express his reservations about the administration's proposals. Von Brentano opposed the composition and function of an International Access Authority. He said Bonn would accept an international organization, provided the four powers occupying Berlin retained the responsibility they currently exercised for the access routes.[90] Von Brentano's visit to Washington suggested that the administration would have to qualify the proposals in some way to obtain consent of all factions in Bonn.

On May 7, Chancellor Adenauer revealed the full depth of the strain in relations between him and President Kennedy's administration. The undercurrent of dissatisfaction in the previous stages of negotiations pushed to the surface in the fourth stage. In West Berlin, he held a long press conference, predicting the failure of the Berlin negotiations.[91] For him to predict their failure was tantamount to assisting their demise. He specifically criticized the proposal for the International Access Authority. A thirteen-member authority would be unworkable, he claimed, because it would leave the power of decision in the hands of the three neutrals. Admitting that the United States did not propose to recognize the DDR formally through an international organization, he thought nonetheless that the East Germans might interpret the proposal as a form of diplomatic recognition. Since the proposal could be misconstrued, he preferred to bar membership for his government in order to prevent membership for the DDR. In ruling out membership for Pankow, he seemed

88. *Ibid.*, April 24, 1962, p. 1.
89. *Ibid.*, May 4, 1962, p. 1.
90. *Ibid.*, May 5, 1962, p. 1.
91. *Ibid.*, May 8, 1962, p. 1. Some observers thought his remarks merely showed his senility. But State Secretary Felix von Eckhardt reiterated them for the government on May 9. *The Bulletin,* Press and Information Office of the German Federal Government, 10 (May 15, 1962), 1-2.

aware that the proposal would lose what attractiveness it had to the Soviet Union.

The fourth stage of negotiations, the decisive stage, never really got under way. Bonn blocked it before it could begin, first by the incident of April 13 and then by Adenauer's press conference. On May 22, the German Foreign Office forwarded a memorandum to American Ambassador Dowling in Bonn, which in effect vetoed stage four and the negotiations.[92] It contained counterproposals that allowed for neither East German membership in the authority nor a decisive place for the neutrals.

Independently of the State Department's preparations for the fourth stage of negotiations and Bonn's reassertion of West German interests, Moscow showed signs of stiffening its position. From the high-water mark of April 20 when Khrushchev spoke of "glimmers of hope for agreement" [93] and of April 24 when Gromyko gave an optimistic report to the Supreme Soviet on the Geneva negotiations [94] to the *Pravda* statement of May 3 in which the Soviets accused the administration of withdrawing from a flexible position on Berlin,[95] the Soviet attitude noticeably changed. The Rusk-Dobrynin meeting of April 27 visibly illustrated a turning point.[96] Since both Khruschev and Gromyko in their statements emphasized withdrawal or alteration of the American garrison in West Berlin as the primary condition for an agreement, Rusk felt he had to stress to Dobrynin that he considered withdrawal out of the question.

The Soviets returned in the fourth stage, as in the second stage, to insist on the free city proposal. The Soviets shifted back to the narrow issues of the second stage of negotiations before Adenauer's

92. *The New York Times*, May 23, 1962, p. 1. For a useful history of Bonn's opposition to negotiations, see Jean Schwoebel, *Les Deux K, Berlin et la Paix* (Paris: René Julliard, 1963), pp. 133-194.

93. Khrushchev said: "I think there are some glimmers of hope for agreement. But the main question remains. It is the presence of Western occupation forces in West Berlin, to which we cannot agree. It cannot be held that agreement is possible without the solution of this question." *An Interview with Nikita Khrushchev by Gardner Cowles*, Moscow, April 20, 1962, p. 26.

94. *Pravda*, April 25, 1962, pp. 5-6.

95. *The New York Times*, May 4, 1962, p. 1.

96. *The New York Times* reported that this meeting was the most intensive of the three meetings to date. *Ibid.*, April 28, 1962, p. 1. Reports appeared, however, as early as April 12 that the Soviets would not make further overtures on the access issue unless the United States discussed military withdrawal from West Berlin. *Ibid.*, April 13, 1962, p. 1.

press conference on May 8.[97] Their broad approach at Geneva, linking arms limitations to Berlin, no longer appeared in evidence. They returned to the central issue of the occupation status of West Berlin. This shift in emphasis made the State Department's five proposals somewhat superfluous since the Department designed them to parallel the Soviet's expanded approach at Geneva. The premature disclosure of the proposals on April 13 informed the Soviets that concessions on the substance of the United States position would not be forthcoming. The administration proposed in an expanded version what it had always proposed since the first stage the previous September—a *modus vivendi* centering on the access issue. Through Dobrynin's inquiry with Rusk on April 27, the Soviets probably concluded that their proposals for an international authority and Central European disarmament had misfired.

Rolling out their propaganda guns, the Soviets pounded away at what they considered the central issue. On May 12, for example, *Izvestiia* accused Adenauer of disrupting the discussions and stated emphatically that the real question in the discussion concerned "turning West Berlin into a free, demilitarized city . . ." [98] In the Rusk-Dobrynin meeting of May 30, the Soviet ambassador dwelt on the "real question" *Izvestiia* described.[99]

A State Department official described the last Rusk-Dobrynin meeting, saying: "They really just keep going around in circles." [100] This description of that one meeting fits the entire record of the Berlin negotiations from September 1961 to June 1962. By June, they had come full circle. Expecting a solution in the fourth stage, the administration, much to its own dismay, witnessed the failure of its best efforts.

In late May, Secretary Rusk announced he would visit Bonn in

97. In the confusion of April and May, 1962, the view developed that the Federal Republic had vetoed the administration's proposals for a settlement, thus overlooking the veto of the Soviet Union as well. As late as December 26, 1963, Sidney Gruson wrote in *The New York Times:* "The American proposals were abandoned as a package because of West German objections which France supported." This impression obscures the Soviets' objection and belies the flaw in the proposals themselves, namely the assumption that a mutual desire to avoid war could be used to create a mutually acceptable *modus vivendi. Ibid.,* December 27, 1963, p. 3.

98. *Izvestiia,* May 21, 1962, p. 5.

99. *The New York Times,* May 31, 1962, p. 1.

100. *Ibid.,* p. 4.

June a few days before Chancellor Adenauer went to Paris.[101] He seemed to be hastening to dissuade Adenauer from going over completely to the French position before de Gaulle could talk to Adenauer. Rusk called in Hervé Alphand, the French ambassador in Washington, to discuss French objections to the administration's Berlin policy. These overtures to Bonn and Paris indicated that the administration had second thoughts about the damage to the alliance incurred by the negotiations. The Soviets decided to switch tracks again, and moved toward new military pressures.

In retrospect, Secretary Rusk admitted that the Berlin negotiations had been misleading. At his press conference on July 12, the following exchange took place:

> Q. Mr. Secretary, are you still sticking to your position that there is no sense talking about internationalization of access routes to Berlin until the Soviets acknowledge the Western rights to remain in West Berlin?
>
> A. Well, the situation on that is that one could talk about a variety of things, but if they are linked to an unacceptable point, such as the one you mentioned, then you could create misunderstandings by seeming to pick up that particular idea of access and talking about it in isolation.[102]

101. *Ibid.*, May 24, 1962, p. 10.
102. *The Department of State Bulletin*, 47 (July 30, 1962), 174.

CHAPTER 7

Khrushchev's Final Bid: The Missile Crisis

THE OUTCOME of the missile crisis terminated the four-year-old Berlin crisis. For the first time, Moscow's lack of caution deprived the administration of reasons for an unmixed response and provided compelling reasons for assuming greater risks. The missile crisis, like Pearl Harbor, temporarily settled an internal debate over administration policy which, if the Soviets had been more knowledgeable or clever or both, they might have preferred to leave unsettled.

Kennedy's willingness to take risks conveyed a message pertinent to Berlin, and possibly, to other issues beyond the immediate one in the Florida Strait. Khrushchev had to admit he miscalculated the determination of the administration to restrain the momentum of Soviet foreign policy. He learned indirectly, although he had been lectured about it many times, that the United States categorically opposed his whole Berlin project. Kennedy deflated Khrushchev's long-standing expectation of Moscow's capacity to extract concessions on Berlin using military power for political payoffs.

After the crisis, the administration no longer had to live in dread that Moscow would move toward war. But Kennedy was lucky, too. First, he learned of Soviet intentions through U-2 flights over the territory of Cuba early enough to intercept additional missile shipments on the high seas and to bring pressure to bear before all the installations in Cuba could be completed. The crisis might have been a very different one if the United States had not discovered the missiles as early as October 14. Second, the Soviets engaged in an out-of-area operation. If they had not been acting out of area, a military demonstration—particularly in an environment of accumulated miscalculation—might not have been sufficient. And third, the United States did not have to invade Cuba because Khrushchev perceived, finally, that Kennedy really would order an invasion. If Khrushchev had not been persuaded, his persistence would have created an extremely risk-laden situation with Moscow trying to get a cease-fire, Washington—with troops ashore—uncertain about moving or holding fire, Cubans firing at the invaders, and the rest of the world alarmed over the irresponsibility of the great powers.

Heavy irony characterizes the terminal phase of the Berlin crisis. Khrushchev pressed his quarrel with Kennedy more vigorously than ever, yet more tenuously because of the change in local setting. Khrushchev's difficulty derived from his decision to make his next move in the Berlin crisis in the Western hemisphere. He squandered what respect he had been able to elicit from Western public opinion in arguing, since 1958, that the Soviet Union generated the Berlin crisis to obtain recognition of the Eastern status quo. Cuba was obviously far removed from the Soviet security area in Eastern Europe. Khrushchev made a move impatiently, exposing at one stroke crude, over-reaching objectives, costing him political capital he had acquired in four years of conflict.

1. *The Berlin Context of the Missile Crisis*

By the summer of 1962, Khrushchev had failed to achieve his objectives in the crisis. Not for lack of trying, he had failed to budge the Western powers through negotiations or through pressure directly on Berlin. But he had learned something of Western reactions when the DDR successfully terminated the quadripartite status of East Berlin in August 1961, and when Soviet aircraft challenged air access to West Berlin in February and March 1962. In the first test, he learned what the administration's Berlin strategy omitted. In the second test, he tried to discover the level of risk the administration would tolerate for its commitment to West Berlin and, if possible, to decrease it. The results of both tests were ambiguous enough to require a further test.

The Cuban crisis was the third occasion of an East-West confrontation within fifteen months. Similar to the first test, it occurred in an area which the United States Berlin strategy had no provisions for, in Cuba geographically far removed from West Berlin. The Soviets did not risk a war by moving the Red Army into West Berlin or by destroying American military aircraft in the corridors. These moves would have flagrantly infringed the declared vital interests of the United States with little opportunity for diplomatic retreat. They chose a more oblique move. But as in the second test, the Soviets struck directly at the administration's tolerance for risk, relevant to Berlin as well as other areas, and tried to lower it drastically. Soviet missiles in Cuba placed Soviet nuclear power to better advantage for Khrushchev to use it to extract political concessions on Berlin. The Soviets, possibly, decided to construct a strawman for testing by analogy the willingness of the administration to take risks before they proposed a final round of negotiations in which the United States would be literally "under the gun" and during which their aims might also be accomplished by moves against West Berlin itself. If this assumption is correct, the danger and importance of the Cuban crisis resided as well in the even greater crisis to which Cuba was a planned prelude. In this sense, the third test of the Berlin strategy was a combination of the previous tests of omission and commission.

Throughout the summer and early autumn, the administration grew uneasy again, fully expecting the Soviets to move against West Berlin. Reportedly, it warned Moscow about the danger of "misjudging" the United States but it had little certainty or confidence that the Soviets were listening. As Khrushchev began to speak once more about the inevitability of a peace treaty, the summer of 1962 increasingly resembled the summer of 1961. The Soviets announced another series of nuclear tests on July 21 [1] and began to harden their missile bases to reduce vulnerability to surprise attack.[2]

Khrushchev proposed a menu of plans again to remove the Western garrisons from West Berlin [3] while Konev administered sporadic

1. *The New York Times*, July 23, 1961, p. 1. The 1961 series lasted from September to November 1961.
2. Hanson Baldwin, *ibid.*, July 26, 1962, p. 1.
3. *Ibid.*, July 11, 1962, p. 1; August 19, 1962, p. 1.

harassment in the air corridors.[4] When the Western powers persisted in proposing a quadripartite meeting in Berlin to prevent further incidents and atrocities at the wall,[5] Khrushchev responded by abolishing the office of the Soviet Commandant in Berlin.[6] His action carried the following message: If you have any complaint about the wall, address your inquiry to Pankow.

On September 5, Moscow declared in a diplomatic note: "The question is not one of discussing incidents and consultations. It is necessary, at long last, to liquidate the occupation regime in West Berlin on the basis of the signing of a German peace treaty, to liquidate the NATO military base, and to withdraw the troops of the three powers from West Berlin." [7]

The administration initially perceived the Soviet shipment of missiles to Cuba in the context of an imminent Berlin crisis. On September 8, Kennedy requested congressional authority to order to active duty 150,000 troops of the ready reserves. He expected to use these troops in a Berlin contingency.[8] Secretary of Defense McNamara inspected NATO forces at the central front September 27-28.[9] On October 10, Rusk reviewed the state of Berlin contingency planning with Schroeder and asked him for a "first hour" commitment making West German troops available for an antiblockade task force if and when a ground blockade went into effect.[10] As late as October 12, Attorney General Kennedy alerted the country to an impending "great crisis" over Berlin.[11]

As the Berlin and Cuban crises converged, the Soviets continued to call attention to Berlin. This factor could be discounted as a diversionary tactic except for certain Soviet intimations to the contrary. Through diplomatic and press sources, the Soviets stated they would insist on renewing negotiations for a German peace treaty.[12] In corridor conversations at the United Nations, they proposed adjusting Soviet influence in Cuba in exchange for concessions in

4. *Ibid.*, July 12, 1962, p. 2; July 24, 1962, p. 4.
5. See *The Department of State Bulletin*, 47 (July 10, 1962), 97-98; *ibid.* (August 27, 1962), pp. 319-320.
6. *The New York Times*, August 23, 1962, p. 1.
7. *The Department of State Bulletin*, 47 (October 15, 1962), 559.
8. *The New York Times*, September 8, 1962, p. 1.
9. *Ibid.*, September 29, 1962, p. 1.
10. *Ibid.*, October 11, 1962, p. 1.
11. *Ibid.*, October 12, 1962, p. 1.
12. *Ibid.*, October 14, 1962, p. 8.

American influence in West Berlin.[13] Rusk went out of his way to reject this linkage saying: "You cannot support freedom in one place by surrendering freedom in another." [14] The most important evidence of ultimate Soviet intentions appeared on September 11 when the Soviet Union indicated that it would not propose new Berlin negotiations until after the congressional elections in the United States in November.[15] In retrospect, the Soviet schedule for missile emplacements would have been completed by mid-December.[16] If new Berlin negotiations had been arranged after the elections, they would have been conducted under severely adverse conditions for the administration.

Parallel to an imminent Berlin crisis, the Soviet Union and Cuba implemented an agreement for the introduction of nuclear weapons into Cuba. Probably when Raul Castro, Cuban Minister of the Armed Forces, visited Moscow in early July, the Soviets prevailed upon him to accept the installation of Soviet missiles on Cuban soil.[17] In late July, the Soviets accelerated the routine delivery of military equipment and personnel to Cuba. By late August, *The New York Times* reported that 3,000–5,000 Soviet military and civilian technicians were busy constructing coastal and air defense installations.[18] On September 2, the Soviets admitted that they had agreed to supply Cuba greater stocks of arms and military training.[19]

On September 11, Moscow tried to discourage any interference with their Cuba trade, issuing a blunt warning that any attempt to prevent access to Cuba for Soviet ships might produce a war nobody could possibly desire. They objected that the presence of Soviet military equipment and personnel in Cuba could be a provocation to any other power.[20] Premier Fidel Castro stridently warned of dire

13. *Ibid.*, October 15, 1962, p. 1.
14. See his press interview in *The Department of State Bulletin*, 47 (October 22, 1962), 598.
15. *The New York Times*, September 12, 1962, p. 1.
16. By October 28, 42 medium range ballistic missiles (MRBM's) were deployed. Judging by the ships that turned back, more missiles were enroute. The intermediate range ballistic missiles (IRBM's) would have been operational by mid-December. Albert and Roberta Wohlstetter, "Controlling the Risks in Cuba," *Adelphi Papers*, Number 17, Institute for Strategic Studies, London, April 1962, p. 11.
17. Cf. *The New York Times*, July 3, 1962, p. 3.
18. *Ibid.*, August 25, 1962, p. 1.
19. *Ibid.*, September 3, 1962, p. 1.
20. *Ibid.*, September 12, 1962, p. 1.

results if the United States intervened. "We are not sardines! The shark should not mistake us to be, because this time it could well be his last mistake." [21] On October 18, Gromyko met at his own request with Kennedy. Gromyko emphasized the urgency of a German peace treaty and underplayed Moscow's agreement with Cuba, calling the increasing Soviet involvement there a "defensive" matter.[22] Generally, the Soviet Union pressed its case on Berlin and simultaneously disclaimed the significance of its actions in Cuba.

Since July, the administration had suspected a discrepancy between Soviet official disclaimers and Soviet intentions in Cuba. According to Arthur Schlesinger, the Central Intelligence Agency alerted Kennedy in "late July" to the surge of activity in Cuban harbors. The intelligence community perceived Soviet actions as a concentrated attempt to bolster Cuban coastal defenses for repelling external attack.[23] Kennedy took note of the growing Soviet presence in Cuba at his August 20 press conference. On September 4 and 13, he issued public reports establishing criteria for what the administration would and would not tolerate. The defensive type of military equipment the Soviets had already shipped to Cuba would be tolerated. But he declared that "this country will do whatever must be done to protect its own security and that of its allies," if an offensive type of military equipment appeared in Cuba.[24]

By mid-September the lines were drawn for the October confrontation. The Soviet Union had declared that interference with Soviet access to Cuba would risk nuclear war. The United States had declared that it would do "whatever must be done" if offensive weapons, intolerable for its own security, appeared in Cuba.

2. Cuba and the Military Balance

At the time of the missile crisis, interpretations varied widely about the reasons for the Soviets' deployment of a number of their

21. *Ibid.*, September 12, 1962, p. 16.
22. *Ibid.*, October 27, 1962, p. 1.
23. Schlesinger, *op. cit.*, pp. 797-798. On the theoretical and practical problems of intelligence involved in discerning the significance of Soviet activity prior to the conclusive disclosure on October 14, see Roberta Wohlstetter, "Cuba and Pearl Harbor: Hindsight and Foresight," *Foreign Affairs*, 43 (July 1965), 691-707; Klaus Knorr, "Failures in National Intelligence Estimates: The Case of the Cuban Missiles," *World Politics*, 16 (April 1964), 455-467.
24. For the two warnings, see *The Department of State Bulletin*, 47 (September 24, 1962), 450; *ibid.* (October 1, 1962), pp. 481-482.

most sophisticated weapon systems to Cuba. The same schools of thought who argued about the nature of Soviet actions in the "deadline crisis" of 1958–1959 reappeared. Some observers read the deployment in the context of Cuba's defensive security requirements. Others emphasized the effects on American security and on the external repercussions of the missile deployments. Khrushchev did not clarify his motives when he argued in December 1962, first, that he deployed the missiles to deter an American invasion of Cuba and, then, that he removed them to deter an American invasion.[25] Castro has offered contradictory explanations of the crisis, on one occasion stating that the Soviets said they needed missile bases in Cuba "to reinforce socialism on the international scale," on another claiming that he requested the missiles.[26] The assumption in this study is that the Soviet move, as in the "deadline crisis" of 1958, simultaneously strengthened a Soviet ally and adversely affected the interests of the West—in the Cuban case, the military balance between the United States and the Soviet Union.

Those who viewed the Cuban missile crisis primarily in the Cuban context believed that the security, power, and prestige of the Castro regime finally would have been consolidated with Castro's acquisition of the capacity to threaten the United States with destruction and, therefore, to prevent any further invasion. Castro had feared an American invasion ever since he had expropriated American property and turned to the Soviet Union for economic support in 1959 and 1960. And they later pointed out that even though Khrushchev failed, Kennedy pledged not to invade Cuba as a result of the missile crisis. This pledge, they argued, altered the status quo to Castro's benefit.[27] As a matter of fact, however, Kennedy made his pledge a conditional one granted in exchange for on-site verification. When

25. See his speech to the Supreme Soviet of December 12, 1962, Reprinted in N. S. Khrushchev, *The Present International Situation and the Foreign Policy of the Soviet Union* (New York: Crosscurrents Press, 1963), pp. 11, 15.

26. He made the first statement to Claude Julien of *Le Monde* in March 1963, the second to Herbert L. Matthews in October, 1963. Arnold Horelick inclined to the *Le Monde* interview as the more accurate of the two. Castro affirmed the first explanation in March 1965. Horelick and Rush, *op. cit.*, pp. 134-135.

27. Council for Correspondence Newsletter, Number 21 (October 1962). Although he stood with the school of thought which emphasized the effects on American security, Robert Crane reached the same conclusion. See his "The Cuban Crisis: A Strategic Analysis of American and Soviet Policy," *Orbis*, 6 (Winter, 1963), 547-548.

Castro refused inspection in October 1962, Kennedy's pledge automatically terminated.[28]

In November 1962, *The New Republic* argued that the missile sites were not militarily significant because of their vulnerability to air attack from the United States.[29] Presumably, however, the Soviets did not believe the sites would be destroyed after installation or they would not have been constructed. Left intact, Soviet missiles and aircraft in Cuba would have constituted a significant threat to the continental defenses of the United States. First, they would have hobbled American nuclear forces, if those forces ever had to attack the Soviet Union, thus complicating a United States strike by a threat from the rear. They would have improved the capability of a Soviet attack because of the shorter range required to reach target. Proximity significantly enhances missile accuracy, reliability, and payload.[30]

Second, what began as a relatively small number of Soviet weapons in Cuba could have been enlarged in the absence of a United States reaction over time to become an imposing threat. Before the Soviets withdrew, American intelligence counted 42 MRBM's and 24–32 IRBM's in Cuba. The number of MRBM's available in the Soviet inventory—although every one probably would not have been shipped to Cuba—totaled 7,500, to say nothing of more IRBM's and Ilyushin 28 bomber aircraft.[31]

More to the point than a potential absolute growth is, third, the consideration that in 1962 the Soviet ICBM inventory was considerably smaller than the United States inventory of strategic nuclear weapons, so that every MRBM or IRBM emplaced in Cuba quickly and substantially added to the Soviet ICBM inventory in terms of the numbers of missiles targeted on the United States. The United States had 96 Polaris missiles and "dozens" of land-based ICBM's, in addition to 600 heavy bombers and attack carrier forces.[32] The Institute of Strategic Studies estimated the Soviets had a force, at the time,

28. Sorensen, *op. cit.*, p. 721.

29. Editorial, *The New Republic*, 147 (November 3, 1962), 4.

30. The Wohlstetters, *op. cit.*, p. 11.

31. *Ibid.*, p. 12.

32. United States Department of Defense, *Department of Defense News Release*, No. 1173-61, Roswell Gilpatric, Address before the Business Council, Hot Springs, Va., October 21, 1961.

of 75 ICBM's.[33] Stewart Alsop reported 100.[34] After the crisis, Khrushchev stated that the Soviet inventory included 80–120 ICBM's.[35] The initial small complement of missiles in Cuba had a disproportionate effect relative to the total inventory of missiles capable of reaching the United States.[36] For this one reason, if for no other, the missile deployment was militarily significant.

The President seemed more concerned that the increment in Cuba to Soviet military power would have far-reaching political repercussions. In his first full-dress meeting on the crisis, he listed three possible political advantages to the Soviets: improving their standing in the world communist movement, strengthening their hand in Berlin, and generally diminishing American prestige abroad.[37]

Further, the administration believed that Khrushchev needed another great test of wills if he expected his effort since 1958 over Berlin to pay off. Throughout the summer and early fall of 1962, officials in Washington sensed that he still did not believe he could not succeed. Kennedy himself sensed this need and belief of his opponent, as he observed the situation of 1962 deteriorating like that of 1961. September 1962 was another low for relations between Moscow and Washington. Worse, this time Kennedy could not press for negotiations to improve the atmosphere, since he had tried and failed with that option between September 1961 and June 1962. Whatever satisfaction the administration derived from Khrushchev's cancellation of the deadline in October 1961 evaporated as the administration dug foxholes ready for the next Soviet offensive. Kennedy's early worries about an inadvertent war returned as Soviet verbal activity directed at Berlin intensified. The discovery of the missiles confirmed his worst fears.

3. *The Third Strategic Test and the Cuba Strategy*

On October 14, a U-2 plane produced film showing the first telltale markings of MRBM sites in Cuba. The intelligence community

33. *The Communist Bloc and the Western Alliances, the Military Balance, 1962–1963*, The Institute of Strategic Studies, London, 1963, p. 3.
34. "Our New Strategy," *The Saturday Evening Post*, December 1, 1962, p. 16.
35. Horelick and Rush, *op. cit.*, p. 99n.
36. The Wohlstetters, *op. cit.*, p. 11.
37. Schlesinger, *op. cit.*, p. 811.

quickly reversed earlier estimates that the Soviets would be acting out of character if they deployed offensive missile systems in Cuba. The Soviet Union had never tried to build foreign bases so distant from its own territory. But after October 14, the evidence multiplied that Moscow was acting in a way the intelligence establishment considered rash and exceedingly dangerous. One could discern the inhibiting effect that this rash behavior had on the administration in the caution and forebearance it used to give the Soviets the opportunity to regain their good sense. Since Moscow did act rashly, the administration did not know for certain that Moscow would react cautiously to countermeasures. Intelligence analysts understood Moscow's action in August 1961, perceiving that, from the Soviet point of view, the refugee traffic had to be terminated. And they knew full well that Moscow probed in the air corridors during the winter of 1962 to see what the United States reaction to harassment would be. They did not believe that these two encounters were irrational considering the circumstances. But they could not adequately explain Moscow's behavior in Cuba.

At least three factors assisted Soviet calculations. First, the Soviets received all the wrong signals. Horelick and Rush note that Soviet activity in Cuba rose steadily after the Bay of Pigs incident in April 1961, proceeding through discernible phases.[38] Pankow constructed the Berlin wall in phases, with the Soviets probably watching the administration's response to each phase. Similarly, in Cuba the Soviets shipped basic conventional weapons in 1961 and 1962 with no extraordinary reaction from Washington. Next, they shipped more elaborate equipment in 1962—coastal patrol boats, motor torpedo boats armed with short range guided missiles, and MIG aircraft. Finally, SA-2 surface-to-air missiles requiring Soviet technicians arrived in August 1962. The administration indicated that it knew of the second- and third-phase shipments when President Kennedy publicly made a distinction between "defensive" and "offensive" systems. Thus, a pattern of unobstructed arms shipment existed, facilitating the Soviets' decision to introduce strategic weapons.[39]

Second, Moscow handled the shipment of MRBM's arriving early in September with great secrecy. The Soviets became more cautious as the importance of the weapons increased. They resorted to night-

38. Horelick and Rush, *op. cit.*, p. 143.
39. *Ibid.*, pp. 143-144.

time unloading and transportation of the SA-2's and MRBM's. Third, speed carried the Soviets across the threshold Kennedy warned them about and into the fourth phase of operational MRBM and IRBM deployment. They anticipated that the offensive systems would be emplaced before the administration could react.[40] In a very few days after October 14, several sites became operational and many more grew rapidly under construction. The tactics of deployment—the success of previous phases, secrecy on arrival, and speed in installation—must have increased the Soviets' confidence in building foreign bases in Cuba.

The Soviets probably thought that if the United States wanted to remove the missiles from Cuba it would have to invade the island, and they did not believe the administration would accept the necessary risks an invasion entailed. When the missile crisis approached a climax, the invasion issue did prove decisive, as Khrushchev admitted afterward. Kennedy's demonstrated reluctance to risk a direct entanglement with Castro in the 1961 Bay of Pigs fiasco probably sustained Khrushchev's hunch that the administration would not invade.

Khrushchev's experience in the Berlin crisis allowed considerable leeway to stage another round. From this point of view, the strategic setting for the missiles in Cuba resembled the setting for the United States confronted in the defense of West Berlin. To defend West Berlin with conventional military forces, the United States had to act as aggressor, invading the DDR if necessary to achieve its objective. With the Soviets in Cuba armed with nuclear weapons, the United States would also have to invade and accept the risks of nuclear war. If the Soviets could structure the situation to favor them, they probably felt confident that the administration would decline to invade, thus compensating for Moscow's problem of operating at great distances from home territory.

The United States—not only the Soviet Union—acted out of character in responding suddenly and massively to the missile deployments. Kennedy provided Moscow with verbal warnings on September 4 and 13 that "offensive" systems would be intolerable for American security. Judging by actions rather than words, the administration did not act—to this point—either in Berlin or in Cuba in a way which even approached the magnitude of its eventual

40. *Ibid.*, pp. 145, 147-149.

response in the Florida Strait. The Soviets, dumbfounded at the energy and movement of the administration from October 22–29, had not even taken the precaution to prepare a fallback position. They floundered for thirteen hours after the President's speech disclosing the missiles in Cuba. Soviet embassies had no instructions. Later in the week the front page of *Izvestiia* carried a statement about the Soviet response to American actions which conflicted with another statement on the inside page on the same subject.[41] In the previous absence of American intervention, the Soviets simply had not been aware they—the Soviets—were acting out of character. After the administration established a naval blockade, four more days elapsed before the Soviets seemed to realize that the United States seriously meant to invade the island. They improvised a way out of the impasse with the aid of U Thant and the forebearance of the administration. Kennedy deliberately weighed his alternatives by trying to anticipate how Khrushchev would react to each one.[42]

In the week between receiving the initial "hard" evidence of offensive weapons in Cuba and Kennedy's public reaction, the administration constructed the higher-risk response it previously declared it would be willing to employ. It borrowed heavily from the military side of the Berlin strategy. Indeed, the Berlin strategy of 1961 served as a model for the Cuba planning. Kennedy still left a wide margin, nevertheless, for negotiating a way out of the crisis. The administration quickly engaged in a very exacting "process of analysis," sifting alternatives and estimating reactions which Under Secretary of State Ball later described as follows:

> During the epic week of day-and-night effort that preceded the President's speech on October 22, we struggled to solve the problem thrust upon us by applying the time-honored methods of comparison, debate, and analysis to test the virtues and disadvantages of first one and then another possible solution, with all their innumerable shades and variants.
> This process entailed canvassing each possibility, grinding considerations against each other, plotting out each apparent course of action with its possible consequences, step by step. It involved estimates as to the possible reaction of the Soviet

41. *Ibid.*, p. 129n.
42. Weintal and Bartlett, *op. cit*, pp. 67-68.

Union to each action we might take. In what seemed endless permutations it then meant devising possible counters to each hypothetical Soviet reaction.[43]

The results of these deliberations appeared in the President's speech. The President spoke to the nation on October 22.[44] October 20 and 21 were consumed by an elaborate orchestration of diplomatic notices and military moves in order that, even as he spoke, a broad and far-reaching effort would be acquiring real momentum. The speech bore a striking resemblance to the President's address of July 25, 1961, setting out a strategy for the missile crisis analogous to the Berlin strategy.

First, he specified the threat to the United States as the presence in Cuba of MRBM and IRBM missiles, and Ilyushin 28 bomber aircraft at sites being constructed by the Soviets "under a cloak of secrecy and deception." "The purpose of these bases can be none other than to provide a nuclear strike capability against the Western Hemisphere." Although the immediate threat emanated from Cuba, Kennedy again set the threat in a worldwide context, specifically linking Cuba to West Berlin. The President said: "Any hostile move anywhere in the world against the safety and freedom of peoples to whom we are committed—including in particular the brave people of West Berlin—will be met by whatever action is needed." [45] The administration felt vulnerable, because if it took decisive action in Cuba, the Soviet Union could easily retaliate against West Berlin.[46] Kennedy did not say so, but the United States had pressed an organized force for an *autobahn* probe into being. After an interview with the President, Reston wrote that the administration had prepared plans for a counterblockade of West Berlin. *The New York Times* reported on October 24: "Berlin held the attention of the administration throughout the preparation of the Cuban blockade."

43. George Ball, "Lawyers and Diplomats," Address before the New York Lawyers' Association, New York City, New York, December 13, 1962, *The Department of State Bulletin*, 47 (December 31, 1962), 989. See Elie Abel's indispensable *The Missile Crisis* (J. B. Lippincott Co., 1966), chapters 3–6 and the posthumous, authoritative account by Robert Kennedy, *Thirteen Days* (New York: W. W. Norton and Company, Inc., 1969).

44. John F. Kennedy, "The Soviet Threat to the Americas," *The Department of State Bulletin*, 47 (November 12, 1962), 716-720.

45. *Ibid.*, p. 718.

46. Sorensen, *op. cit.*, pp. 680, 683, 686, 687, 689, 694.

Officials acknowledged they were ready for a two-front showdown.[47]

Second, Kennedy declared that any use of Cuban-based nuclear weapons against any nation in the Western hemisphere would be regarded as "an attack by the Soviet Union on the United States requiring a full retaliatory response upon the Soviet Union." Identifying the threat exclusively with Soviet missiles in Cuba, it followed that the administration treated the crisis strictly as a Soviet-American affair, not a United States-Cuban affair. The President's statement also underlined the administration's tactically advantageous position in the crisis. It could afford to be bolder in Cuba than in West Berlin because Cuba lay only ninety miles across the Florida Strait from the continental military establishment of the United States. By contrast, the Soviets were handicapped, maintaining shipping routes over an extensive distance of open sea. The greatest advantage, however, lay in the timing of the President's speech. He learned of the shipments before they were completed, before the Soviet Union could compensate for distance by shifting the burden of invasion onto its opponent. Surprising the Soviets before they completed the missile installations, the President fixed them with the risks of responding to a *fait accompli*.

Third, he announced he would order the Navy to impose "a strict quarantine" to prevent further shipment of offensive weapons to Cuba. Since the quarantine could not reach the weapons already shipped, he ordered, in addition, increased aerial surveillance of the construction sites, threatening "further action" if work continued. He wanted to compel the Soviets to withdraw the missiles altogether. This portion of the President's speech drew upon earlier Berlin planning by analogy. The naval blockade—read *autobahn* probe—manifested the administration's determination to counter a Soviet thrust. And it gave the Soviets time to turn their ships around because it would not go into effect until October 23, twenty-four hours after the President spoke. Soviet ships would not undergo any search or seizure unless they made an approach to Cuba. The President's advisers also considered an air strike, but military estimates of the requirements for this option caused it to be confused with the invasion option. For this reason, Kennedy did not feel certain that, without an invasion to accompany it, an air strike could destroy all

47. *The New York Times*, October 23, 1964, p. 19; *ibid.*, October 24, 1962, p. 1.

the missiles. The blockade force consisted of sixteen destroyers, three cruisers, an antisubmarine aircraft carrier, and six auxiliaries. One hundred fifty other ships were on station in the vicinity of Cuba.[48] The use of conventional military forces raised the nuclear threshold. The administration could elect a blockade, air strike, or invasion option and destroy the missile sites in a completely non-nuclear operation. The "further action" Kennedy spoke of seemed credible because of the great numbers of forces being readied. A naval task force bearing ten battalions of Marines operated in the vicinity on "maneuvers." Three Marine battalions were deployed to the Guantanamo naval base at the eastern end of Cuba supported by air and surface units to prevent retaliation against the base. The Army assembled an invasion force of 100,000 troops, ordering an additional 10,000–20,000 to remain in the base area in Florida. The Air Force flew additional tactical air squadrons to Florida bases. McNamara later testified that the force at hand consisted of "several hundred thousand men ready to invade Cuba." [49]

Fourth, Kennedy urged the Soviets toward a line of diplomatic retreat. Having presented Khrushchev with a *fait accompli*, he pressed him to acknowledge the advantages the administration held to halt and reverse base construction. He indicated the United States would accept a negotiated settlement, stressing, however, that he would not restrict his "freedom of action" while negotiating. In other words, he intended to sustain pressure, continuing the quarantine and surveillance until Moscow removed the missiles. The Security Council through the American and Soviet ambassadors to the United Nations in New York provided a working channel of communication to arrange a settlement.[50]

48. Sorensen, *op. cit.*, p. 708.
49. Horelick and Rush, *op. cit.*, p. 153n. See also Kaufmann, *op. cit.*, pp. 271-272; Schlesinger, *op. cit.*, p. 803; *The New York Times*, October 22, 1962, p. 16; October 23, 1962, p. 1.
50. As soon as the President finished speaking, Ambassador Stevenson introduced a draft resolution which read in part:
"*The Security Council*. . . .
1. *Calls* as a provisional measure under Article 40 for the immediate dismantling and withdrawal from Cuba of all missiles and other offensive weapons;
2. *Authorizes and requests* the Acting Secretary General to dispatch to Cuba a United Nations observer corps to assure and report on compliance with this resolution;
3. *Calls* for termination of the measures of quarantine directed against

Analogous to the Berlin strategy, the administration's moves over Cuba fitted an escalation strategy, beginning—in this case—with a naval blockade. Failure of the blockade to convince the Soviets—not only to turn their ships back, but to reverse their entire operation— would lead, eventually, to a combined air strike and invasion. If the Soviets moved against West Berlin, escalation in Europe would match escalation in Cuba. At any one point along the way, either in Cuba or in West Berlin, the administration expected to activate Moscow's desire to avoid war and, therefore, to halt and reverse the spiral of actions.

4. From Miscalculation to Calculation

Moscow responded ambiguously to the President's address. In a statement the next day it simply condemned the blockade, giving no indication whether or how it would retaliate.[51] Signs of confusion appeared in Moscow.[52]

The Soviets had three choices. They could reverse their operation in Cuba in line with Kennedy's insistent demands and negotiate a way out. Second, they could pause and delay further missile shipments, playing for time to complete the bases under construction. In this option, they could salvage a portion of their operation and perhaps still influence the administration with the missiles available in Cuba.[53] Third, the Soviets could challenge the blockade, as Khrushchev asserted, with submarine warfare.[54] This course had the least chance of success given American naval preponderance in the vicinity of Cuba.

---

military shipments to Cuba upon United Nations certification of compliance with Paragraph 1;

4. *Urgently recommends* that the United States of America and the Union of Soviet Socialist Republics confer promptly on measures to remove the existing threat to the security of the Western Hemisphere and the peace of the world, and report thereon to the Security Council." (Italics theirs) *The Department of State Bulletin*, 47 (November 13, 1962), 724.

51. *The New York Times*, October 24, 1962, p. 1.

52. Schlesinger, *op. cit.*, p. 820.

53. Roman Kolkowicz discusses the marshals' pressure on Khrushchev during the crisis, *Conflicts in Soviet Party-Military Relations, 1962–1963*, RM-3760, Rand Corporation, Santa Monica, California, August 1963, pp. 9-15.

54. On October 24, Khrushchev invited William Knox, President of Westinghouse on business in Moscow, to an interview, informing him that Soviet submarines would attack any American ship interferring with Soviet vessels on the high seas. *The New York Times Magazine*, November 18, 1962, p. 32.

To achieve a semblance of their immediate objective—a possibility the blockade alone did not preclude—the Soviets elected to delay further shipments and to accelerate base construction. To succeed, construction had to be completed before the administration marshaled invasion forces in Florida. While the Soviets retained as much ambiguity about their reaction as possible, their decision became evident after October 24 when the ships bearing military equipment to Cuba stopped dead in the water [55] while work on the missile installations continued.[56] The crisis grew into a race between the Soviets striving to activate the bases and the administration gathering the means to remove them.[57]

In awaiting Moscow's reaction to the blockade, the administration granted the Soviets more time to reverse themselves by ordering the blockade line moved closer to Cuba, therefore delaying the necessity for interception.[58] Soviet ships turned back on October 24.[59] Ambassador Adlai Stevenson in the Security Council continued to hammer away at the necessity for negotiations. American naval units let a Soviet tanker and chartered dry cargo ship through—after identification as non-missile-bearing ships—on October 25.[60] The Soviet diplomatic corps now had instructions to inquire about opportunities for a settlement, although Moscow appeared unwilling to halt base construction.

On October 26, Khrushchev—continuing the private correspondence Kennedy initiated in September 1961—sent off a letter to Kennedy, urging him to abandon the blockade to prevent the crisis from degenerating into war. He stated that the shipments had been com-

55. *Ibid.*, October 25, 1962, p. 1.

56. Work at the sites progressed under the steady glare of White House publicity. See the White House statement in *The Department of State Bulletin*, 47 (November 12, 1962), p. 740.

57. Mikoyan continued to deny that Soviet offensive weapons were present in Cuba. Schlesinger, *op. cit.*, p. 820. CIA Director John McCone estimated that all the MRBM's in Cuba would be operational by October 27. Sorensen, *op. cit.*, p. 711.

58. Graham Allison raises a question about whether the blockade line actually did move closer to Cuba, since the Navy did not want to place its aircraft in range of Soviet MIG's in Cuba. "Conceptual Models and the Cuban Missile Crisis," *The American Political Science Review*, 63 (September 1969), 706-707.

59. Schlesinger, *op. cit.*, p. 818. Sorensen indicated that a Soviet ship caused some confusion when it approached the blockade line on October 27. *Op. cit.*, p. 713.

60. Sorensen, *op. cit.*, p. 710.

pleted—a false allegation. Then, he proposed a way out of the crisis: if Kennedy rescinded the blockade and agreed not to invade Cuba, Khrushchev said the Soviet Union would have no need to retain the missiles in Cuba.[61]

Kennedy could interpret this letter to read either that Khrushchev offered a conditional settlement, or that he wanted the administration to reverse its course without agreeing to withdraw the missiles. On the same day, Soviet Ambassador Valerian Zorin in New York submitted the same proposal to U Thant. Also that day, Aleksander Fomin, a Soviet embassy official believed to be the highest KGB (Soviet secret police) official in Washington, proposed to John Scali—the American Broadcasting Company's State Department correspondent—that the Soviets would withdraw the missiles under United Nations inspection if the administration pledged publicly not to invade Cuba. Fomin's proposal clarified Khrushchev's. Fomin asked Scali to relay the proposal to the State Department. In a very few hours, Scali reported Rusk's reply to Fomin. Rusk replied favorably, welcoming a settlement, but he wanted the Soviet Union to understand that, as matters stood at the moment, the United States would have to invade sometime after October 28.

On October 27, the arms race continued unabated. The Soviets destroyed a U-2 overflying their Cuban installations, giving some officials in the administration the impression that the Soviets intended to persist toward a military confrontation.[62] Kennedy received another Khrushchev letter with another proposal: Khrushchev offered to remove Soviet bases in Cuba if the United States dismantled its bases in Turkey—to exchange a base for a base. This letter baffled the administration. Theodore Sorensen believed it came from the Soviet Foreign Ministry rather than from Khrushchev's own hand. Roman Kolkowicz suggests that it represented pressure from the Soviet marshals. The military press consistently took a tougher line during the crisis than *Pravda* and *Izvestiia*, the CPSU and government newspapers respectively. *Krasnaia Zvezda*, organ of the Defense Ministry, expounded editorially on the linkage between bases in Cuba and Turkey.[63] In any event, the administration perceived the proposal

---

61. Schlesinger, *op. cit.*, p. 826. This letter is still unpublished.

62. *Ibid.*, p. 827.

63. Kolkowicz, *op. cit.*, pp. 14-15. See also Kolkowicz, *The Soviet Military and the Communist Party* (Princeton: Princeton University Press, 1967), pp. 210-214.

to trade bases as a case of blackmail intended to weaken Turkey's links with NATO.[64]

Kennedy responded with a letter to Khrushchev, deliberately ignoring Khrushchev's letter of the day in order to single out promising passages in his letter of the previous day—October 26. Kennedy stated that if Khrushchev ordered work stopped on the missile sites and if the United Nations verified stoppage, he would be prepared to negotiate a settlement as Khrushchev proposed: no invasion in exchange for withdrawal of the missiles.[65] Stepping up pressure to indicate the imminence of an invasion, the administration announced that it had called twenty-four troop carrier squadrons of the Air Reserve to active duty.[66] Stevenson warned that the United States would, indeed, take military action against the bases unless construction halted.[67] Scali, because of the setbacks on October 27, accused his embassy contact of deception.

Sorensen believed that Kennedy would have tried to delay the invasion, hoping to give Moscow all the time conceivably possible to come around to a settlement. The Soviets' expectation of an immediate invasion, however, ran ahead of the President's decisions. The stress a State Department briefing officer placed on Kennedy's "further action will be justified" statement in the President's speech of October 22 resulted in boxcar headlines in the American press forecasting an air strike or invasion.[68] Moreover, the Attorney General warned Ambassador Dobrynin that Moscow had to give immediate assurances of withdrawing the missiles if it wanted to prevent an invasion.[69] And, as noted, Rusk through Scali stressed the urgency of a positive Soviet response to Fomin. In the Berlin crisis during 1961, the administration's desire for a settlement got in the way of the message Kennedy tried to convey through partial mobilization. In the missile crisis, a similar contradiction appeared toward the end of the week of crisis, as the eagerness for a settlement naturally rushed in after Kennedy's bold speech on Monday, October 22. This problem did not become acute in the missile crisis because the Soviets per-

---

64. Sorensen, *op. cit.*, p. 714.
65. For the texts of the American and Soviet letters of October 27, see *The Department of State Bulletin*, 47 (November 12, 1962), pp. 741-743.
66. *The New York Times*, October 28, 1962, p. 1.
67. *Ibid.*
68. Sorensen, *op. cit.*, p. 712.
69. *Ibid.*

ceived the invasion to be more imminent than the administration actually planned it to be. Kennedy later noted that Moscow's overreaction provided him with an unexpected advantage.[70]

The Soviets, finally convinced on October 28 that a significant striking force of missiles would not be made operational before an invasion occurred and that Kennedy's proposal of the 27th for a settlement offered an acceptable way out, relented. Time expired. The U-2's premature discovery of the sites stole success from Moscow. If the Soviets had been able to continue a few more weeks, the positions of Moscow and Washington would have been reversed, leaving the administration with the choice of invading or settling for a *fait accompli*, neither one a desirable course of action. The invasion warnings worked because the administration, in conveying the warnings early enough, incurred lesser risks than the Soviets did in persisting, having their military equipment destroyed, and Castro brought down. To deter an invasion of Cuba without abandoning their bases, the Soviets might have reiterated their September 11 threat of nuclear war, but this threat could only have served to increase their risks without measurably reducing the possibility of an invasion.

On December 12, Khrushchev confirmed the decisiveness of the invasion issue in the Kremlin decision:

> However, the Government of the United States of America continued to aggravate the situation. United States militaristic forces were pushing developments towards an attack on Cuba. On the morning of October 27 information from the Cuban comrades and from other sources, which bluntly said that the invasion would be effected in the next two or three days, reached us. We assessed the messages received as a signal of alarm. And this was a well-founded alarm.[71]

On October 28, Khrushchev informed Kennedy that he had ordered construction to halt.[72] For all practical purposes, the Soviet Union followed the lines of diplomatic retreat recommended by the administration.[73] Khrushchev accepted Kennedy's condition that withdrawal

---

70. *Ibid.*, p. 712.

71. Nikita S. Khrushchev, *The Present International Situation and the Foreign Policy of the Soviet Union*, pp. 14-15.

72. This letter was published in *The Department of State Bulletin*, 47 (November 12, 1962), 743-745.

73. In another proposed Security Council resolution, the administration sug-

of the missiles should be verified by the United Nations. In accepting a verification procedure, the Soviets knew well enough that Castro would not tolerate any inspection of Cuban territory.[74] In addition, they themselves moved with great haste to transport the missiles and associated equipment out of Cuba to avoid inspection. Thus, U Thant's meeting with Castro to arrange verification proved fruitless.[75] The Soviets left their bomber aircraft in Cuba; but a few weeks later, at the administration's insistence, they finally removed them as well.[76] On November 20, the administration lifted the naval blockade.[77]

5. The Decisive Issue for Khrushchev

In more than one account of the missile crisis, the blockade is rightly viewed with great satisfaction. For example, Sorensen suggests: "A minimum of force had obtained a maximum gain. The value of conventional strength in the nuclear age had been underlined as never before." [78] The role of the invasion warnings in the crisis is less distinct. Sorensen was less impressed with the possibility of invasion, perhaps because he felt Kennedy was not as immediately prepared to invade as Khrushchev thought. Sorensen implies that Kennedy considered an invasion more a court of last resort which he fortunately avoided.[79] According to Schlesinger, Kennedy worried that an invasion would begin an inexorable process of escalation.[80]

---

gested a three-step program to remove the missiles, each step to be verified by United Nations observers. The first step provided for halting base construction; the second, dismantling the installations constructed; and the third, prohibiting further missile shipments. *The New York Times,* October 27, 1962, p. 6.

74. In his letter of October 28, Khrushchev stated that United Nations inspection would have to be approved by Castro. *The New York Times,* October 29, 1962, p. 16. Castro intervened and insisted on a high price: termination of the American trade embargo and of all American-sponsored subversive activities, coastal attacks, and aerial surveillance. He also demanded United States withdrawal from Guantanamo. *Ibid.,* p. 19.

75. After two days of negotiations in Havana, Thant returned to New York empty-handed. *Ibid.,* November 1, 1962, p. 1.

76. To be consistent, Sorensen said Kennedy would have renewed the crisis if the aircraft had not been removed. Sorensen, *op. cit.,* p. 720.

77. The United States verified removal of the missiles by naval observation and through continued aerial surveillance. *The Department of State Bulletin,* 47 (December 10, 1962), pp. 874-875.

78. *Op. cit.,* p. 711.

79. *Ibid.,* p. 716.

80. Schlesinger, *op. cit.,* p. 830.

Ironically, the administration's willingness to invade impressed Khrushchev more than the blockade did, although—to be sure—the blockade, as a display of resolve, made an invasion seem credible. The Executive Committee managing the crisis clearly rejected invasion as an initial response.[81] But the blockade did not resolve the crisis in Khrushchev's mind, contrary to Sorensen's retrospective statement, "A minimum of force had obtained a maximum gain." [82] The decision to delay the invasion seemed to hamper later consideration of it, perhaps for no other reason than that the Committee members had exhausted themselves working intensively on the first decision for a blockade. As late as October 27, the Committee had not sorted out precisely how the invasion should proceed. Sorensen noted the "rising tempers and irritability" of the participants as they grappled with the question they could no longer avoid.[83]

In retrospect, twelve days of exacting and fatiguing decision-making probably were not the best preparation for the most profound decisions yet to be made.[84] Undoubtedly, the Pentagon had contingency plans for an invasion. But the Executive Committee does not appear to have molded the plans into a clearly defined course of action. The question of an invasion deserved a calmer and more productive consideration than the committee appeared able to give it at the last. The practical application of the fallback position remained relatively unspecified too long, given circumstances which, if the Soviets had been more relentless, would have required urgent decision and action.

The way the Soviets persisted in the missile crisis, even after the blockade, is chilling to contemplate, especially if applied to the immediate Berlin context. If the third strategic test in the Berlin crisis had occurred on the *autobahn* to West Berlin rather than in Cuba, Khrushchev might not have backed down as readily because the Soviet Union had preponderant conventional military forces near the city. President Kennedy acknowledged after the missile crisis that his

---

81. Elie Abel, *op. cit.*, chapter 7; Robert Kennedy, *op. cit.*, pp. 43-46.

82. Acheson criticized the blockade decision for precisely this reason. *The Washington Post*, January 19, 1969, p. B1.

83. Sorensen, *op. cit.*, p. 716.

84. In his comment on Robert Kennedy's memoirs, Acheson referred to the Committee as "a leaderless uninhibited group, many of whom had little knowledge in either the military or diplomatic field." *The Washington Post*, January 19, 1969, p. B1.

success in one area might not apply to other areas where the Soviet Union held a locally superior military position.[85] Perhaps, the equivalent of the Cuban invasion force or something larger would have had to be assembled in Western Europe to engage in a conventional war on the central front before Khrushchev—in a comparable situation to the missile crisis—could be persuaded to back down. The administration planned to build a large force in 1961 for this reason. But Khrushchev did not press for a repeat performance in Europe to learn if the administration would, indeed, apply exactly the same response there. He believed he had the answer by analogy.

85. Schlesinger, *op. cit.*, p. 831.

PART IV

The Crisis in Retrospect

CHAPTER 8

The Political Costs of Berlin Negotiations

THE BERLIN crisis began and ended with a missile crisis. In 1958, Khrushchev objected to the Eisenhower Administration's decision to deploy American IRBM's to Western Europe in response to Khrushchev's own "missile gap" charges. He feared that the NATO agreement of December 1957—reflecting Eisenhower's decision—would allow Bonn to gain access to nuclear weapons. Thus, he stimulated a Berlin crisis to persuade the United States to reverse its plan and prepared a draft peace treaty to win recognition for a nuclear-free zone in Central Europe embracing West Germany. As the crisis evolved, the larger and more central issue concerning limits on West German rearmament tended to be pushed into the background as the test of wills between Washington and Moscow over the immediate issue of Berlin assumed a life of its own. But the Soviet Union's complaint about West Germany's nuclear status surfaced throughout the crisis whenever the subject of a peace treaty for two disarmed and neutral Germanies appeared. As late as October 18, 1962, when Gromyko visited President Kennedy even as the missiles in Cuba were rapidly becoming operational, Gromyko spoke of Soviet purposes in terms of a German peace treaty. Ultimately, and particularly from the Soviet point of view, the Berlin crisis was associated with the issue of West Germany's ability to arm and defend itself indirectly through alliance arrangements.

Three major issues became evident in the protracted crisis. First, the United States response to the crisis, both with Dulles and with Kennedy, seemed inadequate and misleading. Second, Khrushchev did not correctly understand the American response to his initiative and, therefore, miscalculated the potential gains for him in sustaining the crisis for four years. Third, Bonn and Paris did not agree with the way both American administrations managed the crisis, and de Gaulle, at least, broke with the Kennedy Administration over this issue in 1961. All three of these issues were evident at the time, not merely in the light of hindsight.

1. *Washington's Response to the Crisis*

Secretary Dulles started the United States down the negotiations track in the Berlin crisis, a track which remained preferred policy until the Cuban missile crisis. President Kennedy held a two-track policy—introducing partial mobilization in addition to negotiations in 1961—but he preferred to try for a settlement featuring a written agreement covering the Berlin access routes. After the Geneva conference of 1959, the United States perceived the crisis more in terms of the nightmare of a Berlin blockade rather than in terms relevant to West Germany's military status. It moved through the phases of negotiations in 1960, 1961, and 1962 with a consistent interest in postponing a blockade and in arriving at an access agreement to prevent future blockades. The United States defined its interest rather narrowly compared to the nuclear arms issue which motivated Moscow. Bonn, at any rate, considered Washington's response inadequate given the anti-German interest Moscow expressed. Bonn also believed Washington's response would mislead Moscow because Moscow would perceive their moves on the access issue in the context of the Soviet interest to restrict the Federal Republic's role in NATO. Bonn greatly feared that the concessions the West would have to make to obtain a Berlin settlement would alter the juridical and political status of West Berlin and, worse, would force a measure of disarmament upon West Germany without Soviet reciprocity.

The crisis was a nightmare for Bonn because the United States seemed to ignore the larger aims of Soviet policy Bonn perceived. Dulles gave more attention to these aims than his successors, but even he did not oppose them as strenuously as Bonn expected. Two administrations chose to make concessions to Moscow in exchange for an access agreement rather than to focus their efforts exclusively on shielding Bonn from Khrushchev's attack. Admittedly, they made concessions to elicit concessions from Moscow. But the concessions they offered they made over Bonn's misgivings and reluctance. To attract Soviet interest in a Berlin settlement, the United States and Britain proposed to consider arms limitations for Central Europe, thinking these would interest the Soviet Union. Bonn struggled to prevent any linkage between the two subjects or to make the linkage so unappealing for Moscow that the Soviets would reject it out of hand. Bonn objected to linkage in principle because it perceived that arms limitations would seal the division of Germany—a matter only tentatively settled in international law—and because Moscow had not yet forwarded a plan to include a portion of the Soviet Union in a nuclear-free zone. Moscow's plans would make West Germany a nuclear-free zone without touching the military status of the Soviet Union.

Bonn and Washington were estranged by the Berlin negotiations. Bonn discovered itself in an ambiguous role in American foreign policy. The Soviet Union probed diplomatically and militarily in the years of the Berlin crisis to detect fissures or strains in the alliance between Bonn and Washington. The distance the United States kept from Bonn's preferences encouraged Moscow to believe it had something to gain in persisting to generate a crisis atmosphere.[1]

The United States, of course, did not believe that it ignored the larger aims of the Soviet Union in the crisis or the political and legal interests of West Germany at stake. President Kennedy, for example, believed Bonn should be interested in improving the security of the access routes and, beyond that, in stabilizing the *de facto* settlement for Central Europe that had evolved since the Second World War. He did not intend to repudiate Bonn's role in the Atlantic alliance, as Moscow earnestly hoped. Rather he encouraged Bonn to come to terms with the dangers inherent in a situation still tentative and left open sixteen years after the war. The United States, before everything else, wanted stability in the heart of Europe. Contrary to Bonn's misgivings, it intended to honor its commitments there, but it really preferred to place limits on its commitments and to concentrate its efforts

---

1. For the changes in American policy toward West Germany since 1955, see Charles R. Planck, *The Changing Status of German Reunification in Western Diplomacy, 1955–1966* (Baltimore: The Johns Hopkins Press, 1967).

on achieving détente with the Soviet Union through local settlements and arms limitations. Two administrations shared the belief that Washington and Moscow should be able to settle the Berlin crisis or any other local dispute by invoking a mutual interest in preventing nuclear war. Unfortunately, the interest—although a mutual one— was construed divergently by each power and served primarily to place a ceiling on moves to be taken in the crisis. In fact, Moscow misread the administrations' lectures on nuclear war as a sign of preferred noninvolvement and pressed hard to produce American withdrawal from West Berlin and West Germany.

Essentially, the United States calculated the political benefits of the negotiations track without introducing all the relevant cost factors. The cost factors it did use served to reinforce the preference and assumptions favoring negotiations. For example, the Kennedy Administration looked at costs in terms of what would happen if negotiations were not undertaken or if they moved too slowly. Soviet miscalculation would become a real possibility, it predicted, if the political atmosphere became dominated by military moves and countermoves and escalation provoked rash actions by either side. Negotiations were considered a calm means of discourse and the optimal means of communication between parties.

The political costs of negotiating and the benefits of not negotiating were inadequately considered. The United States acted as though it was the only player on the board, as though the negotiations track would be perfectly understood by the other players. But the others did not react as anticipated. They over-reacted by American standards. Moscow got eagerly excited and Bonn frightened. For a very long time, the United States did not take notice of these reactions visible in the game, but fixed its attentions on its own moves, reading others' moves in that context. This way of playing endangers every player in the game because it confuses calculations and may lead to unintended confrontations. The alternative is to play in full consciousness of other players—not to try to play solo, but to consent to play a multiplayer game. To reorient Moscow and to calm Bonn, the United States should have played with them more fully in mind. Judging by the record of their game behavior, each would have understood a mobilization track to mean defense of the status quo and would have calculated their moves accordingly. In the game played between 1958–1962, the attempt by the United States to improve Berlin access was perceived by other players to slight the status quo, suggesting that the United States had little confidence in it. The United States should have hidden its misgivings, made the best of irreversible decisions made years before in 1944 and 1945, and found satisfaction in preventing any further losses in an already uncomfortable situation—in order to adapt to the crisis at hand and to control the reactions of the other players.

Since the interest of the United States lay in the stability and security of the status quo, the two administrations should have defended the status quo—as they found it—more energetically. They should have set about earlier to formulate and implement something like the Berlin strategy later adapted to the missile crisis—leading with a quarantine on Khrushchev's ambitions and reserving negotiations as a way out. The point to criticize is both administrations' preference to lead with negotiations first and to reserve partial mobilization for the last moves. This preference prolonged the Berlin crisis because of the expectation it created among Soviet leaders in Moscow. They did not abandon their effort against West Berlin until the United States reversed its priorities in the missile crisis. Soviet miscalculation and the ruptures in the Atlantic alliance caused by the estrangement with Bonn were a high price to pay for the negotiations track. And the costs would have been higher even for the skillful President in the Cuban missile crisis, if he had not been lucky, too.

2. Khrushchev's Miscalculation

Although Khrushchev reminded Harriman—who was in Moscow in 1963 to negotiate the test ban treaty: 'Remember, I can still step on your corns in Berlin," Khrushchev knew he had miscalculated. At an East German Communist Party Congress in East Berlin on January 16, 1963, Khrushchev officially terminated the Berlin crisis simply by declaring that he had, after all, achieved his objectives:

> And now, if we view the matter from the standpoint of the immediate interests of the socialist countries, the problem of the German peace treaty is not really what it was before the defensive measures were taken on the DDR border with West Berlin.[2]

2. N. S. Khrushchev, *The New Content of Peaceful Coexistence in the Nuclear Age* (New York: Crosscurrents Press, 1963).

He denied that he had lost interest in a peace treaty:

> These are the questions that have to be and, we are sure, will
> soon be solved. But how they are solved does not depend on one
> side only. Given the desire to arrive at a mutually acceptable
> agreement, both sides must act sensibly and show a readiness
> to consider each other's vital interests.[3]

These were words of caution lately acquired.[4]

His miscalculation revealed a serious contradiction in his original
Berlin policy, a contradiction between what he had wanted and what
he had planned to do to get it. He had hammered away at the alliance
binding West Berlin to Bonn and Bonn to Washington, and had relied
on the intimidating tactics of threatening war to make a dent. But his
threats actually had worked against him. If the Western powers regarded his threats seriously and armed themselves accordingly, they
denied him his objectives. Even if the Western powers regarded his
threats as preposterous because of the mutual effects a nuclear war
would wreak, and so did not arm themselves, his efforts fared no
better. In the end, Khrushchev concluded he did not have any feasi-
ble means to move his enemies and contented himself with the Berlin
wall.[5] Peking scornfully declared: "We have never considered that
it was a Marxist-Leninist attitude to brandish nuclear weapons as a
way of settling international disputes." [6]

Peking correctly diagnosed Soviet foreign policy as "adventurist,"
on the one hand, and "capitulationist" on the other.[7] Khrushchev had
alternated between running great risks to give effect to his threats and
retreating at the moment those risks led to an unacceptable state of
affairs. Khrushchev had intended to bring about changes in the status

---

3. *Ibid.*, p. 19.

4. And they were identical—in their sobriety—to Secretary Rusk's remarks at
the conclusion of Berlin negotiations in mid-1962: "Well, the situation on that
[Berlin] is that one could talk about a variety of things, but if they are linked
to an unacceptable point, such as the one you mentioned, then you create
misunderstandings by seeming to pick up that particular idea of access and
talking about it in isolation." *The Department of State Bulletin*, 47 (July 30,
1962), 174.

5. G. F. Hudson, "Russia and China, the Dilemmas of Power," *Foreign
Affairs*, 39 (October 1960), 6, 8; Herbert Dinerstein, "Soviet Goals and Mili-
tary Force," *Orbis*, 5 (Winter, 1962), 430, and "The Soviet Employment of
Military Strength for Political Purposes," *The Annals*, 318 (July 1958), 110.

6. *Peking Review*, January 4, 1963, p. 16.

7. *Ibid.*, September 6, 1963, p. 14.

quo without war. Yet the status quo really could not be changed except by war. Thus, he had locked himself into running in circles. He was reduced, as Peking claimed, to "begging the imperialists" in order to realize any gains at all. Khrushchev's Berlin policy, like Dulles', had no fallback position to cushion his miscalculation.

A primary factor which prompted Khrushchev to "over-react" to the negotiations track followed by the United States and which made that track so costly for the United States was a doctrinaire expectation of change. He read almost every movement in the American negotiating position in favorable terms. He once articulated his philosophy of change—actually a philosophy of history—to Adlai Stevenson:

> You must understand, Mr. Stevenson, that we live in an epoch when one system is giving way to another. When you established your republican system in the eighteenth century, the English did not like it. Now, too, a process is taking place in which the peoples want to live under a new system of society, and it is necessary that one agree and reconcile oneself with this fact. The process should take place without interference.[8]

Khrushchev perceived profound changes occurring on a global scale produced by deep-seated contradictions within the imperialist states, between such states, between those states and the colonial peoples, and between the imperialist and socialist states. He believed changes favored the socialist states because they were historically attuned to the contradictions at work. The West might say that the changes Khrushchev perceived occurring in its midst and in the developing countries were not occurring in the magnitude or in the direction which he ascribed to them. He insisted, however, that the West was doctrinally incapable of perceiving them correctly. Perception was a gift of attunement. The historically unattuned West could not be conscious of its own impending demise.

Khrushchev argued that the advent of the nuclear age, particularly the development of nuclear power by the Soviet Union—the leading socialist state—aggravated the contradictions he perceived. He used nuclear blackmail as a sensitized instrumentality of the age, striking at the West's "weakness," "decay," "rottenness." He did not believe the West could acquire an effective defense against its own contradictions. Yet he had to conclude in 1962 what he once remarked about

8. *The New York Times*, August 28, 1959.

West Berlin: "Evidently the conditions are not ripe as yet for a new scheme of things there. As the saying goes, each vegetable has its season." [9]

3. The Break with de Gaulle

The Berlin crisis coincided with President de Gaulle's first four years of office. He held the view through all those years that the United States mismanaged the Berlin crisis. He publicly warned the Eisenhower Administration in 1959 that the negotiations track would mislead Khrushchev and, when the "spirit of Camp David" seemed to be sowing confusion, he delayed and stiffened the Western negotiating position for the summit at Paris in 1960. Again, Foreign Minister Couve de Murville bluntly told Kennedy in 1961 that the administration's expressions of interest in a Berlin settlement did not fully convey Kennedy's determination to oppose Khrushchev's Berlin project. When Acheson, as Kennedy's emissary, informed de Gaulle of the administration's plans for the missile crisis, de Gaulle predicted the blockade would prove insufficient for removing the missiles.[10] Elie Abel recounts the conclusion de Gaulle drew from the missile crisis: "De Gaulle then asked Acheson why, in his view, the Russians had put missiles into Cuba. Acheson replied that he believed Khrushchev had gambled. The answer might not be flattering to his own government, he said, but the Russians had been led to believe that they could get away with it. De Gaulle nodded in agreement." [11]

At his press conference on January 14, 1963, de Gaulle implied he did not feel supremely confident about American foreign policy. He said recent events had demonstrated two points of interest. First,

> the immediate defense, and one can say privileged defense of Europe, and the military participation of the Europeans, which were once basic factors of their [American] strategy, moved by force of circumstances into second place. We have just witnessed this during the Cuban affair.[12]

The White House informed the allies about decisions taken in the two weeks before President Kennedy's speech of October 22, but it did not consult them before October 22.

9. *Documents*, p. 429.
10. Schlesinger, *op. cit.*, p. 815.
11. Elie Abel, *op. cit.*, p. 113.
12. *Major Addresses, Statements and Press Conferences of General Charles DeGaulle*, p. 217.

Second, it followed that the disposition of American nuclear power "does not necessarily and immediately meet all the eventualities concerning Europe and France." De Gaulle said: "In these conditions, no one in the world—particularly no one in America—can say if, where, when, how and to what extent the American nuclear weapons would be employed to defend Europe."[13] The administration thought the allies would be reassured from the care and success with which it had managed the missile crisis. Instead, de Gaulle observed a pattern of judgment and action he had observed in the Berlin crisis as a whole: a certain ambiguity about the role of Western Europe in American foreign policy generally and a tendency to ignore the interests of France in particular. He did not begrudge the United States having its own policy but he did object to the awkward position in which it placed France and Western Europe.

De Gaulle's break with the Kennedy Administration in the Berlin crisis grew and widened in the post-crisis period over the test ban treaty, the war in Viet Nam, and other issues as well. But Kennedy's inclination to press on, according to Sorensen, with another series of Berlin negotiations in the President's second term did not ease relations with de Gaulle.[14] Conceivably, Kennedy might not have tried again for a Berlin settlement because he admitted after the last round in the spring of 1962 that negotiations had damaged the Atlantic alliance. In December 1962, however, Secretary Rusk said that Berlin policy would not change, implying a continuing preference for negotiations.[15]

13. *Ibid.*
14. Sorensen, *op. cit.*, p. 755.
15. *The Department of State Bulletin,* 47 (December 17, 1962), 911.

Bibliography

OFFICIAL PUBLICATIONS

Berlin Senat, *Studien zur Lage und Entwicklung Westberlins*. Berlin, 1968.

Federal Republic of Germany, *News from the German Embassy*, 2–7. Washington, D.C., 1958–1963.

——, Press and Information Office of the Land Berlin, *Figures, Headlines, Charts*. Berlin, 1962.

——, Press and Information Office of the Federal Government, *Germany and Berlin: An Analysis of the 1959 Geneva Conference*. Bonn, n.d.

——, *The Bulletin*, 6–11. Bonn, 1958–1963.

——, *The Treaty of August 12, 1970*. Wiesbaden, 1970.

France, Ambassade de France, Service de Press et d'Information, *Major Addresses, Statements, and Press Conferences of General Charles de Gaulle, 1958–1964*. New York, 1965.

——, *Statement by French Foreign Minister Maurice Couve de Murville before The Senate on December 5, 1961*, No. 170A. New York, December 6, 1961.

Great Britain, *Defence: Outline of Future Policy*, Cmnd. 124. London, 1957.

——, *Report on Defence, 1961*, Cmnd. 1288. London, 1961.

United States Department of Defense, *Department of Defense News Release*, No. 1173–61, Roswell L. Gilpatric, Address before the Business Council, Hot Springs, Va., October 21, 1961.

————, *Department of Defense News Release*, No. 919–61, Paul H. Nitze, Address before the Association of the United States Army, Washington, D.C., September 7, 1961.

United States Department of State, *Bulletin*, 38–47. Washington, 1958–1962.

————, *Foreign Ministers Meeting, May–August, 1959, Geneva*, Publication 6882. Washington, 1959.

————, *President Eisenhower's Report to the Nation, May 25, 1960; Secretary Herter's Report to the Senate Foreign Relations Committee, May 27, 1960*, Publication 7010. Washington, 1960.

————, *The Soviet Note on Berlin: An Analysis*, Publication 6757. Washington, 1959.

United States Senate, Committee on Armed Services, Preparedness Investigating Subcommittee, *Investigation of the Preparedness Program: Interim Report on the Cuban Military Buildup*, 88th Cong., 1st Sess., 1963.

————, Committee on Foreign Relations, *Background Documents on Events Incident to the Summit Conference*, 86th Cong., 2nd Sess. Washington, 1960.

————, *Documents on Germany, 1944–1961*, 87th Cong., 1st Sess. Washington, 1961.

————, *Hearings, Events Incident to the Summit Conference*, 86th Cong., 2nd Sess. Washington, 1960.

————, *Khrushchev on the Shifting Balance of World Forces: A Special Study*, 86th Cong., 1st Sess. Washington, 1959.

————, *Report, Events Relating to the Summit Conference*, 86th Cong., 2nd Sess. Washington, 1960.

BOOKS AND MONOGRAPHS

Abel, Elie, *The Missile Crisis*. New York: J. B. Lippincott Co., 1966.

Adenauer, Konrad, *Erinnerungen, 1953–1955*. Stuttgart: Deutsche Verlags-Anstalt, 1966.

————, *Erinnerungen, 1955–1959*. Stuttgart: Deutsche Verlags-Anstalt, 1967.

————, *Erinnerungen, 1959–1963*. Stuttgart: Deutsche Verlags-Anstalt, 1968.

Beal, John Robinson, *John Foster Dulles*. New York: Harper & Brothers, 1957.

Berding, Andrew H., *Dulles on Diplomacy*. Princeton: D. Van Nostrand Co., Inc., 1963.

Brzezinski, Zbigniew K., *Ideology and Power in Soviet Politics*. New York: Frederick A. Praeger, Inc., 1962.

Buchan, Alastair, *Crisis Management: The New Diplomacy*, Atlantic Papers, NATO Series II, Boulogne-Sur-Seine, April, 1966.

———, *NATO in the 1960's*. New York: Frederick A. Praeger, 1960.

Buchan, Alastair, and Philip Windsor, *Arms and Stability in Europe*. New York: Frederick A. Praeger, Inc., 1963.

Burns, James MacGregor, *John F. Kennedy, A Political Profile*. New York: Harcourt, Brace, World, 1961.

Clay, Lucius D., *Decision in Germany*. Doubleday and Company, Inc., 1950.

Conquest, Robert, *Power and Policy in the U.S.S.R., The Study of Soviet Dynastics*. London: MacMillan & Company, Ltd., 1962.

Craig, Gordon, *From Bismarck to Adenauer: Aspects of German Statecraft*. Baltimore: The Johns Hopkins Press, 1958.

Dallin, David J., *Soviet Foreign Policies After Stalin*. Philadelphia: J. B. Lippincott Company, 1961.

Dalma, Alfons, *Hintergründe der Berlin-Krise*. Karlsruhe: Condor Verlag, 1962.

Davison, W. Phillips, *The Berlin Blockade: A Study in Cold War Politics*. Princeton: Princeton University Press, 1958.

Deutsch, Karl, and Lewis J. Edinger, *Germany Rejoins the Powers*. Stanford: Stanford University Press, 1959.

Dinerstein, Herbert S., *War and the Soviet Union*. New York: Frederick A. Praeger, Inc., 1959.

Donlon, Michael, *The Ideas of American Foreign Policy*. London: Chapman and Hall, Ltd., 1963.

Donner, Jörn, *Report from Berlin*, trans. Alvin T. Anderson. Bloomington: Indiana University Press, 1961.

Drummond, Roscoe and Gaston Coblenz, *Duel at the Brink: John Foster Dulles' Command of American Power*. New York: Doubleday and Company, Inc., 1960.

Dulles, Eleanor Lansing, *John Foster Dulles: The Last Year*. New York: Harcourt, Brace & World, Inc., 1963.

Dulles, John Foster, *War or Peace*. New York: Macmillan and Company, 1948.

———, *War, Peace and Change*. New York: Harper & Brothers, 1939.

Eisenhower, Dwight D., *The White House Years, Waging Peace 1956–1960*. New York: Doubleday and Company, Inc., 1965.

Embree, George D. (ed.), *The Soviet Union and the German Question, September, 1958–June, 1961*. The Hague: Martinus Nijhoff, 1963.

Feld, Werner, *Reunification and West German-Soviet Relations*. The Hague: Martinus Nijhoff, 1963.

Freund, Gerald, *Germany Between Two Worlds*. New York: Harcourt, Brace, and Company, 1961.

Furniss, Edgar S., Jr., "France under de Gaulle," *Headline Series*. Number 139, Council on Foreign Relations, New York, January–February, 1960.

Garthoff, Raymond, *Soviet Military Policy: An Historical Analysis*. New York: Frederick A. Praeger, Inc., 1966.

———, *Soviet Strategy in the Nuclear Age*. New York: Frederick A. Praeger, Inc., 1958.

———, *The Soviet Image of Future War*. Washington: Public Affairs Press, 1959.

Gould-Adams, Richard, *The Time of Power, A Reappraisal of John Foster Dulles*. London: Weidenfeld and Nicolson, 1962.

Grewe, Wilhelm G., *Deutsche Aussenpolitik der Nachkriegszeit*. Stuttgart: Deutsche Verlag-Anstalt, 1960.

Grosser, Alfred, *French Foreign Policy under de Gaulle, trans.* Lois Ames Pattison. Boston: Little, Brown & Company, 1967.

Gruliow, Leo (ed.), *Current Soviet Policies, III*. New York: Columbia University Press, 1960.

Hangen, Welles, *The Muted Revolution: East Germany's Challenge to Russia and the West*. New York: Alfred A. Knopf, Inc., 1966.

Hanhardt, Arthur M., Jr., *The German Democratic Republic*. Baltimore: The Johns Hopkins Press, 1968.

Hanrieder, Wolfram F., *West German Foreign Policy, 1949–1963: International Pressure and Domestic Response*. Stanford: Stanford University Press, 1967.

Harriman, Averell, *Peace with Russia*. New York: Simon and Schuster, 1959.

Heidelmeyer, Wolfgang, and Günter Hindrichs (eds.), *Documents on Berlin, 1943–1963*. München: R. Oldenbourg Verlag, 1963. (An abridgement and translation of *Dokumente zur Berlin-Frage, 1944–1962*. München: R. Oldenbourg Verlag, 1962.)

Heller, Deane and David, *The Berlin Wall*. New York: Walker, 1962.

Henkin, Louis, *The Berlin Crisis and the United Nations*. Carnegie Endowment for International Peace, New York, 1959.

Hinterhoff, Eugene, *Disengagement*. London: Stevens and Sons, Ltd., 1959.

Horelick, Arnold L., and Myron Rush, *Strategic Power and Soviet Foreign Policy*. Chicago: University of Chicago Press, 1966.

Howley, Frank L., *Berlin Command*. New York: G. D. Putnam's Sons, 1950.

Hudson, G. F., Richard Löwenthal, and Roderick MacFarquhar, *The Sino-Soviet Dispute*. New York: Frederick A. Praeger, Inc., 1961.

Hughes, Emrys, *Pilgrims' Progress in Russia*. London: Housman's Publishers, 1959.

Iklé, Fred Charles, *How Nations Negotiate*. New York: Harper and Row, 1964.

Kahn, Herman, *On Escalation: Metaphors and Scenarios*. New York: Frederick A. Praeger, Inc., 1965.

Kaiser, Karl, *German Foreign Policy in Transition, Bonn between East and West*. Oxford: Oxford University Press, 1968.

Kaufmann, William W., *The McNamara Strategy*. New York: Harper and Row, 1964.

Keller, John W., *Germany, the Wall and Berlin: Internal Politics during an International Crisis*. New York: Vantage Press, 1964.

Kennan, George F., *On Dealing with the Communist World*. New York: Harper and Row, 1964.

Kennedy, John F., *The Strategy of Peace* (ed. Allan Nevins). New York: Harper & Brothers, 1960.

Khrushchev, Nikita S., *Khrushchev in America*. New York: Cross-currents Press, 1960.

———, *For Victory in Peaceful Competition with Capitalism*. New York: E. P. Dutton & Company, Inc., 1960.

———, *Statement and Replies to Questions, Gorky Park, Moscow, May 11, 1960*. New York: Crosscurrents Press, 1960.

———, *The New Content of Peaceful Coexistence in the Nuclear Age*. New York: Crosscurrents Press, 1963.

———, *The Present International Situation and the Foreign Policy of the Soviet Union*. New York: Crosscurrents Press, 1963.

———, *The Soviet Stand on Germany*. New York: Crosscurrents Press, 1961.

Kolkowicz, Roman, *The Soviet Military and the Communist Party*. Princeton: Princeton University Press, 1967.

Kroll, Hans, *Lebenserinnerungen eines Botschafters*. Köln und Berlin: Verlag Kiepenheuer und Witsch, 1967.

Legien, Rudolf, *The Four Power Agreements on Berlin, Alternative Solutions to the Status Quo?*, trans. Trevor Davies. Carl Heymanns: Berlin, n.d.

Lippmann, Walter, *The Coming Tests with Russia*. Boston: Little, Brown and Company, 1961.

———, *The Communist World and Ours*. Boston: Little, Brown and Company, 1959.

Leonhard, Wolfgang, *Child of the Revolution*, trans. C. M. Woodhouse. Chicago: H. Regnery Co., 1958.

McDermott, Geoffrey, *Berlin: Success of a Mission?* New York: Harper and Row, 1963.

MacKintosh, J. M., *Strategy and Tactics of Soviet Foreign Policy*. London: Oxford University Press, 1963.

Mander, John, *Berlin, Hostage for the West*. Baltimore: Penguin Books, Inc., 1962.

Marcuse, Herbert, *Soviet Marxism: A Critical Analysis*. New York: Columbia University Press, 1958.

Marshall, Charles Burton, *Two Communist Manifestoes*, Johns Hopkins University, Washington Center of Foreign Policy Research, Washington, D.C., 1961.

Meyer, Alfred G., *Marxism, the Unity of Theory and Practice*. Cambridge: Harvard University Press, 1964.

Mosely, Philip E., *The Kremlin and World Politics*. New York: Vintage Books, Inc., 1961.

Murphy, Robert, *Diplomat Among Warriors*. New York: Doubleday and Company, Inc., 1964.

Nicolaevsky, Boris, *Power and the Soviet Elite: "The Letter of an Old Bolshevik" and Other Essays*, ed. Janet D. Zagoria. New York: Frederick A. Praeger, Inc., 1965.

Osgood, Robert E., *NATO: The Entangling Alliance*. Chicago: University of Chicago Press, 1962.

Pickles, Dorothy, *The Uneasy Entente, French Foreign Policy and Franco-British Misunderstandings*. London: Oxford University Press, 1966.

Planck, Charles R., *The Changing Status of German Reunification in Western Diplomacy, 1955–1966*. Baltimore: The Johns Hopkins Press, 1967.

Richardson, James L., *Germany and the Atlantic Alliance: The Interaction of Strategy and Politics*. Cambridge: Harvard University Press, 1966.

Rush, Myron, *The Rise of Khrushchev*. Washington: Public Affairs Press, 1958.

Schlesinger, Arthur M., Jr., *A Thousand Days: John F. Kennedy in the White House*. Boston: Houghton Mifflin Company, 1965.

Schmidt, Helmut, *Defense or Retaliation—A German View*. New York: Frederick A. Praeger, Inc., 1962.

Schwoebel, Jean, *Les Deux K, Berlin et la Paix*. Paris: René Julliard, 1963.

Shell, Kurt L., *Bedrohung und Bewährung: Führung und Bevölkerung in der Berlin Krise*. Köln und Opladen, Westdeutscher Verlag, 1965.

Shulman, Marshall D., *Stalin's Foreign Policy Reappraised*. Cambridge: Harvard University Press, 1963.

Skriver, Ansgor (ed.), *Berlin und Keine Illusion*. Hamburg: Rütten und Loening Verlag, 1962.

Smith, Bruce L. R., "The Governance of Berlin," *International Conciliation*, Number 525, November 1959.

Smith, Jean Edward, *The Defense of Berlin*. Baltimore: The Johns Hopkins Press, 1963.

Snyder, William P., *The Politics of British Defense Policy, 1945–1962*. Columbus: The Ohio State University Press, 1964.

Sokolovsky, Marshal V. D., *Military Strategy, Soviet Doctrine and Concepts*, ed. Raymond L. Garthoff. New York: Frederick A. Praeger, Inc., 1963.

Sorensen, Theodore C., *Kennedy*. New York: Harper and Row, 1965.

Speier, Hans, *Divided Berlin: The Anatomy of Soviet Political Blackmail*. New York: Frederick A. Praeger, Inc., 1961.

———, *German Rearmament and Atomic War: The Views of German Military and Political Leaders*. Evanston: Row, Peterson and Company, 1957.

Speier, Hans, and W. P. Davison (eds.), *West German Leadership and Foreign Policy*. Evanston: Row, Peterson and Company, 1957.

Stanger, Roland J. (ed.), *West Berlin: The Legal Context*. Columbus: Ohio State University Press, 1966.

Stern, Carola, *Ulbricht: A Political Biography*. New York: Frederick A. Praeger, Inc., 1965.

Triska, Jan, and David D. Finley, *Soviet Foreign Policy*. New York: The Macmillan Company, 1968.

Vali, Ferenc, *The Quest for a United Germany*. Baltimore: The Johns Hopkins Press, 1967.

Von Brentano, Heinrich, *Germany and Europe: Reflections on German Foreign Policy*, trans. Edward FitzGerald. New York: Frederick A. Praeger, Inc., 1962.

Watt, D. C., *Britain Looks to Germany: British Opinion and Policy toward Germany since 1945*. London: Oswald Wolff, 1965.

Weymar, Paul, *Adenauer: His Authorized Biography*. New York: E. P. Dutton and Company, 1957.

Wighton, Charles, *Adenauer—Democratic Dictator*. London: Frederick Muller Ltd., 1963.

Windsor, Philip, *City on Leave: A History of Berlin, 1945–1962*. Frederick A. Praeger, Inc., 1963.

Wise, David, and Thomas B. Ross, *The U-2 Affair*. New York: Random House, 1962.

Wolfe, James H., *Indivisible Germany, Illusion or Reality?* The Hague: Martinus Nijhoff, 1963.

Wolfe, Thomas W., *Soviet Strategy at the Crossroads*. Cambridge: Harvard University Press, 1964.

Ydit, Meir, *Internationalized Territories, from the "Free City of Cracow" to the "Free City of Berlin."* Leyden: A. W. Sythoff, 1961.

Zagoria, Donald S., *The Sino-Soviet Conflict, 1956–1961*. New York: Atheneum, 1964.

Zolling, Hermann, and Uwe Bahnsen, *Kalter Winter im August*. Oldenburg und Hamburg: Gerhard Stalling Verlag, 1967.

ARTICLES, PAPERS, RESEARCH MEMORANDA, AND MSS

Acheson, Dean, "Wishing Won't Hold Berlin," *Saturday Evening Post*, March 7, 1959, pp. 32–36.

———, "Acheson Says Luck Saved JFK on Cuba," *The Washington Post*, January 19, 1969, p. B1.

Adenauer, Konrad, "The German Problem, A World Problem," *Foreign Affairs*, 41 (October 1962), 59–65.

Allemann, Fritz René, "Berlin in Search of a Purpose," *Survey*, 61 (October 1966), 129–138.

Alsop, Stewart, "Our New Strategy," *The Saturday Evening Post*, December 1, 1962, pp. 13–19.

Anderson, Evelyn, "East Germany," *Survey*, 42 (June 1962), 96–106.

Ausland, John C., "The Struggle over Access to Berlin," unpublished MS, 1966.

Ausland, John C., and Col. Hugh F. Richardson, "Crisis Management: Berlin, Cyprus, Laos," *Foreign Affairs*, 44 (January 1966), 291–303.

Bailey, George, "The Gentle Erosion of Berlin," *The Reporter*, April 26, 1962, pp. 18–19.

Baylis, Thomas A., "The New Economic System" *Survey*, 61 (October 1966), 139–152.

Beaton, Leonard, *The Western Alliance and the McNamara Doctrine*, Adelphi Papers, Number 4, Institute for Strategic Studies, London, August 1964.

Ben, Philippe, "Communist Officials Worry about the Berlin Crisis," *Translations of Political Interest 1962–1963*, ed. Horst Mendershausen, RM-3078, Rand Corporation, Santa Monica, California, 1964, pp. 42–48.

"Berlin," *Der Spiegel*, October 9, 1967.

Brodie, Bernard, "The McNamara Phenomenon," *World Politics*, 17 (July 1965), 672–686.

Burin, Frederic S., "The Communist Doctrine of the Inevitability of War," *American Political Science Review*, 57 (March 1963), 334–354.

Clay, Lucius, "Berlin," *Foreign Affairs*, 41 (October 1962), 47–58.

Craig, Gordon A., "Techniques of Negotiation," *Russian Foreign Policy, Essays in Historical Perspective*, ed. Ivo J. Lederer. New Haven: Yale University Press, 1962.

Crane, Robert D., "The Cuban Crisis: A Strategic Analysis of American and Soviet Policy," *Orbis*, 6 (Winter, 1963), 547–548.

Croan, Melvin, "Party Politics and the Wall," *Survey*, 61 (October 1966), 38–46.

Dalma, Alfons, "The Risks of a Détente Policy to Central Europe," *Changing East-West Relations and the Unity of the West*, (ed.) Arnold Wolfers. Baltimore: Johns Hopkins Press, 1964.

Delcour, Roland, "Germany Behind the Wall," *Translations of Political Interest, 1962–1963*, (ed.) Horst Mendershausen, RM-3078, Rand Corporation, Santa Monica, California, 1964, pp. 1–27.

Democratic Advisory Council, *Democratic Programs for Action*, Number 4, June, 1959.

DeWeerd, H. A., *Britain's Defense New Look Five Years Later*, P-2562, Rand Corporation, Santa Monica, California, March, 1962.

Dinerstein, Herbert S., "Soviet Goals and Military Force," *Orbis*, 5 (Winter, 1962), 425–36.

———, "The Soviet Employment of Military Strength for Political Purposes," *The Annals of the American Academy of Political and Social Science* (July 1958), pp. 104–112.

Dulles, John Foster, "Challenge and Response in United States Policy," *Foreign Affairs*, 36 (October 1957), 25–43.

———, "Policy for Security and Peace," *Foreign Affairs*, 32 (April 1954), 353–364.

Eisenhower, Dwight D., "My Views on Berlin," *Saturday Evening Post*, December 9, 1961, pp. 19–28.

Epstein, Klaus, "The Adenauer Era in German History," *A New Europe?* ed. Stephen R. Graubard. Boston: Houghton Mifflin Co., 1964.

Erler, Fritz, "Les Aspects politiques de l'action sovietique a Berlin," *Politique étrangère*, 27 (1963), 5–14.

Fainsod, Merle, "The Twenty-second Party Congress," *Russia under Khrushchev*, ed. Abraham Brumberg. New York: Frederick A. Praeger, Inc., 1962.

Franklin, William M., "Zonal Boundaries and Access to Berlin," *World Politics*, 16 (October 1963), 1–31.

George, Alexander L., "The 'Operational Code': A Neglected Approach to the Study of Political Leaders and Decision-Making," *International Studies Quarterly*, 13 (June 1969), 190–222.

Grewe, Wilhelm G., "The Eastern Problems in German Foreign Policy," 1959 (mimeograph).

———, "Other Legal Aspects of the Berlin Crisis," *American Journal of International Law*, 56 (April 1962), 510–513.

Griffith, William E., "The German Problem and American Policy," *Survey*, 61 (October, 1966), 104–117.

Hadik, Laszlo, "The Berlin Question 1942–1961, A Historical Summary," unpublished MS, Institute for Defense Analyses, Washington, D.C., 1961.

Haffner, Sebastian, "The Berlin Crisis," *Survey*, 44/45 (October 1962), 37–44.

Halpern, A. M., "Communist China and Peaceful Coexistence," *China Quarterly*, 3 (July–September 1960), 16–31.

Harriman, Averell, "My Alarming Interview with Khrushchev," *Life*, July 8, 1959.

Hilsman, Roger, "On NATO Strategy," *Alliance Policy in the Cold War*, ed. Arnold Wolfers. Baltimore: Johns Hopkins Press, 1959.

————, "The Developing Strategic Context," *NATO and American Security*, ed. Klaus Knorr. Princeton: Princeton University Press, 1959.

Holsti, Ole R., "Cognitive Dynamics and Images of the Enemy: Dulles and Russia," *Enemies in Politics* (with David J. Finley and Richard R. Fagen). Chicago: Rand McNally and Company, 1967.

Horelick, Arnold L., "The Cuban Missile Crisis: An Analysis of Soviet Calculations and Behavior," *World Politics*, 16 (April 1964), 363–389.

Hudson, G. F., "Russia and China, the Dilemmas of Power," *Foreign Affairs*, 39 (October 1960), 1–10.

Johnstone, Paul H., *American Policy-Making Practices and the Origins of the U.S. Commitment to the West Berlin Enclave*, Research Paper P-279, Institute for Defense Analyses, Washington, September 1966.

Kennedy, John F., "A Democrat Looks at Foreign Policy," *Foreign Affairs*, 36 (October 1957), 44–59.

————, "The Soviet Threat to the Americas," *Department of State Bulletin*, 47 (November 12, 1962), 716–720.

Khrushchev, Nikita S., "On Peaceful Coexistence," *Foreign Affairs*, 38 (October 1959), 1–18.

King, James E., Jr., "The Berlin Controversy, What Are We Prepared to Defend?" *The New Republic*, April 13, 1959, pp. 10–15.

————, "The Berlin Controversy II: What is the United States Prepared to Defend?" *The New Republic*, April 20, 1959, pp. 9–13.

Kluge, Franz, "The Economic Viability of Berlin," *Berlin-Pivot of German Destiny*, trans. and ed. Charles B. Robson. Chapel Hill: The University of North Carolina Press, 1960.

Knorr, Klaus, "Failures in National Intelligence Estimates: The Case of the Cuban Missiles," *World Politics*, 16 (April 1964), 455–467.

Kolkowicz, Roman, *Conflicts in Soviet Party-Military Relations, 1962–1963*, RM-3760, Rand Corporation, Santa Monica, California, August 1963.

Komarov, M., "Coexistence of the Two German States and the Peace Treaty," *International Affairs* (Moscow), 7 (July 1962), 6–10.

Lippmann, Walter, "Cuba and the Nuclear Risk," *The Atlantic*, February 1963, pp. 55–58.

Löwenthal, Richard, "The Impossible Defensive," *Encounter*, 17 (November 1961), 22–23.

———, "The Nature of Khrushchev's Power," *Russia under Khrushchev*, ed. Abraham Brumberg. New York: Frederick A. Praeger, Inc., 1963.

MacKintosh, J. M., "Soviet Motives in Cuba," *Survival*, January–February, 1963, pp. 16–18.

McNamara, Robert S., "Defense Arrangements of the North Atlantic Community," *Department of State Bulletin*, 47 (July 10, 1962), 64–69.

Marshall, Charles Burton, "Making Foreign Policy on the New Frontier," *Administration of National Security, Selected Papers*, Subcommittee on National Security Policy Machinery, Committee on Government Operations, U.S. Senate, 87th Congress, 2nd Session, Washington, 1962.

Mendershausen, Horst, *A View of U.S.-European Relations in 1964*, RM-4334, Rand Corporation, Santa Monica, California, November, 1964.

———, *Dependence of East Germany on Western Imports*, RM-2414, Rand Corporation, Santa Monica, California, July 1959.

———, *Interzonal Trade in Germany, Part I: The Trade and the Contractual Relations*, RM-3686, Rand Corporation, Santa Monica, California, July 1963.

———, *Interzonal Trade in Germany, Part II: Interaction With Early Berlin Conflicts*, RM-3686 (Part II), Rand Corporation, Santa Monica, California, November 1963.

Merkl, Peter H., "Equilibrium, Structure of Interests and Leadership: Adenauer's Survival as Chancellor," *The American Political Science Review*, 56 (September 1962), 634–650.

Morgenthau, Hans J., "End of an Illusion," *Commentary*, November 1961, pp. 422–425.

Prittie, Terence, "Berlin Crisis, Tactics and Strategy," *Nation*, December 6, 1958, pp. 424–426.

Rauschning, Dietrich, "Die Berlin-Frage in Neueren Schrifttum," *Europa Archiv* 16 (November 1961), 663–674.

Rovere, Richard H., "Letter from Washington," *The New Yorker*, September 23, 1961, pp. 82–88.

Reddaway, P. B., "The Fall of Khrushchev," *Survey*, 56 (July 1965), 11–30.

Shell, Kurt L., "Berlin and the German Problem," *World Politics*, 16 (October 1963), 137–146.

Smith, Jean Edward, "Berlin: The Erosion of a Principle," *The Reporter*, November 21, 1963, pp. 32–37.

Speier, Hans, "Soviet Atomic Blackmail and the North Atlantic Alliance," *World Politics*, 19 (April 1957), 307–328.

Steiniger, Peter Alfons, "Rechtsprobleme der Entmilitarisierten Freien Stadt West Berlin," *Problems des Volkerrechts*, Band 2. Berlin: Veb Deutscher Zentral Verlag, 1962.

Tatu, Michel, "Khrushchev's Miscalculation in Cuba," *Translations of Political Interest, 1962–1963* (ed.) Horst Mendershausen, RM-3078, Rand Corporation, Santa Monica, California, 1964, pp. 49–55.

Thomas, Stephen, "Beyond the Wall," *Survey*, 44/45 (October 1962), 54–65.

Tudyka, Kurt P., "The Foreign Policy of the G.D.R." *Survey*, 61 (October 1962), 56–69.

Whelan, Joseph G., "Berlin: A Chronological Summary, September 12, 1944–July 17, 1961," Library of Congress, Legislative Reference Service, Washington, D.C., 1961 (mimeograph).

Wohlstetter, Albert, and Roberta Wohlstetter, *Controlling the Risks in Cuba*, Adelphi Papers, Number 17, Institute for Strategic Studies, London, April 1965.

Wohlstetter, Roberta, "Cuba and Pearl Harbor—Hindsight and Foresight," *Foreign Affairs*, 43 (July 1965), 691–707.

Wright, Quincy, "Some Legal Aspects of the Berlin Crisis," *The American Journal of International Law*, 55 (October 1961), 959–965.

INDEX

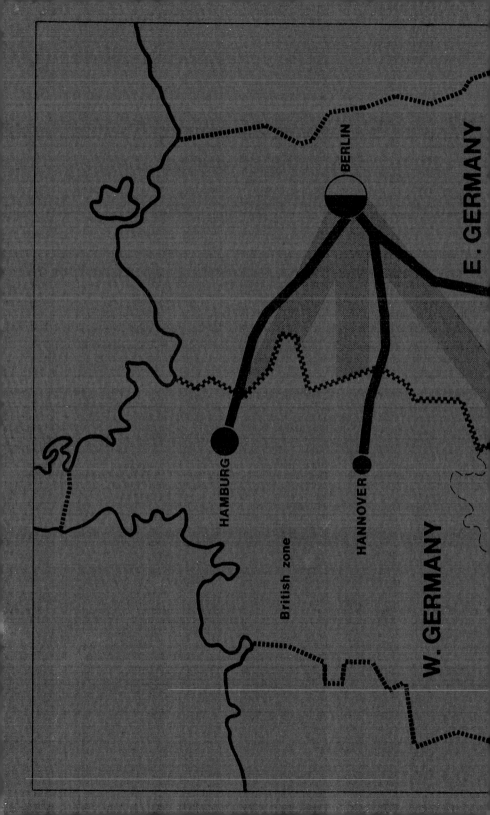